THE LECTURES, ESSAYS AND LITERARY CRITICISM OF VIRGINIA WOOLF

By

VIRGINIA WOOLF

Read &' Co.

Copyright © 2021 Read & Co. Great Essays

This edition is published by Read & Co. Great Essays,
an imprint of Read & Co.

British Library Cataloguing-in-Publication Data
A catalogue record for this book is available
from the British Library.

Read & Co. is part of Read Books Ltd.
For more information visit
www.readandcobooks.co.uk

CONTENTS

VIRGINIA WOOLF

Virginia Woolf was born Adeline Virginia Stephen in Kensington, London, England in 1882. Her father, Leslie Stephen, was a respected man of letters, and as a young girl Woolf was introduced to many literary figures, including Henry James. Woolf also made great use of the family home's vast library, working her way through much of the English literary canon as a teenager. Her summers were spent in St. Ives, Cornwall, which would later form the setting for her famous novel, *To the Lighthouse.*

In 1895, when Woolf was just thirteen, her mother died, triggering the first of her many mental breakdowns. Despite this, between 1897 and 1901 she was able to take courses in Greek, Latin, German and history at the Ladies' Department of King's College London. She even began publishing work with the *Times Literary Supplement.* However, in 1904, following the death of her father, Woolf suffered another breakdown which saw her briefly institutionalised.

Following her discharge, Woolf and her sisters moved from their family home to a new abode in Bloomsbury. It was here that Woolf met Lytton Strachey, John Maynard Keynes, E. M. Forster and various other writers and intellectuals, who together would form the famous Bloomsbury Set. In 1912, Woolf married author Leonard Woolf, who nursed her through another breakdown and suicide attempt. Woolf published her first novel, *The Voyage Out*, in 1915. This, as well as various essays, quickly established her as a major public intellectual.

During the twenties, Woolf published the novels that established her as a leading figure of modernism and one of the greatest British novelists of the 20th century: *Jacob's Room* (1922), *Mrs. Dalloway* (1925), *To the Lighthouse* (1927) and *Orlando* (1928). Stylistically, Woolf experimented with a lyrical stream-of-consciousness narrative mode, and is now considered – along with fellow modernist James Joyce – one of the finest innovators in the English language. Her work has been translated into fifty languages, and her major novels have never been out of print.

After completing her last novel, *Between the Acts*, Woolf fell into a period of deep depression – exacerbated by the the onset of World War ii and the destruction of her home during the Blitz. In 1941, fearing a total mental collapse, Woolf committed suicide. She was 59 years old.

THE LECTURES, ESSAYS AND LITERARY CRITICISM OF VIRGINIA WOOLF

JOSEPH CONRAD

Written in August, 1914

Suddenly, without giving us time to arrange our thoughts or prepare our phrases, our guest has left us; and his withdrawal without farewell or ceremony is in keeping with his mysterious arrival, long years ago, to take up his lodging in this country. For there was always an air of mystery about him. It was partly his Polish birth, partly his memorable appearance, partly his preference for living in the depths of the country, out of ear-shot of gossips, beyond reach of hostesses, so that for news of him one had to depend upon the evidence of simple visitors with a habit of ringing door-bells who reported of their unknown host that he had the most perfect manners, the brightest eyes, and spoke English with a strong foreign accent.

Still, though it is the habit of death to quicken and focus our memories, there clings to the genius of Conrad something essentially, and not accidentally, difficult of approach. His reputation of later years was, with one obvious exception, undoubtedly the highest in England; yet he was not popular. He was read with passionate delight by some; others he left cold and lustreless. Among his readers were people of the most opposite ages and sympathies. Schoolboys of fourteen, driving their way through Marryat, Scott, Henty, and Dickens, swallowed him down with the rest; while the seasoned and the fastidious, who in process of time have eaten their way to the heart of literature and there turn over and over a few precious crumbs, set Conrad scrupulously upon their banqueting table. One source of difficulty and disagreement is, of course, to be found where men have at all times found it, in his beauty. One opens his pages and feels as Helen must have felt when she looked in her glass and realised that, do what she would, she could never in any circumstances pass for a plain woman. So Conrad had been gifted, so he had schooled himself, and such was his obligation to a strange language wooed characteristically for its Latin qualities rather than its Saxon that it seemed impossible for him to make an ugly or insignificant movement of the pen. His mistress, his style, is a little somnolent sometimes in repose. But let somebody speak to her, and then how magnificently she bears down upon us, with what colour, triumph, and majesty! Yet it is arguable that Conrad would have gained both in credit and in popularity if he had written what he had to write without this incessant care for appearances. They block and impede and distract, his critics say, pointing to those famous passages which it is becoming the habit to lift from their context and exhibit among other cut flowers of English prose. He was self-conscious and stiff and ornate, they complain, and the sound of his own voice was dearer to him than the voice of humanity in its anguish. The criticism is familiar, and as difficult to refute as the remarks of deaf people when *Figaro* is played. They see the orchestra; far off they hear a dismal scrape of sound; their own remarks are interrupted, and, very naturally, they conclude that the ends of life would be better served if instead of scraping Mozart those fifty fiddlers broke stones upon the road. That beauty teaches, that beauty is a disciplinarian, how are we to convince them, since her teaching is inseparable from the sound of her voice and to that they are deaf? But read Conrad, not in birthday books but in the bulk, and he must be lost indeed to the meaning of words who does not hear in that rather stiff and sombre music, with its reserve, its pride, its vast and implacable integrity, how it is better to be good than bad, how loyalty is good and honesty and courage, though ostensibly Conrad is concerned merely to show us the beauty of a night at sea. But it is ill work dragging such intimations from their element.

Dried in our little saucers, without the magic and mystery of language, they lose their power to excite and goad; they lose the drastic power which is a constant quality of Conrad's prose.

For it was by virtue of something drastic in him, the qualities of a leader and captain, that Conrad kept his hold over boys and young people. Until *Nostromo* was written his characters, as the young were quick to perceive, were fundamentally simple and heroic, however subtle the mind and indirect the method of their creator. They were seafarers, used to solitude and silence. They were in conflict with Nature, but at peace with man. Nature was their antagonist; she it was who drew forth honour, magnanimity, loyalty, the qualities proper to man; she who in sheltered bays reared to womanhood beautiful girls unfathomable and austere. Above all, it was Nature who turned out such gnarled and tested characters as Captain Whalley and old Singleton, obscure but glorious in their obscurity, who were to Conrad the pick of our race, the men whose praises he was never tired of celebrating:

> They had been strong as those are strong who know neither doubts nor hopes. They had been impatient and enduring, turbulent and devoted, unruly and faithful. Well-meaning people had tried to represent these men as whining over every mouthful of their food, as going about their work in fear of their lives. But in truth they had been men who knew toil, privation, violence, debauchery—but knew not fear, and had no desire of spite in their hearts. Men hard to manage, but easy to inspire; voiceless men— but men enough to scorn in their hearts the sentimental voices that bewailed the hardness of their fate. It was a fate unique and their own; the capacity to bear it appeared to them the privilege of the chosen!

> Their generation lived inarticulate and indispensable, without knowing the sweetness of affections or the refuge

11

of a home—and died free from the dark menace of a narrow grave. They were the everlasting children of the mysterious sea.

Such were the characters of the early books—*Lord Jim, Typhoon, The Nigger of the "Narcissus", Youth*; and these books, in spite of the changes and fashions, are surely secure of their place among our classics. But they reach this height by means of qualities which the simple story of adventure, as Marryat told it, or Fenimore Cooper, has no claim to possess. For it is clear that to admire and celebrate such men and such deeds, romantically, whole-heartedly and with the fervour of a lover, one must be possessed of the double vision; one must be at once inside and out. To praise their silence one must possess a voice. To appreciate their endurance one must be sensitive to fatigue. One must be able to live on equal terms with the Whalleys and the Singletons and yet hide from their suspicious eyes the very qualities which enable one to understand them. Conrad alone was able to live that double life, for Conrad was compound of two men; together with the sea captain dwelt that subtle, refined, and fastidious analyst whom he called Marlow. "A most discreet, understanding man", he said of Marlow.

Marlow was one of those born observers who are happiest in retirement. Marlow liked nothing better than to sit on deck, in some obscure creek of the Thames, smoking and recollecting; smoking and speculating; sending after his smoke beautiful rings of words until all the summer's night became a little clouded with tobacco smoke. Marlow, too, had a profound respect for the men with whom he had sailed; but he saw the humour of them. He nosed out and described in masterly fashion those livid creatures who prey successfully upon the clumsy veterans. He had a flair for human deformity; his humour was sardonic. Nor did Marlow live entirely wreathed in the smoke of his own cigars. He had a habit of opening his eyes suddenly and looking—at a rubbish heap, at a port, at a shop counter—and then complete in its burning ring of light that thing is flashed bright upon the mysterious background. Introspective and analytical, Marlow was aware of this peculiarity. He said the power came to him suddenly. He might, for instance, overhear a French officer murmur "Mon Dieu, how the time passes!"

> Nothing [he comments] could have been more commonplace than this remark; but its utterance coincided for me with a moment of vision. It's extraordinary how we go through life with eyes half shut, with dull ears, with dormant thoughts. . . . Nevertheless, there can be but few of us who had never known one of these rare moments of awakening, when we see, hear, understand, ever so much—everything—in a flash, before we fall back again into our agreeable somnolence. I raised my eyes when he spoke, and I saw him as though I had never seen him before.

Picture after picture he painted thus upon that dark background; ships first and foremost, ships at anchor, ships flying before the storm, ships in harbour; he painted sunsets and dawns; he painted the night; he painted the sea in every aspect; he painted the gaudy brilliancy of Eastern ports, and men and women, their houses and their attitudes. He was an accurate and unflinching observer, schooled to that "absolute loyalty towards his feelings and sensations", which, Conrad wrote, "an author should keep hold of in his most exalted moments of creation". And very quietly and compassionately Marlow sometimes lets fall a few words of epitaph which remind us, with all that beauty and brilliancy before our eyes, of the darkness of the background.

Thus a rough-and-ready distinction would make us say that it is Marlow who comments, Conrad who creates. It would lead us, aware that we are on dangerous ground, to account for that change which, Conrad tells us, took place when he had finished

13

the last story in the *Typhoon* volume—"a subtle change in the nature of the inspiration"—by some alteration in the relationship of the two old friends. ". . . it seemed somehow that there was nothing more in the world to write about." It was Conrad, let us suppose, Conrad the creator, who said that, looking back with sorrowful satisfaction upon the stories he had told; feeling as he well might that he could never better the storm in *The Nigger of the "Narcissus"*, or render more faithful tribute to the qualities of British seamen than he had done already in *Youth* and *Lord Jim*. It was then that Marlow, the commentator, reminded him how, in the course of nature, one must grow old, sit smoking on deck, and give up seafaring. But, he reminded him, those strenuous years had deposited their memories; and he even went so far perhaps as to hint that, though the last word might have been said about Captain Whalley and his relation to the universe, there remained on shore a number of men and women whose relationships, though of a more personal kind, might be worth looking into. If we further suppose that there was a volume of Henry James on board and that Marlow gave his friend the book to take to bed with him, we may seek support in the fact that it was in 1905 that Conrad wrote a very fine essay upon that master.

For some years, then, it was Marlow who was the dominant partner. *Nostromo, Chance, The Arrow of Gold* represent that stage of the alliance which some will continue to find the richest of all. The human heart is more intricate than the forest, they will say; it has its storms; it has its creatures of the night; and if as novelist you wish to test man in all his relationships, the proper antagonist is man; his ordeal is in society, not solitude. For them there will always be a peculiar fascination in the books where the light of those brilliant eyes falls not only upon the waste of waters but upon the heart in its perplexity. But it must be admitted that, if Marlow thus advised Conrad to shift his angle of vision, the advice was bold. For the vision of a novelist is both complex and specialised; complex, because behind his characters and apart from them must stand something stable to which he relates them; specialised because since he is a single person with one sensibility the aspects of life in which he can believe with conviction are strictly limited. So delicate a balance is easily disturbed. After the middle period Conrad never again was able to bring his figures into perfect relation with their background. He never believed in his later, and more highly sophisticated characters as he had believed in his early seamen. When he had to indicate their relation to that other unseen world of novelists, the world of values and convictions, he was far less sure what those values were. Then, over and over again, a single phrase, "He steered with care", coming at the end of a storm, carried in it a whole morality. But in this more crowded and complicated world such terse phrases became less and less appropriate. Complex men and women of many interests and relations would not submit to so summary a judgement; or, if they did, much that was important in them escaped the verdict. And yet it was very necessary to Conrad's genius, with its luxuriant and romantic power, to have some law by which its creations could be tried. Essentially—such remained his creed—this world of civilised and self-conscious people is based upon "a few very simple ideas"; but where, in the world of thoughts and personal relations, are we to find them? There are no masts in drawing-rooms; the typhoon does not test the worth of politicians and business men. Seeking and not finding such supports, the world of Conrad's later period has about it an involuntary obscurity, an inconclusiveness, almost a disillusionment which baffles and fatigues. We lay hold in the dusk only of the old nobilities and sonorities: fidelity, compassion, honour, service—beautiful always, but now a little wearily reiterated, as if times had changed. Perhaps it was Marlow who was at fault. His habit of mind was a trifle sedentary. He had sat upon deck too long; splendid in soliloquy, he was less apt in the give and take of conversation; and those "moments of vision" flashing and fading, do not serve as well as steady lamplight to illumine the ripple of life and its long, gradual years. Above all, perhaps, he did not take into account how, if Conrad was to create, it was essential first that he should believe.

Therefore, though we shall make expeditions into the later books and bring back wonderful trophies, large tracts of them will remain by most of us untrodden. It is the earlier books— *Youth, Lord Jim, Typhoon, The Nigger of the "Narcissus"*— that we shall read in their entirety. For when the question is asked, what of Conrad will survive and where in the ranks of novelists we are to place him, these books, with their air of telling us something very old and perfectly true, which had lain hidden but is now revealed, will come to mind and make such questions and comparisons seem a little futile. Complete and still, very chaste and very beautiful, they rise in the memory as, on these hot summer nights, in their slow and stately way first one star comes out and then another.

"JANE EYRE" AND
"WUTHERING HEIGHTS"

Written in 1916

Of the hundred years that have passed since Charlotte Brontë was born, she, the centre now of so much legend, devotion, and literature, lived but thirty-nine. It is strange to reflect how different those legends might have been had her life reached the ordinary human span. She might have become, like some of her famous contemporaries, a figure familiarly met with in London and elsewhere, the subject of pictures and anecdotes innumerable, the writer of many novels, of memoirs possibly, removed from us well within the memory of the middle-aged in all the splendour of established fame. She might have been wealthy, she might have been prosperous. But it is not so. When we think of her we have to imagine some one who had no lot in our modern world; we have to cast our minds back to the 'fifties of the last century, to a remote parsonage upon the wild Yorkshire moors. In that parsonage, and on those moors, unhappy and lonely, in her poverty and her exaltation, she remains for ever.

These circumstances, as they affected her character, may have left their traces on her work. A novelist, we reflect, is bound to build up his structure with much very perishable material which begins by lending it reality and ends by cumbering it with rubbish. As we open *Jane Eyre* once more we cannot stifle the suspicion that we shall find her world of imagination as antiquated, mid-Victorian, and out of date as the parsonage on the moor, a place only to be visited by the curious, only preserved by the pious. So we open *Jane Eyre*; and in two pages every doubt is swept clean from our minds.

> Folds of scarlet drapery shut in my view to the right hand; to the left were the clear panes of glass, protecting, but not separating me from the drear November day. At intervals, while turning over the leaves of my book, I studied the aspect of that winter afternoon. Afar, it offered a pale blank of mist and cloud; near, a scene of wet lawn and storm-beat shrub, with ceaseless rain sweeping away wildly before a long and lamentable blast.

There is nothing there more perishable than the moor itself, or more subject to the sway of fashion than the "long and lamentable blast". Nor is this exhilaration short-lived. It rushes us through the entire volume, without giving us time to think, without letting us lift our eyes from the page. So intense is our absorption that if some one moves in the room the movement seems to take place not there but up in Yorkshire. The writer has us by the hand, forces us along her road, makes us see what she sees, never leaves us for a moment or allows us to forget her. At the end we are steeped through and through with the genius, the vehemence, the indignation of Charlotte Brontë. Remarkable faces, figures of strong outline and gnarled feature have flashed upon us in passing; but it is through her eyes that we have seen them. Once she is gone, we seek for them in vain. Think of Rochester and we have to think of Jane Eyre. Think of the moor, and again there is Jane Eyre. Think of the drawing-room[1], even, those "white carpets on which seemed

---

1   Charlotte and Emily Brontë had much the same sense of colour. ". . . we saw—ah! it was beautiful—a splendid place carpeted with crimson, and crimson-covered chairs and tables, and a pure white ceiling bordered by gold, a shower of glass drops hanging in silver chains from the centre, and

laid brilliant garlands of flowers", that "pale Parian mantelpiece" with its Bohemia glass of "ruby red" and the "general blending of snow and fire"—what is all that except Jane Eyre?

The drawbacks of being Jane Eyre are not far to seek. Always to be a governess and always to be in love is a serious limitation in a world which is full, after all, of people who are neither one nor the other. The characters of a Jane Austen or of a Tolstoi have a million facets compared with these. They live and are complex by means of their effect upon many different people who serve to mirror them in the round. They move hither and thither whether their creators watch them or not, and the world in which they live seems to us an independent world which we can visit, now that they have created it, by ourselves. Thomas Hardy is more akin to Charlotte Brontë in the power of his personality and the narrowness of his vision. But the differences are vast. As we read *Jude the Obscure* we are not rushed to a finish; we brood and ponder and drift away from the text in plethoric trains of thought which build up round the characters an atmosphere of question and suggestion of which they are themselves, as often as not, unconscious. Simple peasants as they are, we are forced to confront them with destinies and questionings of the hugest import, so that often it seems as if the most important characters in a Hardy novel are those which have no names. Of this power, of this speculative curiosity,

shimmering with little soft tapers" (*Wuthering Heights*). "Yet it was merely a very pretty drawing-room, and within it a boudoir, both spread with white carpets, on which seemed laid brilliant garlands of flowers; both ceiled with snowy mouldings of white grapes and vine leaves, beneath which glowed in rich contrast crimson couches and ottomans; while the ornaments on the pale Parian mantelpiece were of sparkling Bohemia glass, ruby red; and between the windows large mirrors repeated the general blending of snow and fire" (*Jane Eyre*).

19

Charlotte Brontë has no trace. She does not attempt to solve the problems of human life; she is even unaware that such problems exist; all her force, and it is the more tremendous for being constricted, goes into the assertion, "I love", "I hate", "I suffer".

For the self-centred and self-limited writers have a power denied the more catholic and broad-minded. Their impressions are close packed and strongly stamped between their narrow walls. Nothing issues from their minds which has not been marked with their own impress. They learn little from other writers, and what they adopt they cannot assimilate. Both Hardy and Charlotte Brontë appear to have founded their styles upon a stiff and decorous journalism. The staple of their prose is awkward and unyielding. But both with labour and the most obstinate integrity, by thinking every thought until it has subdued words to itself, have forged for themselves a prose which takes the mould of their minds entire; which has, into the bargain, a beauty, a power, a swiftness of its own. Charlotte Brontë, at least, owed nothing to the reading of many books. She never learnt the smoothness of the professional writer, or acquired his ability to stuff and sway his language as he chooses. "I could never rest in communication with strong, discreet, and refined minds, whether male or female", she writes, as any leader-writer in a provincial journal might have written; but gathering fire and speed goes on in her own authentic voice "till I had passed the outworks of conventional reserve and crossed the threshold of confidence, and won a place by their hearts' very hearthstone". It is there that she takes her seat; it is the red and fitful glow of the heart's fire which illumines her page. In other words, we read Charlotte Brontë not for exquisite observation of character—her characters are vigorous and elementary; not for comedy—hers is grim and crude; not for a philosophic view of life—hers is that of a country parson's daughter; but for her poetry. Probably that is so with all writers who have, as she has, an overpowering personality, so that, as we say in real life, they have only to open the door to make themselves felt. There is in them some untamed ferocity perpetually at war with the accepted order of things which makes them desire to create instantly rather than to observe patiently. This very ardour, rejecting half shades and other minor impediments, wings its way past the daily conduct of ordinary people and allies itself with their more inarticulate passions. It makes them poets, or, if they choose to write in prose, intolerant of its restrictions. Hence it is that both Emily and Charlotte are always invoking the help of nature. They both feel the need of some more powerful symbol of the vast and slumbering passions in human nature than words or actions can convey. It is with a description of a storm that Charlotte ends her finest novel *Villette*. "The skies hang full and dark—a wrack sails from the west; the clouds cast themselves into strange forms." So she calls in nature to describe a state of mind which could not otherwise be expressed. But neither of the sisters observed nature accurately as Dorothy Wordsworth observed it, or painted it minutely as Tennyson painted it. They seized those aspects of the earth which were most akin to what they themselves felt or imputed to their characters, and so their storms, their moors, their lovely spaces of summer weather are not ornaments applied to decorate a dull page or display the writer's powers of observation—they carry on the emotion and light up the meaning of the book.

The meaning of a book, which lies so often apart from what happens and what is said and consists rather in some connection which things in themselves different have had for the writer, is necessarily hard to grasp. Especially this is so when, like the Brontës, the writer is poetic, and his meaning inseparable from his language, and itself rather a mood than a particular observation. *Wuthering Heights* is a more difficult book to understand than *Jane Eyre*, because Emily was a greater poet than Charlotte. When Charlotte wrote she said with eloquence and splendour and passion "I love", "I hate", "I suffer". Her experience, though more intense, is on a level with our own. But there is no "I" in *Wuthering Heights*. There are no governesses.

21

There are no employers. There is love, but it is not the love of men and women. Emily was inspired by some more general conception. The impulse which urged her to create was not her own suffering or her own injuries. She looked out upon a world cleft into gigantic disorder and felt within her the power to unite it in a book. That gigantic ambition is to be felt throughout the novel—a struggle, half thwarted but of superb conviction, to say something through the mouths of her characters which is not merely "I love" or "I hate", but "we, the whole human race" and "you, the eternal powers . . ." the sentence remains unfinished. It is not strange that it should be so; rather it is astonishing that she can make us feel what she had it in her to say at all. It surges up in the half-articulate words of Catherine Earnshaw, "If all else perished and *he* remained, I should still continue to be; and if all else remained and he were annihilated, the universe would turn to a mighty stranger; I should not seem part of it". It breaks out again in the presence of the dead. "I see a repose that neither earth nor hell can break, and I feel an assurance of the endless and shadowless hereafter—the eternity they have entered—where life is boundless in its duration, and love in its sympathy and joy in its fulness." It is this suggestion of power underlying the apparitions of human nature and lifting them up into the presence of greatness that gives the book its huge stature among other novels. But it was not enough for Emily Brontë to write a few lyrics, to utter a cry, to express a creed. In her poems she did this once and for all, and her poems will perhaps outlast her novel. But she was novelist as well as poet. She must take upon herself a more laborious and a more ungrateful task. She must face the fact of other existences, grapple with the mechanism of external things, build up, in recognisable shape, farms and houses and report the speeches of men and women who existed independently of herself. And so we reach these summits of emotion not by rant or rhapsody but by hearing a girl sing old songs to herself as she rocks in the branches of a tree; by watching the moor sheep crop the turf; by listening to the soft wind breathing through the grass. The life at the farm with all its absurdities and its improbability is laid open to us. We are given every opportunity of comparing *Wuthering Heights* with a real farm and Heathcliff with a real man. How, we are allowed to ask, can there be truth or insight or the finer shades of emotion in men and women who so little resemble what we have seen ourselves? But even as we ask it we see in Heathcliff the brother that a sister of genius might have seen; he is impossible we say, but nevertheless no boy in literature has a more vivid existence than his. So it is with the two Catherines; never could women feel as they do or act in their manner, we say. All the same, they are the most lovable women in English fiction. It is as if she could tear up all that we know human beings by, and fill these unrecognisable transparences with such a gust of life that they transcend reality. Hers, then, is the rarest of all powers. She could free life from its dependence on facts; with a few touches indicate the spirit of a face so that it needs no body; by speaking of the moor make the wind blow and the thunder roar.

HENRY JAMES:
THE OLD ORDER

Written in 1917

With this small volume,[2] which brings us down to about the year 1870, the memories of Henry James break off. It is more fitting to say that they break off than that they come to an end, for although we are aware that we shall hear his voice no more, there is no hint of exhaustion or of leave-taking; the tone is as rich and deliberate as if time were unending and matter infinite; what we have seems to be but the prelude to what we are to have, but a crumb, as he says, of a banquet now forever withheld. Someone speaking once incautiously in his presence of his "completed" works drew from him the emphatic assertion that never, never so long as he lived could there be any talk of completion; his work would end only with his life; and it seems in accord with this spirit that we should feel ourselves pausing, at the end of a paragraph, while in imagination the next great wave of the wonderful voice curves into fullness.

All great writers have, of course, an atmosphere in which they seem most at their ease and at their best; a mood of the great general mind which they interpret and indeed almost discover, so that we come to read them rather for that than for any story or character or scene of separate excellence. For ourselves Henry James seems most entirely in his element, doing that is to say what everything favours his doing, when it is a question of recollection. The mellow light which swims over the past, the

2   *The Middle Years.* By Henry James.

25

beauty which suffuses even the commonest little figures of that time, the shadow in which the detail of so many things can be discerned which the glare of day flattens out, the depth, the richness, the calm, the humour of the whole pageant—all this seems to have been his natural atmosphere and his most abiding mood. It is the atmosphere of all those stories in which aged Europe is the background for young America. It is the half light in which he sees most, and sees farthest. To Americans, indeed, to Henry James and to Hawthorne, we owe the best relish of the past in our literature—not the past of romance and chivalry, but the immediate past of vanished dignity and faded fashions. The novels teem with it; but wonderful as they are, we are tempted to say that the memories are yet more wonderful, in that they are more exactly Henry James, and give more precisely his tone and his gesture. In them his benignity is warmer, his humour richer, his solicitude more exquisite, his recognition of beauty, fineness, humanity more instant and direct. He comes to his task with an indescribable air of one so charged and laden with precious stuff that he hardly knows how to divest himself of it all—where to find space to set down this and that, how to resist altogether the claims of some other gleaming object in the background; appearing so busy, so unwieldy with ponderous treasure that his dexterity in disposing of it, his consummate knowledge of how best to place each fragment, afford us the greatest delight that literature has had to offer for many a year. The mere sight is enough to make anyone who has ever held a pen in his hand consider his art afresh in the light of this extraordinary example of it. And our pleasure at the mere sight soon merges in the thrill with which we recognize, if not directly then by hearsay, the old world of London-life which he brings out of the shades and sets tenderly and solidly before us as if his last gift were the most perfect and precious of the treasures hoarded in "the scented chest of our savings."

After the absence from Europe of about nine years which is recorded in *Notes of a Son and Brother*, he arrived in Liverpool on March 1st, 1869, and found himself "in the face of an opportunity that affected me then and there as the happiest, the most interesting, the most alluring and beguiling that could ever have opened before a somewhat disabled young man who was about to complete his twenty-sixth year." He proceeded to London, and took up his lodging with a "kind slim celibate," a Mr. Lazarus Fox—every detail is dear to him—who let out slices of his house in Half Moon Street to gentlemen lodgers. The London of that day, as Henry James at once proceeded to ascertain with those amazingly delicate and tenacious tentacles of his, was an extremely characteristic and uncompromising organism. "The big broom of change" had swept it hardly at all since the days of Byron at least. She was still the "unaccommodating and unaccommodated city . . . the city too indifferent, too proud, too unaware, too stupid even if one will, to enter any lists that involved her moving from her base and that thereby . . . enjoyed the enormous 'pull,' for making her impression, of ignoring everything but her own perversities and then of driving these home with an emphasis not to be gainsaid." The young American ("brooding monster that I was, born to discriminate à tout propos") was soon breakfasting with the gentleman upstairs (Mr. Albert Rutson), eating his fried sole and marmalade with other gentlemen from the Home Office, the Foreign Office, the House of Commons, whose freedom to lounge over that meal impressed him greatly, and whose close questioning as to the composition of Grant's first Cabinet embarrassed him not a little. The whole scene, which it would be an impiety to dismember further, has the very breath of the age in it. The whiskers, the leisure, the intentness of those gentlemen upon politics, their conviction that the composition of Cabinets was the natural topic for the breakfast-table, and that a stranger unable, as Henry James found himself, to throw light upon it was "only not perfectly ridiculous because perfectly insignificant"—all this provides a picture that many of us will be able to see again as we saw it once perhaps from the perch of an obliging pair of shoulders.

The main facts about that London, as all witnesses agree in testifying, were its smallness compared with our city, the limited number of distractions and amusements available, and the consequent tendency of all people worth knowing to know each other and to form a very accessible and, at the same time, highly enviable society. Whatever the quality that gained you admittance, whether it was that you had done something or showed yourself capable of doing something worthy of respect, the compliment was not an empty one. A young man coming up to London might in a few months claim to have met Tennyson, Browning, Matthew Arnold, Carlyle, Froude, George Eliot, Herbert Spencer, Huxley, and Mill. He had met them; he had not merely brushed against them in a crowd. He had heard them talk; he had even offered something of his own. The conditions of those days allowed a kind of conversation which, so the survivors always maintain, is an art unknown in what they are pleased to call our chaos. What with recurring dinner parties and Sunday calls, and country visits lasting far beyond the week-ends of our generation, the fabric of friendship was solidly built up and carefully preserved. The tendency perhaps was rather to a good fellowship in which the talk was wide-sweeping, extremely well informed, and impersonal than to the less formal, perhaps more intense and indiscriminate, intimacies of to-day. We read of little societies of the sixties, the Cosmopolitan and the Century, meeting on Wednesday and on Sunday evenings to discuss the serious questions of the times, and we have the feeling that they could claim a more representative character than anything of the sort we can show now. We are left with the impression that whatever went forward in those days, either among the statesmen or among the men of letters—and there was a closer connection than there is now—was promoted or inspired by the members of this group. Undoubtedly the resources of the day—and how magnificent they were!—were better organized; and it must occur to every reader of their memoirs that a reason is to be found in the simplicity which accepted the greatness of certain names and imposed something like order on their immediate neighbourhood. Having crowned their kin they worshipped him with the most whole-hearted loyalty. Groups of people would come together at Freshwater, in that old garden where the houses of Melbury Road now stand, or in various London centres, and live as it seems to us for months at a time, some of them indeed for the duration of their lives, in the mood of the presiding genius. Watts and Burne-Jones in one quarter of the town, Carlyle in another, George Eliot in a third, almost as much as Tennyson in his island, imposed their laws upon a circle which had spirit and beauty to recommend it as well as an uncritical devotion.

Henry James, of course, was not a person to accept laws or to make one of any circle in a sense which implies the blunting of the critical powers. Happily for us, he came over not only with the hoarded curiosity of years, but also with the detachment of the stranger and the critical sense of the artist. He was immensely appreciative, but he was also immensely observant. Thus it comes about that his fragment revives, indeed stamps afresh, the great figures of the epoch, and, what is no less important, illumines the lesser figures by whom they were surrounded. Nothing could be happier than his portrait of Mrs. Greville, "with her exquisite good nature and her innocent fatuity," who was, of course, very much an individual, but also a type of the enthusiastic sisterhood which, with all its extravagances and generosities and what we might unkindly, but not without the authority of Henry James, call absurdity, now seems extinct. We shall not spoil the reader's impression of the superb passage describing a visit arranged by Mrs. Greville to George Eliot by revealing what happened on that almost tragic occasion. It is more excusable to dwell for a moment upon the drawing-room at Milford Cottage, the most embowered retreat for social innocence that it was possible to conceive . . . The red candles in the red shades have remained with me, inexplicably, as a vivid note of this pitch, shedding their rosy light, with the autumn gale, the averted reality, all shut out, upon such felicities of feminine helplessness as I couldn't have prefigured in advance, and as exemplified, for further gathering in, the possibilities of the old tone.

The drawn curtains, the "copious service," the second volume of the new novel "half-uncut" laid ready to hand, "the exquisite head and incomparable brush of the domesticated collie"—that is the familiar setting. He recalls the high-handed manner in which these ladies took their way through life, baffling the very stroke of age and disaster with their unquenchable optimism, ladling out with both hands every sort of gift upon their passage, and bringing to port in their tow the most incongruous and battered of derelicts. No doubt "a number of the sharp truths that one might privately apprehend beat themselves beautifully in vain" against such defences. Truth, so it seems to us, was not so much disregarded as flattered out of countenance by the energy with which they pursued the beautiful, the noble, the poetic, and ignored the possibility of another side of things. The extravagant steps which they would take to snare whatever grace or atmosphere they desired at the moment lend their lives in retrospect a glamour of adventure, aspiration, and triumph such as seems for good or for evil banished from our conscious and much more critical day. Was a friend ill? A wall would be knocked down to admit the morning sun. Did the doctor prescribe fresh milk? The only perfectly healthy cow in England was at your service. All this personal exuberance Henry James brings back in the figure of Mrs. Greville, "friend of the super-eminent" and priestess at the different altars. Cannot we almost hear the "pleasant growling note of Tennyson" answering her "mild extravagance of homage" with "Oh, yes, you may do what you like—so long as you don't kiss me before the cabman!"

And then with the entrance of Lady Waterford, Henry James ponders lovingly the quality which seems to hang about those days and people as the very scent of the flower—"the quality of personal beauty, to say nothing of personal accomplishment as our fathers were appointed to enjoy it . . . Scarce to be sated that form of wonder, to my own imagination I confess." Were they as beautiful as we like to remember them, or was it that the whole atmosphere made a beautiful presence, any sort of distinction or eminence indeed, felt in a way no longer so carefully arranged for, or so unquestionably accepted? Was it not all a part of the empty London streets, of the four-wheelers even, lined with straw, of the stuffy little boxes of the public dining rooms, of the protectedness, of the leisure? But if they had merely to stand and be looked at, how splendidly they did it! A certain width of space seems to be a necessary condition for the blooming of such splendid plants as Lady Waterford, who, when she had dazzled sufficiently with her beauty and presence, had only to take up her brush to be acclaimed the equal of Titian or of Watts.

Personality, whatever one may mean by it, seems to have been accorded a licence for the expression of itself for which we can find no parallel in the present day. The gift if you had it was encouraged and sheltered beyond the bounds of what now seems possible. Tennyson, of course, is the supreme example of what we mean, and happily for us Henry James was duly taken to that shrine and gives with extraordinary skill a new version of the mystery which in our case will supersede the old. "The fond prefigurements of youthful piety are predestined, more often than not, I think, experience interfering, to strange and violent shocks . . . Fine, fine, fine, could he only be . . . " So he begins, and so continuing for some time leads us up to the pronouncement that "Tennyson was not Tennysonian." The air one breathed at Aldworth was one in which nothing but "the blest obvious, or at least the blest outright, could so much as attempt to live . . . It was a large and simple and almost empty occasion . . . He struck me in truth as neither knowing nor communicating knowledge." He recited *Locksley Hall* and "Oh dear, oh dear . . . I heard him in cool surprise take even more out of his verse than he had put in." And so by a series of qualifications which are all beautifully adapted to sharpen the image without in the least destroying it, we are led to the satisfactory and convincing conclusion, "My critical reaction hadn't in the least invalidated our great man's being a Bard—it had in fact made him and left him more a Bard than ever." We see, really for the first time, how obvious and simple and almost empty it was, how "the glory was without history," the poetic character "more worn than paid for, or at least more saved than spent," and yet somehow the great man revives and flourishes in the new conditions and dawns upon us more of a Bard than we had got into the habit of thinking him. The same service of defining, limiting, and restoring to life he performs as beautifully for the ghost of George Eliot, and proclaims himself, as the faithful will be glad to hear, "even a very Derondist of Derondists."

And thus looking back into the past which is all changed and gone (he could mark, he said, the very hour or the change) Henry James performs a last act of piety which is supremely characteristic of him. The English world of that day was very clear to him; it had a fineness and a distinction which he professed half humorously not to find in our "vast monotonous mob." It had given him friendship and opportunity and much else, no doubt, that it had no consciousness of giving. Such a gift he of all people could never forget; and this book of memories sounds to us like a superb act of thanksgiving. What could he do to make up for it all, he seems to have asked himself. And then with all the creative power at his command he summons back the past and makes us a present of that. If we could have had the choice, that is what we should have chosen, not entirely for what it gives us of the dead, but also for what it gives us of him. Many will hear his voice again in these pages; they will perceive once more that solicitude for others, that immense desire to help which had its origin, one might guess, in the aloofness and loneliness of the artist's life. It seemed as if he were grateful for the chance of taking part in the ordinary affairs of the world, of assuring himself that, in spite of his absorption with the fine and remote things of the imagination, he had not lost touch with human interests. To acknowledge any claim that was in the least connected with the friends or memories of the past gave him, for this reason, a peculiar joy; and we can believe that if he could have chosen, his last words would have been like these, words of recollection and of love.

MODERN FICTION

First published in 1919

In making any survey, even the freest and loosest, of modern
fiction, it is difficult not to take it for granted that the modern
practice of the art is somehow an improvement upon the old.
With their simple tools and primitive materials, it might be said,
Fielding did well and Jane Austen even better, but compare their
opportunities with ours! Their masterpieces certainly have a
strange air of simplicity. And yet the analogy between literature
and the process, to choose an example, of making motor cars
scarcely holds good beyond the first glance. It is doubtful
whether in the course of the centuries, though we have learnt
much about making machines, we have learnt anything about
making literature. We do not come to write better; all that we
can be said to do is to keep moving, now a little in this direction,
now in that, but with a circular tendency should the whole
course of the track be viewed from a sufficiently lofty pinnacle.
It need scarcely be said that we make no claim to stand, even
momentarily, upon that vantage ground. On the flat, in the
crowd, half blind with dust, we look back with envy to those
happier warriors, whose battle is won and whose achievements
wear so serene an air of accomplishment that we can scarcely
refrain from whispering that the fight was not so fierce for them
as for us. It is for the historian of literature to decide; for him to
say if we are now beginning or ending or standing in the middle
of a great period of prose fiction, for down in the plain little is
visible. We only know that certain gratitudes and hostilities
inspire us; that certain paths seem to lead to fertile land, others

to the dust and the desert; and of this perhaps it may be worth while to attempt some account.

Our quarrel, then, is not with the classics, and if we speak of quarrelling with Mr. Wells, Mr. Bennett, and Mr. Galsworthy, it is partly that by the mere fact of their existence in the flesh their work has a living, breathing, everyday imperfection which bids us take what liberties with it we choose. But it is also true that, while we thank them for a thousand gifts, we reserve our unconditional gratitude for Mr. Hardy, for Mr. Conrad, and in a much lesser degree for the Mr. Hudson of *The Purple Land, Green Mansions,* and *Far Away and Long Ago.* Mr. Wells, Mr. Bennett, and Mr. Galsworthy have excited so many hopes and disappointed them so persistently that our gratitude largely takes the form of thanking them for having shown us what they might have done but have not done; what we certainly could not do, but as certainly, perhaps, do not wish to do. No single phrase will sum up the charge or grievance which we have to bring against a mass of work so large in its volume and embodying so many qualities, both admirable and the reverse. If we tried to formulate our meaning in one word we should say that these three writers are materialists. It is because they are concerned not with the spirit but with the body that they have disappointed us, and left us with the feeling that the sooner English fiction turns its back upon them, as politely as may be, and marches, if only into the desert, the better for its soul. Naturally, no single word reaches the centre of three separate targets. In the case of Mr. Wells it falls notably wide of the mark. And yet even with him it indicates to our thinking the fatal alloy in his genius, the great clod of clay that has got itself mixed up with the purity of his inspiration. But Mr. Bennett is perhaps the worst culprit of the three, inasmuch as he is by far the best workman. He can make a book so well constructed and solid in its craftsmanship that it is difficult for the most exacting of critics to see through what chink or crevice decay can creep in. There is not so much as a draught between the frames of the windows, or a crack in the boards. And yet—if life should refuse to live there? That is a risk which the creator of *The Old Wives' Tale*, George Cannon, Edwin Clayhanger, and hosts of other figures, may well claim to have surmounted. His characters live abundantly, even unexpectedly, but it remains to ask how do they live, and what do they live for? More and more they seem to us, deserting even the well-built villa in the Five Towns, to spend their time in some softly padded first-class railway carriage, pressing bells and buttons innumerable; and the destiny to which they travel so luxuriously becomes more and more unquestionably an eternity of bliss spent in the very best hotel in Brighton. It can scarcely be said of Mr. Wells that he is a materialist in the sense that he takes too much delight in the solidity of his fabric. His mind is too generous in its sympathies to allow him to spend much time in making things shipshape and substantial. He is a materialist from sheer goodness of heart, taking upon his shoulders the work that ought to have been discharged by Government officials, and in the plethora of his ideas and facts scarcely having leisure to realise, or forgetting to think important, the crudity and coarseness of his human beings. Yet what more damaging criticism can there be both of his earth and of his Heaven than that they are to be inhabited here and hereafter by his Joans and his Peters? Does not the inferiority of their natures tarnish whatever institutions and ideals may be provided for them by the generosity of their creator? Nor, profoundly though we respect the integrity and humanity of Mr. Galsworthy, shall we find what we seek in his pages.

If we fasten, then, one label on all these books, on which is one word materialists, we mean by it that they write of unimportant things; that they spend immense skill and immense industry making the trivial and the transitory appear the true and the enduring.

We have to admit that we are exacting, and, further, that we find it difficult to justify our discontent by explaining what it is that we exact. We frame our question differently at different times. But it reappears most persistently as we drop the finished novel on the crest of a sigh—Is it worth while? What is the point of it all? Can it be that, owing to one of those little deviations which the human spirit seems to make from time to time, Mr. Bennett has come down with his magnificent apparatus for catching life just an inch or two on the wrong side? Life escapes; and perhaps without life nothing else is worth while. It is a confession of vagueness to have to make use of such a figure as this, but we scarcely better the matter by speaking, as critics are prone to do, of reality. Admitting the vagueness which afflicts all criticism of novels, let us hazard the opinion that for us at this moment the form of fiction most in vogue more often misses than secures the thing we seek. Whether we call it life or spirit, truth or reality, this, the essential thing, has moved off, or on, and refuses to be contained any longer in such ill-fitting vestments as we provide. Nevertheless, we go on perseveringly, conscientiously, constructing our two and thirty chapters after a design which more and more ceases to resemble the vision in our minds. So much of the enormous labour of proving the solidity, the likeness to life, of the story is not merely labour thrown away but labour misplaced to the extent of obscuring and blotting out the light of the conception. The writer seems constrained, not by his own free will but by some powerful and unscrupulous tyrant who has him in thrall, to provide a plot, to provide comedy, tragedy, love interest, and an air of probability embalming the whole so impeccable that if all his figures were to come to life they would find themselves dressed down to the last button of their coats in the fashion of the hour. The tyrant is obeyed; the novel is done to a turn. But sometimes, more and more often as time goes by, we suspect a momentary doubt, a spasm of rebellion, as the pages fill themselves in the customary way. Is life like this? Must novels be like this?

Look within and life, it seems, is very far from being "like this". Examine for a moment an ordinary mind on an ordinary day. The mind receives a myriad impressions—trivial, fantastic, evanescent, or engraved with the sharpness of steel. From all sides they come, an incessant shower of innumerable atoms; and as they fall, as they shape themselves into the life of Monday or Tuesday, the accent falls differently from of old; the moment of importance came not here but there; so that, if a writer were a free man and not a slave, if he could write what he chose, not what he must, if he could base his work upon his own feeling and not upon convention, there would be no plot, no comedy, no tragedy, no love interest or catastrophe in the accepted style, and perhaps not a single button sewn on as the Bond Street tailors would have it. Life is not a series of gig lamps symmetrically arranged; life is a luminous halo, a semi-transparent envelope surrounding us from the beginning of consciousness to the end. Is it not the task of the novelist to convey this varying, this unknown and uncircumscribed spirit, whatever aberration or complexity it may display, with as little mixture of the alien and external as possible? We are not pleading merely for courage and sincerity; we are suggesting that the proper stuff of fiction is a little other than custom would have us believe it.

It is, at any rate, in some such fashion as this that we seek to define the quality which distinguishes the work of several young writers, among whom Mr. James Joyce is the most notable, from that of their predecessors. They attempt to come closer to life, and to preserve more sincerely and exactly what interests and moves them, even if to do so they must discard most of the conventions which are commonly observed by the novelist. Let us record the atoms as they fall upon the mind in the order in which they fall, let us trace the pattern, however disconnected and incoherent in appearance, which each sight or incident scores upon the consciousness. Let us not take it for granted that life exists more fully in what is commonly thought big than in what is commonly thought small. Any one who has read *The Portrait of the Artist as a Young Man* or, what promises to be a far more interesting work, *Ulysses*[3], now appearing in the *Little Review*, will have hazarded some theory of this nature as to Mr. Joyce's intention. On our part, with such a fragment before us, it is hazarded rather than affirmed; but whatever the intention of the whole, there can be no question but that it is of the utmost sincerity and that the result, difficult or unpleasant as we may judge it, is undeniably important. In contrast with those whom we have called materialists, Mr. Joyce is spiritual; he is concerned at all costs to reveal the flickerings of that innermost flame which flashes its messages through the brain, and in order to preserve it he disregards with complete courage whatever seems to him adventitious, whether it be probability, or coherence, or any other of these signposts which for generations have served to support the imagination of a reader when called upon to imagine what he can neither touch nor see. The scene in the cemetery, for instance, with its brilliancy, its sordidity, its incoherence, its sudden lightning flashes of significance, does undoubtedly come so close to the quick of the mind that, on a first reading at any rate, it is difficult not to acclaim a masterpiece. If we want life itself, here surely we have it. Indeed, we find ourselves fumbling rather awkwardly if we try to say what else we wish, and for what reason a work of such originality yet fails to compare, for we must take high examples, with *Youth* or *The Mayor of Casterbridge*. It fails because of the comparative poverty of the writer's mind, we might say simply and have done with it. But it is possible to press a little further and wonder whether we may not refer our sense of being in a bright yet narrow room, confined and shut in, rather than enlarged and set free, to some limitation imposed by the method as well as by the mind. Is it the method that inhibits the creative power? Is it due to the method that we feel neither jovial nor magnanimous, but centred in a self which, in spite of its tremor of susceptibility, never embraces or creates what is outside itself

3   Written April 1919.

and beyond? Does the emphasis laid, perhaps didactically, upon indecency, contribute to the effect of something angular and isolated? Or is it merely that in any effort of such originality it is much easier, for contemporaries especially, to feel what it lacks than to name what it gives? In any case it is a mistake to stand outside examining "methods". Any method is right, every method is right, that expresses what we wish to express, if we are writers; that brings us closer to the novelist's intention if we are readers. This method has the merit of bringing us closer to what we were prepared to call life itself; did not the reading of *Ulysses* suggest how much of life is excluded or ignored, and did it not come with a shock to open *Tristram Shandy* or even *Pendennis* and be by them convinced that there are not only other aspects of life, but more important ones into the bargain.

However this may be, the problem before the novelist at present, as we suppose it to have been in the past, is to contrive means of being free to set down what he chooses. He has to have the courage to say that what interests him is no longer "this" but "that": out of "that" alone must he construct his work. For the moderns "that", the point of interest, lies very likely in the dark places of psychology. At once, therefore, the accent falls a little differently; the emphasis is upon something hitherto ignored; at once a different outline of form becomes necessary, difficult for us to grasp, incomprehensible to our predecessors. No one but a modern, no one perhaps but a Russian, would have felt the interest of the situation which Tchekov has made into the short story which he calls "Gusev". Some Russian soldiers lie ill on board a ship which is taking them back to Russia. We are given a few scraps of their talk and some of their thoughts; then one of them dies and is carried away; the talk goes on among the others for a time, until Gusev himself dies, and looking "like a carrot or a radish" is thrown overboard. The emphasis is laid upon such unexpected places that at first it seems as if there were no emphasis at all; and then, as the eyes accustom themselves to twilight and discern the shapes of things in a room we see how complete the story is, how profound, and how truly in obedience to his vision Tchekov has chosen this, that, and the other, and placed them together to compose something new. But it is impossible to say "this is comic", or "that is tragic", nor are we certain, since short stories, we have been taught, should be brief and conclusive, whether this, which is vague and inconclusive, should be called a short story at all.

The most elementary remarks upon modern English fiction can hardly avoid some mention of the Russian influence, and if the Russians are mentioned one runs the risk of feeling that to write of any fiction save theirs is waste of time. If we want understanding of the soul and heart where else shall we find it of comparable profundity? If we are sick of our own materialism the least considerable of their novelists has by right of birth a natural reverence for the human spirit. "Learn to make yourself akin to people. . . . But let this sympathy be not with the mind— for it is easy with the mind—but with the heart, with love towards them." In every great Russian writer we seem to discern the features of a saint, if sympathy for the sufferings of others, love towards them, endeavour to reach some goal worthy of the most exacting demands of the spirit constitute saintliness. It is the saint in them which confounds us with a feeling of our own irreligious triviality, and turns so many of our famous novels to tinsel and trickery. The conclusions of the Russian mind, thus comprehensive and compassionate, are inevitably, perhaps, of the utmost sadness. More accurately indeed we might speak of the inconclusiveness of the Russian mind. It is the sense that there is no answer, that if honestly examined life presents question after question which must be left to sound on and on after the story is over in hopeless interrogation that fills us with a deep, and finally it may be with a resentful, despair. They are right perhaps; unquestionably they see further than we do and without our gross impediments of vision. But perhaps we see something that escapes them, or why should this voice of protest mix itself with our gloom? The voice of protest is the voice of another and an ancient civilisation which seems to have bred in us the instinct to enjoy and fight rather than to suffer and understand. English fiction from Sterne to Meredith bears witness to our natural delight in humour and comedy, in the beauty of earth, in the activities of the intellect, and in the splendour of the body. But any deductions that we may draw from the comparison of two fictions so immeasurably far apart are futile save indeed as they flood us with a view of the infinite possibilities of the art and remind us that there is no limit to the horizon, and that nothing—no "method", no experiment, even of the wildest—is forbidden, but only falsity and pretence. "The proper stuff of fiction" does not exist; everything is the proper stuff of fiction, every feeling, every thought; every quality of brain and spirit is drawn upon; no perception comes amiss. And if we can imagine the art of fiction come alive and standing in our midst, she would undoubtedly bid us break her and bully her, as well as honour and love her, for so her youth is renewed and her sovereignty assured.

DEFOE

Written 1919

The fear which attacks the recorder of centenaries lest he should find himself measuring a diminishing spectre and forced to foretell its approaching dissolution is not only absent in the case of *Robinson Crusoe* but the mere thought of it is ridiculous. It may be true that *Robinson Crusoe* is two hundred years of age upon the twenty-fifth of April 1919, but far from raising the familiar speculations as to whether people now read it and will continue to read it, the effect of the bi-centenary is to make us marvel that *Robinson Crusoe*, the perennial and immortal, should have been in existence so short a time as that. The book resembles one of the anonymous productions of the race rather than the effort of a single mind; and as for celebrating its centenary we should as soon think of celebrating the centenaries of Stonehenge itself. Something of this we may attribute to the fact that we have all had *Robinson Crusoe* read aloud to us as children, and were thus much in the same state of mind towards Defoe and his story that the Greeks were in towards Homer. It never occurred to us that there was such a person as Defoe, and to have been told that *Robinson Crusoe* was the work of a man with a pen in his hand would either have disturbed us unpleasantly or meant nothing at all. The impressions of childhood are those that last longest and cut deepest. It still seems that the name of Daniel Defoe has no right to appear upon the title-page of *Robinson Crusoe,* and if we celebrate the bi-centenary of the book we are making a slightly unnecessary allusion to the fact that, like Stonehenge, it is still in existence.

The great fame of the book has done its author some injustice; for while it has given him a kind of anonymous glory it has obscured the fact that he was a writer of other works which, it is safe to assert, were not read aloud to us as children. Thus when the Editor of the *Christian World* in the year 1870 appealed to "the boys and girls of England" to erect a monument upon the grave of Defoe, which a stroke of lightning had mutilated, the marble was inscribed to the memory of the author of *Robinson Crusoe*. No mention was made of *Moll Flanders*. Considering the topics which are dealt with in that book, and in *Roxana, Captain Singleton, Colonel Jack* and the rest, we need not be surprised, though we may be indignant, at the omission. We may agree with Mr. Wright, the biographer of Defoe, that these "are not works for the drawing-room table". But unless we consent to make that useful piece of furniture the final arbiter of taste, we must deplore the fact that their superficial coarseness, or the universal celebrity of *Robinson Crusoe,* has led them to be far less widely famed than they deserve. On any monument worthy of the name of monument the names of *Moll Flanders* and *Roxana,* at least, should be carved as deeply as the name of Defoe. They stand among the few English novels which we can call indisputably great. The occasion of the bicentenary of their more famous companion may well lead us to consider in what their greatness, which has so much in common with his, may be found to consist.

Defoe was an elderly man when he turned novelist, many years the predecessor of Richardson and Fielding, and one of the first indeed to shape the novel and launch it on its way. But it is unnecessary to labour the fact of his precedence, except that he came to his novel-writing with certain conceptions about the art which he derived partly from being himself one of the first to practise it. The novel had to justify its existence by telling a true story and preaching a sound moral. "This supplying a story by invention is certainly a most scandalous crime", he wrote. "It is a sort of lying that makes a great hole in the heart, in which by degrees a habit of lying enters in." Either in the preface or in the text of each of his works, therefore, he takes pains to insist that he has not used his invention at all but has depended upon facts, and that his purpose has been the highly moral desire to convert the vicious or to warn the innocent. Happily these were principles that tallied very well with his natural disposition and endowments. Facts had been drilled into him by sixty years of varying fortunes before he turned his experience to account in fiction. "I have some time ago summed up the Scenes of my life in this distich," he wrote:

No man has tasted differing fortunes more,
And thirteen times I have been rich and poor.

He had spent eighteen months in Newgate and talked with thieves, pirates, highwaymen, and coiners before he wrote the history of Moll Flanders. But to have facts thrust upon you by dint of living and accident is one thing; to swallow them voraciously and retain the imprint of them indelibly, is another. It is not merely that Defoe knew the stress of poverty and had talked with the victims of it, but that the unsheltered life, exposed to circumstances and forced to shift for itself, appealed to him imaginatively as the right matter for his art. In the first pages of each of his great novels he reduces his hero or heroine to such a state of unfriended misery that their existence must be a continued struggle, and their survival at all the result of luck and their own exertions. Moll Flanders was born in Newgate of a criminal mother; Captain Singleton was stolen as a child and sold to the gipsies; Colonel Jack, though "born a gentleman, was put 'prentice to a pickpocket"; Roxana starts under better auspices, but, having married at fifteen, she sees her husband go bankrupt and is left with five children in "a condition the most deplorable that words can express".

Thus each of these boys and girls has the world to begin and the battle to fight for himself. The situation thus created was entirely to Defoe's liking. From her very birth or with half a year's respite at most, Moll Flanders, the most notable of them, is goaded by "that worst of devils, poverty", forced to earn her living as soon as she can sew, driven from place to place, making no demands upon her creator for the subtle domestic atmosphere which he was unable to supply, but drawing upon him for all he knew of strange people and customs. From the outset the burden of proving her right to exist is laid upon her. She has to depend entirely upon her own wits and judgement, and to deal with each emergency as it arises by a rule-of-thumb morality which she has forged in her own head. The briskness of the story is due partly to the fact that having transgressed the accepted laws at a very early age she has henceforth the freedom of the outcast. The one impossible event is that she should settle down in comfort and security. But from the first the peculiar genius of the author asserts itself, and avoids the obvious danger of the novel of adventure. He makes us understand that Moll Flanders was a woman on her own account and not only material for a succession of adventures. In proof of this she begins, as Roxana also begins, by falling passionately, if unfortunately, in love. That she must rouse herself and marry some one else and look very closely to her settlements and prospects is no slight upon her passion, but to be laid to the charge of her birth; and, like all Defoe's women, she is a person of robust understanding. Since she makes no scruple of telling lies when they serve her purpose, there is something undeniable about her truth when she speaks it. She has no time to waste upon the refinements of personal affection; one tear is dropped, one moment of despair allowed, and then "on with the story". She has a spirit that loves to breast the storm. She delights in the exercise of her own powers. When she discovers that the man she has married in Virginia is her own brother she is violently disgusted; she insists upon leaving him; but as soon as she sets foot in Bristol, "I took the diversion of going to Bath, for as I was still far from being old so my humour, which was always gay; continued so to an extreme". Heartless she is not, nor can any one charge her with levity; but life delights her, and a heroine who lives has us all in tow. Moreover, her ambition has that slight strain of imagination in it which puts it in the category of the noble passions. Shrewd and practical of necessity, she is yet haunted by a desire for romance and for the quality which to her perception makes a man a gentleman. "It was really a true gallant spirit he was of, and it was the more grievous to me. 'Tis something of relief even to be undone by a man of honour rather than by a scoundrel", she writes when she had misled a highwayman as to the extent of her fortune. It is in keeping with this temper that she should be proud of her final partner because he refuses to work when they reach the plantations but prefers hunting, and that she should take pleasure in buying him wigs and silver-hilted swords "to make him appear, as he really was, a very fine gentleman". Her very love of hot weather is in keeping, and the passion with which she kissed the ground that her son had trod on, and her noble tolerance of every kind of fault so long as it is not "complete baseness of spirit, imperious, cruel, and relentless when uppermost, abject and low-spirited when down". For the rest of the world she has nothing but good-will.

Since the list of the qualities and graces of this seasoned old sinner is by no means exhausted we can well understand how it was that Borrow's apple-woman on London Bridge called her "blessed Mary" and valued her book above all the apples on her stall; and that Borrow, taking the book deep into the booth, read till his eyes ached. But we dwell upon such signs of character only by way of proof that the creator of Moll Flanders was not, as he has been accused of being, a mere journalist and literal recorder of facts with no conception of the nature of psychology. It is true that his characters take shape and substance of their own accord, as if in despite of the author and not altogether to his liking. He never lingers or stresses any point of subtlety or pathos, but presses on imperturbably as if they came there without his knowledge. A touch of imagination, such as that when the Prince sits by his son's cradle and Roxana observes how "he loved to look at it when it was asleep", seems to mean much more to us than to him. After the curiously modern dissertation upon the need of communicating matters of importance to a second person lest, like the thief in Newgate, we should talk of it in our sleep, he apologises for his digression. He seems to have taken his characters so deeply into his mind that he lived them without exactly knowing how; and, like all unconscious artists, he leaves more gold in his work than his own generation was able to bring to the surface.

The interpretation that we put on his characters might therefore well have puzzled him. We find for ourselves meanings which he was careful to disguise even from his own eye. Thus it comes about that we admire Moll Flanders far more than we blame her. Nor can we believe that Defoe had made up his mind as to the precise degree of her guilt, or was unaware that in considering the lives of the abandoned he raised many deep questions and hinted, if he did not state, answers quite at variance with his professions of belief. From the evidence supplied by his essay upon the "Education of Women" we know that he had thought deeply and much in advance, of his age upon the capacities of women, which he rated very high, and the injustice done to them, which he rated very harsh.

> I have often thought of it as one of the most barbarous customs in the world, considering us as a civilised and a Christian country, that we deny the advantages of learning to women. We reproach the sex every day with folly and impertinence; which I am confident, had they the advantages of education equal to us, they would be guilty of less than ourselves.

The advocates of women's rights would hardly care, perhaps, to claim Moll Flanders and Roxana among their patron saints;

and yet it is clear that Defoe not only intended them to speak some very modern doctrines upon the subject, but placed them in circumstances where their peculiar hardships are displayed in such a way as to elicit our sympathy. Courage, said Moll Flanders, was what women needed, and the power to "stand their ground"; and at once gave practical demonstration of the benefits that would result. Roxana, a lady of the same profession, argues more subtly against the slavery of marriage. She "had started a new thing in the world" the merchant told her; "it was a way of arguing contrary to the general practise". But Defoe is the last writer to be guilty of bald preaching. Roxana keeps our attention because she is blessedly unconscious that she is in any good sense an example to her sex and is thus at liberty to own that part of her argument is "of an elevated strain which was really not in my thoughts at first, at all". The knowledge of her own frailties and the honest questioning of her own motives, which that knowledge begets, have the happy result of keeping her fresh and human when the martyrs and pioneers of so many problem novels have shrunken and shrivelled to the pegs and props of their respective creeds.

But the claim of Defoe upon our admiration does not rest upon the fact that he can be shown to have anticipated some of the views of Meredith, or to have written scenes which (the odd suggestion occurs) might have been turned into plays by Ibsen. Whatever his ideas upon the position of women, they are an incidental result of his chief virtue, which is that he deals with the important and lasting side of things and not with the passing and trivial. He is often dull. He can imitate the matter-of-fact precision of a scientific traveller until we wonder that his pen could trace or his brain conceive what has not even the excuse of truth to soften its dryness. He leaves out the whole of vegetable nature, and a large part of human nature. All this we may admit, though we have to admit defects as grave in many writers whom we call great. But that does not impair the peculiar merit of what remains. Having at the outset limited his scope and confined his ambitions he achieves a truth of insight which is far rarer and more enduring than the truth of fact which he professed to make his aim. Moll Flanders and her friends recommended themselves to him not because they were, as we should say, "picturesque"; nor, as he affirmed, because they were examples of evil living by which the public might profit. It was their natural veracity, bred in them by a life of hardship, that excited his interest. For them there were no excuses; no kindly shelter obscured their motives. Poverty was their taskmaster. Defoe did not pronounce more than a judgement of the lips upon their failings. But their courage and resource and tenacity delighted him. He found their society full of good talk, and pleasant stories, and faith in each other, and morality of a home-made kind. Their fortunes had that infinite variety which he praised and relished and beheld with wonder in his own life. These men and women, above all, were free to talk openly of the passions and desires which have moved men and women since the beginning of time, and thus even now they keep their vitality undiminished. There is a dignity in everything that is looked at openly. Even the sordid subject of money, which plays so large a part in their histories, becomes not sordid but tragic when it stands not for ease and consequence but for honour, honesty, and life itself. You may object that Defoe is humdrum, but never that he is engrossed with petty things.

He belongs, indeed, to the school of the great plain writers, whose work is founded upon a knowledge of what is most persistent, though not most seductive, in human nature. The view of London from Hungerford Bridge, grey, serious, massive, and full of the subdued stir of traffic and business, prosaic if it were not for the masts of the ships and the towers and domes of the city, brings him to mind. The tattered girls with violets in their hands at the street corners, and the old weather-beaten women patiently displaying their matches and bootlaces beneath the shelter of arches, seem like characters from his books. He is of the school of Crabbe and of Gissing, and not merely a fellow-pupil in the same stern place of learning, but its founder and master.

ADDISON

Written in 1919

In July, 1843, Lord Macaulay pronounced the opinion that Joseph Addison had enriched our literature with compositions "that will live as long as the English language". But when Lord Macaulay pronounced an opinion it was not merely an opinion. Even now, at a distance of seventy-six years, the words seem to issue from the mouth of the chosen representative of the people. There is an authority about them, a sonority, a sense of responsibility, which put us in mind of a Prime Minister making a proclamation on behalf of a great empire rather than of a journalist writing about a deceased man of letters for a magazine. The article upon Addison is, indeed, one of the most vigorous of the famous essays. Florid, and at the same time extremely solid, the phrases seem to build up a monument, at once square and lavishly festooned with ornament, which should serve Addison for shelter so long as one stone of Westminster Abbey stands upon another. Yet, though we may have read and admired this particular essay times out of number (as we say when we have read anything three times over), it has never occurred to us, strangely enough, to believe that it is true. That is apt to happen to the admiring reader of Macaulay's essays. While delighting in their richness, force, and variety, and finding every judgement, however emphatic, proper in its place, it seldom occurs to us to connect these sweeping assertions and undeniable convictions with anything so minute as a human being. So it is with Addison. "If we wish", Macaulay writes, "to find anything more vivid than Addison's best portraits, we must go either to Shakespeare or to Cervantes". "We have not the least doubt that if Addison had written a novel on an extensive plan it would have been superior to any that we possess." His essays, again, "fully entitle him to the rank of a great poet"; and, to complete the edifice, we have Voltaire proclaimed "the prince of buffoons", and together with Swift forced to stoop so low that Addison takes rank above them both as a humorist.

Examined separately, such flourishes of ornament look grotesque enough, but in their place—such is the persuasive power of design—they are part of the decoration; they complete the monument. Whether Addison or another is interred within, it is a very fine tomb. But now that two centuries have passed since the real body of Addison was laid by night under the Abbey floor, we are, through no merit of our own, partially qualified to test the first of the flourishes on that fictitious tombstone to which, though it may be empty, we have done homage, in a formal kind of way, these sixty-seven years. The compositions of Addison will live as long as the English language. Since every moment brings proof that our mother tongue is more lusty and lively than sorts with complete sedateness or chastity, we need only concern ourselves with the vitality of Addison. Neither lusty nor lively is the adjective we should apply to the present condition of the *Tatler* and the *Spectator*. To take a rough test, it is possible to discover how many people in the course of a year borrow Addison's works from the public library, and a particular instance affords us the not very encouraging information that during nine years two people yearly take out the first volume of the *Spectator*. The second volume is less in request than the first. The inquiry is not a cheerful one. From certain marginal comments and pencil marks it seems that these rare devotees seek out only the famous passages and, as their habit is, score what we are bold enough to consider the least admirable phrases. No; if Addison lives at all, it is not in the public libraries. It is in libraries that are markedly private, secluded, shaded by lilac trees and brown with folios, that he still draws his faint, regular breath. If any man or woman is going to solace himself with a page of Addison before the June sun is out of the sky to-day, it is in some such pleasant retreat as this.

Yet all over England at intervals, perhaps wide ones, we may be sure that there are people engaged in reading Addison, whatever the year or season. For Addison is very well worth reading. The temptation to read Pope on Addison, Macaulay on Addison, Thackeray on Addison, Johnson on Addison rather than Addison himself is to be resisted, for you will find, if you study the *Tatler* and the *Spectator,* glance at *Cato,* and run through the remainder of the six moderate-sized volumes, that Addison is neither Pope's Addison nor anybody else's Addison, but a separate, independent individual still capable of casting a clear-cut shape of himself upon the consciousness, turbulent and distracted as it is, of nineteen hundred and nineteen. It is true that the fate of the lesser shades is always a little precarious. They are so easily obscured or distorted. It seems so often scarcely worth while to go through the cherishing and humanising process which is necessary to get into touch with a writer of the second class who may, after all, have little to give us. The earth is crusted over them; their features are obliterated, and perhaps it is not a head of the best period that we rub clean in the end, but only the chip of an old pot. The chief difficulty with the lesser writers, however, is not only the effort. It is that our standards have changed. The things that they like are not the things that we like; and as the charm of their writing depends much more upon taste than upon conviction, a change of manners is often quite enough to put us out of touch altogether. That is one of the most troublesome barriers between ourselves and Addison. He attached great importance to certain qualities. He had a very precise notion of what we are used to call "niceness" in man or woman. He was extremely fond of saying that men ought not to be atheists, and that women ought not to wear large petticoats. This directly inspires in us not so much a sense of distaste as a sense of difference. Dutifully, if at all, we strain our imaginations to conceive the kind of audience to whom these precepts were addressed. The *Tatler* was published in 1709; the *Spectator* a year or two later. What was the state of England at that particular moment? Why was Addison so anxious to insist upon the necessity of a decent and cheerful religious belief? Why did he so constantly, and in the main kindly, lay stress upon the foibles of women and their reform? Why was he so deeply impressed with the evils of party government? Any historian will explain; but it is always a misfortune to have to call in the services of any historian. A writer should give us direct certainty; explanations are so much water poured into the wine. As it is, we can only feel that these counsels are addressed to ladies in hoops and gentlemen in wigs—a vanished audience which has learnt its lesson and gone its way and the preacher with it. We can only smile and marvel and perhaps admire the clothes.

And that is not the way to read. To be thinking that dead people deserved these censures and admired this morality, judged the eloquence, which we find so frigid, sublime, the philosophy to us so superficial, profound, to take a collector's joy in such signs of antiquity, is to treat literature as if it were a broken jar of undeniable age but doubtful beauty, to be stood in a cabinet behind glass doors. The charm which still makes *Cato* very readable is much of this nature. When Syphax exclaims,

> So, where our wide Numidian wastes extend,
> Sudden, th'impetuous hurricanes descend,
> Wheel through the air, in circling eddies play,
> Tear up the sands, and sweep whole plains away.
> The helpless traveller, with wild surprise,
> Sees the dry desert all around him rise,
> And smother'd in the dusty whirlwind dies,

we cannot help imagining the thrill in the crowded theatre, the feathers nodding emphatically on the ladies' heads, the gentlemen leaning forward to tap their canes, and every one exclaiming to his neighbour how vastly fine it is and crying "Bravo!" But how can *we* be excited? And so with Bishop Hurd and his notes—his "finely observed", his "wonderfully exact, both in the sentiment and expression", his serene confidence that when "the present humour of idolising Shakespeare is over", the time will come when *Cato* is "supremely admired by all candid and judicious critics". This is all very amusing and productive of pleasant fancies, both as to the faded frippery of our ancestors' minds and the bold opulence of our own. But it is not the intercourse of equals, let alone that other kind of intercourse, which as it makes us contemporary with the author, persuades us that his object is our own. Occasionally in *Cato* one may pick up a few lines that are not obsolete; but for the most part the tragedy which Dr. Johnson thought "unquestionably the noblest production of Addison's genius" has become collector's literature.

Perhaps most readers approach the essays also with some suspicion as to the need of condescension in their minds. The question to be asked is whether Addison, attached as he was to certain standards of gentility, morality, and taste, has not become one of those people of exemplary character and charming urbanity who must never be talked to about anything more exciting than the weather. We have some slight suspicion that the *Spectator* and the *Tatler* are nothing but talk, couched in perfect English, about the number of fine days this year compared with the number of wet the year before. The difficulty of getting on to equal terms with him is shown by the little fable which he introduces into one of the early numbers of the *Tatler,* of "a young gentleman, of moderate understanding, but great vivacity, who . . . had got a little smattering of knowledge, just enough to make an atheist or a freethinker, but not a philosopher, or a man of sense". This young gentleman visits his father in the country, and proceeds "to enlarge the narrowness of the country notions; in which he succeeded so well, that he had seduced the butler by his table-talk, and staggered his eldest sister. . . . 'Till one day, talking of his setting dog . . . said 'he did not question but Tray was as immortal as any one of the family'; and in the heat of the argument told his father, that for his own part, 'he expected to die like a dog'. Upon which, the old man, starting up in a very great passion, cried out, 'Then, sirrah, you shall live like one'; and taking his cane in his hand, cudgelled him out of his system. This had so good an effect upon him, that he took up from that day, fell to reading good books, and is now a bencher in the Middle-Temple". There is a good deal of Addison in that story: his dislike of "dark and uncomfortable prospects"; his respect for "principles which are the support, happiness, and glory of all public societies, as well as private persons"; his solicitude for the butler; and his conviction that to read good books and become a bencher in the Middle-Temple is the proper end for a very vivacious young gentleman. This Mr. Addison married a countess, "gave his little senate laws", and, sending for young Lord Warwick, made that famous remark about seeing how a Christian can die which has fallen upon such evil days that our sympathies are with the foolish, and perhaps fuddled, young peer rather than with the frigid gentleman, not too far gone for a last spasm of self-complacency, upon the bed.

Let us rub off such incrustations, so far as they are due to the corrosion of Pope's wit or the deposit of mid-Victorian lachrymosity, and see what, for us in our time, remains. In the first place, there remains the not despicable virtue, after two centuries of existence, of being readable. Addison can fairly lay claim to that; and then, slipped in on the tide of the smooth, well-turned prose, are little eddies, diminutive waterfalls, agreeably diversifying the polished surface. We begin to take note of whims, fancies, peculiarities on the part of the essayist which light up the prim, impeccable countenance of the moralist and convince us that, however tightly he may have pursed his lips, his eyes are very bright and not so shallow after all. He is alert to his finger-tips. Little muffs, silver garters, fringed gloves draw his attention; he observes with a keen, quick glance, not unkindly, and full rather of amusement than of censure. To be sure, the age was rich in follies. Here were coffee-houses packed with politicians talking of Kings and Emperors and letting their own small affairs go to ruin. Crowds applauded the Italian opera every night without understanding a word of it. Critics discoursed of the unities. Men gave a thousand pounds for a handful of tulip roots. As for women—or "the fair sex", as Addison liked to call them—their follies were past counting. He did his best to count them, with a loving particularity which roused the ill-humour of Swift. But he did it very charmingly, with a natural relish for the task, as the following passage shows:

> I consider woman as a beautiful romantic animal, that may be adorned with furs and feathers, pearls and diamonds, ores and silks. The lynx shall cast its skin at her feet to make her a tippet; the peacock, parrot, and swan, shall pay contributions to her muff; the sea shall be searched for shells, and the rocks for gems; and every part of nature furnish out its share towards the embellishment of a creature that is the most consummate work of it. All this I shall indulge them in; but as for the petticoat I have been speaking of, I neither can nor will allow it.

In all these matters Addison was on the side of sense and taste and civilisation. Of that little fraternity, often so obscure and yet so indispensable, who in every age keep themselves alive to the importance of art and letters and music, watching, discriminating, denouncing and delighting, Addison was one— distinguished and strangely contemporary with ourselves. It would have been, so one imagines, a great pleasure to take him a manuscript; a great enlightenment, as well as a great honour, to have his opinion. In spite of Pope, one fancies that his would have been criticism of the best order, open-minded and generous to novelty, and yet, in the final resort, unfaltering in its standards. The boldness which is a proof of vigour is shown by his defence of "Chevy Chase". He had so clear a notion of what he meant by the "very spirit and soul of fine writing" as to track it down in an old barbarous ballad or rediscover it in "that divine work" "Paradise Lost". Moreover, far from being a connoisseur only of the still, settled beauties of the dead, he was aware of the present; a severe critic of its "Gothic taste", vigilant in protecting the rights and honours of the language, and all in favour of simplicity and quiet. Here we have the Addison of Will's and Button's, who, sitting late into the night and drinking more than was good for him, gradually overcame his taciturnity and began to talk. Then he "chained the attention of every one to him". "Addison's conversation", said Pope, "had something in it more charming than I have found in any other man." One can well believe it, for his essays at their best preserve the very cadence of easy yet exquisitely modulated conversation—the smile checked before it has broadened into laughter, the thought lightly turned from frivolity or abstraction, the ideas springing, bright, new, various, with the utmost spontaneity. He seems to speak what comes into his head, and is never at the trouble of raising his voice. But he has described himself in the character of the lute better than any one can do it for him.

> The lute is a character directly opposite to the drum, that sounds very finely by itself, or in a very small concert. Its notes are exquisitely sweet, and very low, easily drowned in a multitude of instruments, and even lost among a few, unless you give a particular attention to it. A lute is seldom heard in a company of more than five, whereas a drum will show itself to advantage in an assembly of 500. The lutanists, therefore, are men of a fine genius, uncommon reflection, great affability, and esteemed chiefly by persons of a good taste, who are the only proper judges of so delightful and soft a melody.

Addison was a lutanist. No praise, indeed, could be less appropriate than Lord Macaulay's. To call Addison on the strength of his essays a great poet, or to prophesy that if he had written a novel on an extensive plan it would have been "superior to any that we possess", is to confuse him with the drums and trumpets; it is not merely to overpraise his merits, but to overlook them. Dr. Johnson superbly, and, as his manner is, once and for all has summed up the quality of Addison's poetic genius:

> His poetry is first to be considered; of which it must be confessed that it has not often those felicities of diction which give lustre to sentiments, or that vigour of sentiment that animates diction; there is little of ardour, vehemence, or transport; there is very rarely the awfulness of grandeur, and not very often the splendour of elegance. He thinks justly; but he thinks faintly.

The Sir Roger de Coverley papers are those which have the most resemblance, on the surface, to a novel. But their merit consists in the fact that they do not adumbrate, or initiate, or anticipate anything; they exist, perfect, complete, entire in themselves. To read them as if they were a first hesitating experiment containing the seed of greatness to come is to miss the peculiar point of them. They are studies done from the outside by a quiet spectator. When read together they compose a portrait of the Squire and his circle all in characteristic positions—one with his rod, another with his hounds—but each can be detached from the rest without damage to the design or harm to himself. In a novel, where each chapter gains from the one before it or adds to the one that follows it, such separations would be intolerable. The speed, the intricacy, the design, would be mutilated. These particular qualities are perhaps lacking, but nevertheless Addison's method has great advantages. Each of these essays is very highly finished. The characters are defined by a succession of extremely neat, clean strokes. Inevitably, where the sphere is so narrow—an essay is only three or four pages in length—there is not room for great depth or intricate subtlety. Here, from the *Spectator,* is a good example of the witty and decisive manner in which Addison strikes out a portrait to fill the little frame:

> Sombrius is one of these sons of sorrow. He thinks himself obliged in duty to be sad and disconsolate. He looks on a sudden fit of laughter as a breach of his baptismal vow. An innocent jest startles him like blasphemy. Tell him of one who is advanced to a title of honour, he lifts up his hands and eyes; describe a public ceremony, he shakes his head; shew him a gay equipage, he blesses himself. All the little ornaments of life are pomps and vanities. Mirth is wanton, and wit profane. He is scandalized at youth for being lively, and at childhood for being playful. He sits at a christening, or at a marriage-feast, as at a funeral; sighs at the conclusion of a merry story, and grows devout when the rest of the company grow pleasant. After all Sombrius is a religious man, and would have behaved himself very properly, had he lived when Christianity was under a general persecution.

The novel is not a development from that model, for the good reason that no development along these lines is possible. Of its kind such a portrait is perfect; and when we find, scattered up and down the *Spectator* and the *Tatler,* numbers of such little masterpieces with fancies and anecdotes in the same style, some doubt as to the narrowness of such a sphere becomes inevitable. The form of the essay admits of its own particular perfection; and if anything is perfect the exact dimensions of its perfection become immaterial. One can scarcely settle whether, on the whole, one prefers a raindrop to the River Thames. When we have said all that we can say against them—that many are dull, others superficial, the allegories faded, the piety conventional, the morality trite—there still remains the fact that the essays of

Addison are perfect essays. Always at the highest point of any art there comes a moment when everything seems in a conspiracy to help the artist, and his achievement becomes a natural felicity on his part of which he seems, to a later age, half-unconscious. So Addison, writing day after day, essay after essay, knew instinctively and exactly how to do it. Whether it was a high thing, or whether it was a low thing, whether an epic is more profound or a lyric more passionate, undoubtedly it is due to Addison that prose is now prosaic—the medium which makes it possible for people of ordinary intelligence to communicate their ideas to the world. Addison is the respectable ancestor of an innumerable progeny. Pick up the first weekly journal and the article upon the "Delights of Summer" or the "Approach of Age" will show his influence. But it will also show, unless the name of Mr. Max Beerbohm, our solitary essayist, is attached to it, that we have lost the art of writing essays. What with our views and our virtues, our passions and profundities, the shapely silver drop, that held the sky in it and so many bright little visions of human life, is now nothing but a hold-all knobbed with luggage packed in a hurry. Even so, the essayist will make an effort, perhaps without knowing it, to write like Addison.

In his temperate and reasonable way Addison more than once amused himself with speculations as to the fate of his writings. He had a just idea of their nature and value. "I have new-pointed all the batteries of ridicule", he wrote. Yet, because so many of his darts had been directed against ephemeral follies, "absurd fashions, ridiculous customs, and affected forms of speech", the time would come, in a hundred years, perhaps, when his essays, he thought, would be "like so many pieces of old plate, where the weight will be regarded, but the fashion lost". Two hundred years have passed; the plate is worn smooth; the pattern almost rubbed out; but the metal is pure silver.

HENRY JAMES:
WITHIN THE RIM

Written in 1919

It would be easy to justify the suspicion which the sight of *Within the Rim* aroused, and to make it account for the tepid and formal respect with which we own to have approached the book. Essays about the war contributed to albums and books with a charitable object even by the most distinguished of writers bear for the most part such traces of perfunctory composition, such evidence of genius forcibly harnessed to the wagon of philanthropy and sullen and stubborn beneath the lash, that one is inclined for the sake of the writer to leave them unread. But we should not have said this unless we intended immediately and completely to unsay it. The process of reading these essays was a process of recantation. It is possible that the composition of some of them was an act of duty, in the sense that the writing of a chapter of a novel was not an act of duty. But the duty was imposed upon Henry James not by the persuasions of a committee nor by the solicitations of friends, but by a power much more commanding and irresistible—a power so large and of such immense significance to him that he scarcely succeeds with all his range of expression in saying what it was or all that it meant to him. It was Belgium, it was France, it was above all England and the English tradition, it was everything that he had ever cared for of civilization, beauty and art threatened with destruction and arrayed before his imagination in one figure of tragic appeal.

Perhaps no other elderly man existed in August 1914 so well

qualified to feel imaginatively all that the outbreak of war meant as Henry James. For years he had been appreciating ever more and more finely what he calls "the rare, the sole, the exquisite England": he had relished her discriminatingly as only the alien, bred to different sounds and sights and circumstances, could relish others so distinct and so delightful in their distinctness. Knowing so well what she had given him, he was the more tenderly and scrupulously grateful to her for the very reason that she seemed to him to bestow her gifts half in ignorance of their value. Thus when the news came that England was in danger he wandered in the August sunshine half overwhelmed with the vastness of what had happened, reckoning up his debt, conscious to the verge of agony of the extent to which he had committed his own happiness to her, and analysing incessantly and acutely just what it all meant to the world and to him. At first, as he owned, he had "an elderly dread of a waste of emotion . . . my house of the spirit amid everything around me had become more and more the inhabited, adjusted, familiar home"; but before long he found himself building additions and upper storeys, throwing out extensions and protrusions, indulging even, all recklessly, in gables and pinnacles and battlements—things that had presently transformed the unpretending place into I scarce know what to call it, a fortress of the faith, a palace of the soul, an extravagant, bristling, flag-flying structure which had quite as much to do with the air as with the earth.

In a succession of images not to be torn from their context he paints the state of his mind confronted by one aspect after another of what appeared to him in so many diverse lights of glory and of tragedy. His gesture as of one shrinking from the sight of the distress, combined with an irresistible instinct of pity drawing him again and again to its presence, recalls to the present writer his reluctance to take a certain road in Rye because it led past the workhouse gates and forced to his notice the dismal line of tramps waiting for admittance. But in the case of the wounded and the fugitive his humanity forced him again and again to face the sight, and brought him the triumphant reward of finding that the beauty emerging from such conditions more than matched the squalor. " . . . their presence," he wrote of the wounded soldier, "is a blest renewal of faith."

A moralist perhaps might object that terms of beauty and ugliness are not the terms in which to speak of so vast a catastrophe, nor should a writer exhibit so keen a curiosity as to the tremors and vibrations of his own spirit in face of the universal calamity. Yet, of all books describing the sights of war and appealing for our pity, this largely personal account is the one that best shows the dimensions of the whole. It is not merely or even to any great extent that we have been stimulated intellectually by the genius of Henry James to analyse shades and subtleties; but rather that for the first and only time, so far as we are aware, someone has reached an eminence sufficiently high above the scene to give it its grouping and standing in the universal. Read, for instance, the scene of the arrival of the Belgian refugees by night at Rye, which we will not curtail and thus rob of its completeness. It is precisely the same little scene of refugees hurrying by in silence, save for the cry of a woman carrying her child, which, in its thousand varieties, a thousand pens have depicted during the past four years. They have done their best, and left us acknowledging their effort, but feeling it to be a kind of siege or battering ram laid to the emotions, which have obstinately refused to yield their fruits. That it is altogether otherwise with the scene painted for us by Henry James might perhaps be credited to his training as a novelist. But when, in his stately way, diminishing his stature not one whit and majestically rolling the tide of his prose over the most rocky of obstacles, he asks us for the gift of a motor-car, we cannot help feeling that if all philanthropies had such advocates our pockets would never be anything but empty. It is not that our emotions have been harassed by the sufferings of the individual case. That he can do upon occasion with beautiful effect. But what he does in this little book of less than a hundred and twenty pages is, so it seems to us, to present the best statement yet made of the largest point of view. He makes us understand what civilization meant to him and should mean to us. For him it was a spirit that overflowed the material bounds of countries, but it is in France that he sees it most plainly personified:

> . . . what happens to France happens to all that part of ourselves which we are most proud, and most finely advised, to enlarge and cultivate and consecrate . . . She is sole and single in this, that she takes charge of those of the 'interests' of man which most dispose him to fraternize with himself, to pervade all his possibilities and to taste all his faculties, and in consequence to find and to make the earth a friendlier, an easier, and especially a more various sojourn.

If all our counsellors, we cannot help exclaiming, had spoken with that voice!

THE LETTERS
OF HENRY JAMES

Written in 1920

Who, on stepping from the cathedral dusk, the growl and boom of the organ still in the ears, and the eyes still shaded to observe better whatever intricacy of carving or richness of marble may there be concealed, can breast the stir of the street and instantly and briskly sum up and deliver his impressions? How discriminate, how formulate? How, Henry James may be heard grimly asking, dare you pronounce any opinion whatever upon me? In the first place only by taking cover under some such figure as implies that, still dazed and well-nigh drowned, our gesture at the finish is more one of exclamation than of interpretation. To soothe and to inspirit there comes, a moment later, the consciousness that, although in the eyes of Henry James our attempt is foredoomed to failure, nevertheless his blessing is upon it. Renewal of life, on such terms as we can grant it, upon lips, in minds, here in London, here among English men and women, would receive from him the most generous acknowledgment; and with a royal complacency, he would admit that our activities could hardly be better employed. Nor are we left to grope without a guide. It would not be easy to find a difficult task better fulfilled than by Mr. Percy Lubbock in his introduction and connecting pararaphs.[4] It seems to us, and this not only before reading the letters but more emphatically afterwards, that the lines of interpretation he lays down are the

4   *The Letters of Henry James.* Edited by Percy Lubbock.

true ones. They end—as he is the first to declare—in the heart of darkness; but any understanding that we may have won of a difficult problem is at every point fortified and corrected by the help of his singularly thoughtful and intimate essay. His intervention is always illuminating.

It must be admitted that these remarks scarcely seem called for by anything specially abstruse in the first few chapters. If ever a young American proved himself capable of giving a clear and composed account of his experiences in Europe during the seventies of the last century that young American was Henry James. He recounts his seeings and doings, his dinings out and meetings, his country house visits, like a guest too well-bred to show surprise even if he feels it. A "cosmopolitanized American," as he calls himself, was far more likely, it appears, to find things flat than to find them surprising; to sink into the depths of English civilization as if it were a soft feather bed inducing sleep and warmth and security rather than shocks and sensations. Henry James, of course, was much too busy recording impressions to fall asleep; it only appears that he never did anything, and never met anyone, in those early days, capable of rousing him beyond the gay and sprightly mood so easily and amusingly sustained in his letters home. Yet he went everywhere; he met everyone, as the sprinkling of famous names and great occasions abundantly testify. Let one fair specimen suffice:

Yesterday I dined with Lord Houghton—with Gladstone, Tennyson, Dr. Schliemann (the excavator of old Mycenae, &c.), and half a dozen other men of "high culture." I sat next but one to the Bard and heard most of his talk, which was all about port wine and tobacco; he seems to know much about them, and can drink a whole bottle of port at a sitting with no incommodity. He is very swarthy and scraggy, and strikes one' at first as much less handsome than his photos: but gradually you see that it's a face of genius. He had I know not what simplicity, speaks with a strange rustic accent and seemed altogether like a creature of some primordial English stock, a thousand miles away from

American manufacture. Behold me after dinner conversing affably with Mr. Gladstone-not by my own seeking, but by the almost importunate affection of Lord H. But I was glad of a chance to feel the "personality" of a great political leader—or as G. is now thought here even, I think, by his partisans, ex-leader. That of Gladstone is very fascinating—his urbanity extreme-his eye that of a man of genius—and his apparent self-surrender to what he is talking of without a flaw. He made a great impression on me—greater than anyone I have seen here: though 'tis perhaps owing to my *naïveté*, and unfamiliarity with statesmen . . .

And so to the Oxford and Cambridge boat-race. The impression is well and brightly conveyed; what we miss, perhaps, is any body of resistance to the impression—any warrant for thinking that the receiving mind is other than a stretched white sheet. The best comment upon that comes in his own words a few pages later. "It is something to have learned how to write." If we look upon many of these early pages as experiments in the art of writing by one whose standard of taste exacts that small things must be done perfectly before big things are even attempted, we shall understand that their perfection is of the inexpressive kind that often precedes a late maturity. He is saying all that his means allow him to say. Moreover, he is saying it already, as most good letter writers learn to say it, not to an individual but to a chosen assembly. "It is, indeed, I think, the very essence of a good letter to be shown," he wrote; "it is wasted if it is kept for *one* . . . I give you full leave to read mine aloud at your soirees!" Therefore, if we refrain from quotation, it is not that passages of the necessary quality are lacking. It is, rather, that while he writes charmingly, intelligently and adequately of this, that and the other, we begin by guessing and end by resenting the fact that his mind is elsewhere. It is not the dinner parties—a hundred and seven in one season—nor the ladies and gentlemen, nor even the Tennysons and the Gladstones that interest him primarily; the pageant passes before him: the impressions ceaselessly descend; and yet as we watch we also wait for the clue, the secret of it all.

It is, indeed, clear that if he discharged the duties of his position with every appearance of equanimity the choice of the position itself was one of momentous importance, constantly requiring examination, and, with its promise of different possibilities, harassing his peace till the end of time. On what spot of the civilized globe was he to settle? His vibrations and vacillations in front of that problem suffer much in our report of them, but in the early days the case against America was simply that " . . . it takes an old civilization to set a novelist in motion."

Next, Italy presented herself; but the seductions of "the golden climate" were fatal to work. Paris had obvious advantages, but the drawbacks were equally positive—"I have seen almost nothing of the literary fraternity, and there are fifty reasons why I should not become intimate with them. I don't like their wares, and they don't like any others; and, besides, they are not *accueillants*." London exercised a continuous double pressure of attraction and repulsion to which finally he succumbed, to the extent of making his headquarters in the metropolis without shutting his eyes to her faults. "I am attracted to London in spite of the long list of reasons why I should not be; I think it, on the whole, the best point of view in the world . . . But the question is interminable." When he wrote that, he was thirty-seven; a mature age; an age at which the native growing confidently in his own soil is already putting forth whatever flower fate ordains and natural conditions allow. But Henry James had neither roots nor soil; he was of the tribe of wanderers and aliens; a winged visitant, ceaselessly circling and seeking, unattached, uncommitted, ranging hither and thither at his own free will, and only at length precariously settling and delicately inserting his proboscis in the thickset lusty blossoms of the old garden beds.

Here, then, we distinguish one of the strains, always to some extent present in the letters before us, from which they draw their unlikeness to any others in the language, and, indeed, bring us at times to doubt whether they are "in the language" at all. If London is primarily a point of view, if the whole field of human activity is only a prospect and a pageant, then we cannot help asking, as the store of impressions heaps itself up, what is the aim of the spectator, what is the purpose of his hoard? A spectator, alert, aloof, endlessly interested, endlessly observant, Henry James undoubtedly was; but as obviously, though not so simply, the long drawn process of adjustment and preparation was from first to last controlled and manipulated by a purpose which, as the years went by, only dealt more powerfully and completely with the treasures of a more complex sensibility. Yet, when we look to find the purpose expressed, to see the material in the act of transmutation, we are met by silence, we are blindly waved outside. "To write a series of good little tales I deem ample work for a life time. It's at least a relief to have arranged one's life time." The words are youthful, perhaps intentionally light but few and frail as they are, they have almost alone to bear the burden built upon them, to answer the questions and quiet the suspicions of those who insist that a writer must have a mission and proclaim it aloud. Scarcely for a moment does Henry James talk of his writing; never for an instant is the thought of it absent from his mind. Thus, in the letters to Stevenson abroad we hear behind everything else a brooding murmur of amazement and horror at the notion of living with savages. How, he seems to be asking himself, while on the surface all is admiration and affection, can he endure it—how could I write my books if I lived in Samoa with savages? All refers to his writing; all points in to that preoccupation. But so far as actual statement goes the books might have sprung as silently and spontaneously as daffodils in spring. No notice is taken of their birth. Nor does it matter to him what people say. Their remarks are probably wide of the point, or if they have a passing truth they are uttered in unavoidable ignorance of the fact that each book is a step onward in a gradual process of evolution, the plan of which is onward only to the author himself. He remains inscrutable. silent, and assured.

How, then, are we to explain the apparent inconsistency of his disappointment when, some years later, the failure of *The Bostonians* and *Princess Casamassima* brought him face to face with the fact that he was not destined to be a popular novelist—

> . . . I am still staggering [he wrote] a good deal under the mysterious and to me inexplicable injury wrought—apparently—upon my situation by my two last novels, the *Bostonians* and the *Princess*, from which I expected so much and derived so little. They have reduced the desire, and the demand, for my productions to zero—as I judge from the fact that though I have for a good while past been writing a number of good short things, I remain irremediably unpublished.

Compensations at once suggested themselves; he was "really in better form then ever" and found himself "holding the 'critical world' at large in singular contempt" but we have Mr. Lubbock's authority for supposing that it was chiefly a desire to retrieve the failure of the novels that led him to strive so strenuously, and in the end so disastrously, for success upon the stage. Success and failure upon the lips of a man who never for a moment doubted the authenticity of his genius or for a second lowered his standard of the artist's duty have not their ordinary meaning. Perhaps we may hold that failure in the sense that Henry James used it meant, more than anything, failure on the part of the public to receive. That was the public's fault, but that did not lessen the catastrophe or make less desirable the vision of an order of things where the public gratefully and with understanding accepts at the artists' hands what is, after all, the finest essence, transmuted and returned, of the public itself. When *Guy Domville* failed, and Henry James for one "abominable quarter of an hour" faced the "yelling barbarians" and "learned what could be the savagery of their disappointment that one wasn't perfectly the *same* as everything else they had ever seen" he had no doubt of his genius; but he went home to reflect:

> I have felt for a long time past that I have fallen upon evil
> days—every sign and symbol of one's being in the least
> wanted, anywhere or by anyone, having so utterly failed. A
> new generation, that I know not, and mainly prize not, has
> taken universal possession.

The public henceforward appeared to him, so far as it appeared at all, a barbarian crowd incapable of taking in their rude paws the beauty and delicacy that he had to offer. More and more was he confirmed in his conviction that an artist can neither live with the public, write for it, nor seek his material in the midst of it. A select group, representative of civilization, had at the same time protested its devotion, but how far can one write for a select group? Is not genius itself restricted, or at least influenced in its very essence by the consciousness that its gifts are to the few, its concern with the few, and its revelation apparent only to scattered enthusiasts who may be the advance guard of the future or only a little band strayed from the high road and doomed to extinction while civilization marches irresistibly elsewhere? All this Henry James poised, pondered, and held in debate. No doubt the influence upon the direction of his work was profound. But for all that he went serenely forward; bought a house, bought a typewriter, shut himself up, surrounded himself with furniture of the right period, and was able at the critical moment by the timely, though rash, expenditure of a little capital to ensure that certain hideous new cottages did not deface his point of view. One admits to a momentary malice. The seclusion is so deliberate; the exclusion so complete. All within the sanctuary is so prosperous and smooth. No private responsibilities harassed him; no public duties claimed him; his health was excellent and his income, in spite of his protests to the contrary, more than adequate to his needs. The voice that issued from the hermitage might well speak calmly, subtly, of exquisite emotions, and yet now and then we are warned by something exacting and even acid in its tone that the effects of seclusion are not altogether benign. "Yes. Ibsen is ugly, common, hard, prosaic, bottomlessly bourgeois. . . ." "But, oh, yes, dear Louis, [*Tess of The D'urbervilles*] is vile. The pretence of 'sexuality' is only equalled by the absence of it, and the abomination of the language by the author's reputation for style." The lack of "aesthetic curiosity" in Meredith and his circle was highly to be deplored. The artist in him "was nothing to the good citizen and liberalized bourgeois." The works of Tolstoy and Dostoevsky are "fluid puddings" and "when you ask me if I don't feel Dostoevsky's 'mad jumble, that flings things down in a heap,' nearer truth and beauty than the picking up and composing that you instance in Stevenson, I reply with emphasis that I feel nothing of the sort." It is true that in order to keep these points at their sharpest one has had to brush aside a mass of qualification and explanation which make each the apex of a formidable body of criticism. It is only for a moment that the seclusion seems cloistered, and the feelings of an artist confounded with those of a dilettante.

Yet as that second flits across the mind, with the chill of a shadow brushing the waves, we realize what a catastrophe for all of us it would have been if the prolonged experiment, the struggle and the solitude of Henry James's life had ended in failure. Excuses could have been found both for him and for us. It is impossible, one might have said, for the artist not to compromise, or, if he persists in his allegiance, then, almost inevitably, he must live apart, for ever alien, slowly perishing in his isolation. The history of literature is strewn with examples of both disasters. When, therefore, almost perceptibly at a given moment, late in the story, something yields, something is overcome, something dark and dense glows in splendour, it is as if the beacon flamed bright on the hilltop; as if before our eyes the crown of long deferred completion and culmination swung slowly into place. Not columns but pages, and not pages but chapters, might be filled with comment and attempted analysis of this late and mighty flowering, this vindication, this crowded gathering together and superb welding into shape of all the separate strands, alien instincts, irreconcilable desires of the twofold nature. For, as we dimly perceive, here at last two warring forces have coalesced; here, by a prodigious efflort of concentration, the field of human activity is brought into fresh focus, revealing new horizons, new landmarks, and new lights upon it of right and wrong.

But it is for the reader at leisure to delve in the rich material of the later letters and build up from it the complex figure of the artist in his completeness. If we choose two passages—one upon conduct, the other upon the gift of a leather dressing case—to represent Henry James in his later mood we purposely brush aside a thousand others which have innumerable good claims to be put in their place.

If there be a wisdom in not feeling—to the last throb—the great things that happen to us, it is a wisdom that I shall never either know or esteem. Let your soul live—it's the only life that isn't on the whole a sell . . .

That [the dressing case] is the grand fact of the situation— that is the tawny lion, portentous creature in my path. I can't get past him, I can't get round him, and on the other hand he stands glaring at me, refusing to give way and practically blocking all my future. I can't live with him, you see; because I can't live *up* to him. His claims, his pretensions, his dimensions, his assumptions and consumptions, above all the manner in which he causes every surrounding object (on my poor premises or within my poor range) to tell a dingy, or deplorable tale—all this makes him the very scourge of my life, the very blot on my scutcheon. He doesn't regild that rusty metal—he simply takes up an attitude of gorgeous swagger, straight in front of all the rust and the rubbish, which makes me look as if I had stolen *somebody else's* (regarnished *blason*) and were trying to palm it off as my own . . . *he is out of the picture*—out of *mine*; and behold me condemned to live for ever with that canvas turned to the wall. Do you know what that means?

And so on and so on. There, portentous and prodigious, we hear unmistakably the voice of Henry James. There, to our thinking, we have exploded in our ears the report of his enormous, sustained, increasing, and overwhelming love of life. It issues from whatever tortuous channels and dark tunnels like a flood at its fullest. There is nothing too little, too large, too remote, too queer for it not to flow round, float off and make its own. Nothing in the end has chilled or repressed him; everything has fed and filled him; the saturation is complete. The labours of the morning might be elaborate and austere. There remained an irrepressible fund of vitality which the flying hand at midnight addressed fully and affectionately to friend after friend, each sentence, from the whole fling of his person to the last snap of his fingers, firmly fashioned and throwing out at its swiftest well nigh incredible felicities of phrase.

The only difficulty, perhaps, was to find an envelope that would contain the bulky product, or any reason, when two sheets were blackened, for not filling a third. Truly, Lamb House was no sanctuary, but rather a "small, crammed and wholly unlucrative hotel," and the hermit no meagre solitary but a tough and even stoical man of the world, English in his humour, Johnsonian in his sanity, who lived every second with insatiable gusto and in the flux and fury of his impressions obeyed his own injunction to remain "as solid and fixed and dense as you can." For to be as subtle as Henry James one must also be as robust; to enjoy his power of exquisite selection one must have "lived and loved and cursed and floundered and enjoyed and suffered," and, with the appetite of a giant, have swallowed the whole.

Yet, if he shared with magnanimity, if he enjoyed hugely, there remained something incommunicable, something reserved, as if in the last resort, it was not to us that he turned, nor from us that he received, nor into our hands that he placed his offerings. There they stand, the many books, products of "an inexhaustible sensibility," all with the final seal upon them of artistic form, which, as it imposes its stamp, sets apart the object thus consecrated and makes it no longer part of ourselves. In this impersonality the maker himself desired to share—"to take it," as he said, "wholly, exclusively with the pen (the style, the genius) and absolutely not at all with the person," to be "the mask without the face," the alien in our midst, the worker who when his work is done turns even from that and reserves his confidence for the solitary hour, like that at midnight when, alone on the threshold of creation, Henry James speaks aloud to himself "and the prospect clears and flushes, and my poor blest old genius pats me so admirably and lovingly on the back that I turn, I screw round, and bend my lips to passionately, in my gratitude, kiss its hands." So that is why, perhaps, as life swings and clangs, booms and reverberates, we have the sense of an altar of service, of sacrifice, to which, as we pass out, we bend the knee.

SIR WALTER SCOTT.
THE ANTIQUARY

Written in 1924

There are some writers who have entirely ceased to influence others, whose fame is for that reason both serene and cloudless, who are enjoyed or neglected rather than criticised and read. Among them is Scott. The most impressionable beginner, whose pen oscillates if exposed within a mile of the influence of Stendhal, Flaubert, Henry James, or Chekhov, can read the Waverley Novels one after another without altering an adjective. Yet there are no books perhaps upon which at this moment more thousands of readers are brooding and feasting in a rapture of uncritical and silent satisfaction. And if this is the mood in which the Waverley Novels are read, the inference is perhaps that there is something vicious about such a pleasure; it cannot be defended; it must be enjoyed in secret. Let us run through *The Antiquary* again and make a note or two as we go. The first charge that is levelled against Scott is that his style is execrable. Every page of the novel, it is true, is watered down with long languid Latin words—peruse, manifest, evince. Old metaphors out of the property box come flapping their dusty wings across the sky. The sea in the heat of a crisis is "the devouring element". A gull on the same occasion is a "winged denizen of the crag". Taken from their context it is impossible to deny that such expressions sound wrong, though a good case might be made against the snobbery which insists upon preserving class distinctions even among words. But read currently in their places, it is difficult either to notice or to condemn them. As

Scott uses them they fulfil their purpose and merge perfectly in their surroundings. Great novelists who are going to fill seventy volumes write after all in pages, not in sentences, and have at their command, and know when to use, a dozen different styles of varying intensities. The genteel pen is a very useful pen in its place. These slips and slovenlinesses serve as relaxations; they give the reader breathing space and air the book. Let us compare Scott the slovenly with Stevenson the precise. "It was as he said: there was not a breath stirring; a windless stricture of frost had bound the air; and as we went forth in the shine of the candles, the blackness was like a roof over our heads." One may search the Waverley Novels in vain for such close writing as this. But if we get from Stevenson a much closer idea of a single object, we get from Scott an incomparably larger impression of the whole. The storm in *The Antiquary,* made up as it is of stage hangings and cardboard screens, of "denizens of the crags" and "clouds like disasters round a sinking empire", nevertheless roars and splashes and almost devours the group huddled on the crag; while the storm in *Kidnapped,* for all its exact detail and its neat dapper adjectives, is incapable of wetting the sole of a lady's slipper.

The much more serious charge against Scott is that he used the wrong pen, the genteel pen, not merely to fill in the background and dash off a cloud piece, but to describe the intricacies and passions of the human heart. But what language to use of the Lovels and Isabellas, the Darsies, Ediths, and Mortons! As well talk of the hearts of seagulls and the passions and intricacies of walking-sticks and umbrellas; for indeed these ladies and gentlemen are scarcely to be distinguished from the winged denizens of the crag. They are equally futile; equally impotent; they squeak; they flutter; and a strong smell of camphor exudes from their poor dried breasts when, with a dismal croaking and cawing, they emit the astonishing language of their love-making.

"Without my father's consent, I will never entertain the addresses of anyone; and how totally impossible it is that he should countenance the partiality with which you honour me, you are yourself fully aware," says the young lady. "Do not add to the severity of repelling my sentiments the rigour of obliging me to disavow them," replies the young gentleman; and he may be illegitimate, and he may be the son of a peer, or he may be both one and the other, but it would take a far stronger inducement than that to make us care a straw what happens to Lovel and his Isabella.

But then, perhaps, we are not meant to care a straw. When Scott has pacified his conscience as a magistrate by alluding to the sentiments of the upper classes in tones of respect and esteem, when he has vindicated his character as a moralist by awakening "the better feelings and sympathies of his readers by strains of generous sentiment and tales of fictitious woe", he was quit both of art and of morals, and could scribble endlessly for his own amusement. Never was a change more emphatic; never one more wholly to the good. One is tempted, indeed, to suppose that he did it, half-consciously, on purpose—he showed up the languor of the fine gentlemen who bored him by the immense vivacity of the common people whom he loved. Images, anecdotes, illustrations drawn from sea, sky, and earth, race and bubble from their lips. They shoot every thought as it flies, and bring it tumbling to the ground in metaphor. Sometimes it is a phrase—"at the back of a dyke, in a wreath o' snaw, or in the wame o' a wave"; sometimes a proverb—"he'll no can haud down his head to sneeze, for fear o' seeing his shoon"; always the dialogue is sharpened and pointed, by the use of that Scottish dialect which is at once so homely and so pungent, so colloquial and so passionate, so shrewd and so melancholy into the bargain. And the result is strange. For since the sovereigns who should preside have abdicated, since we are afloat on a broad and breezy sea without a pilot, the Waverley Novels are as unmoral as Shakespeare's plays. Nor, for some readers, is it the least part of their astonishing freshness, their perennial vitality, that you may read them over and over again, and never know for certain what Scott himself was or what Scott himself thought.

We know, however, what his characters are, and we know it almost as we know what our friends are by hearing their voices and watching their faces simultaneously. However often one may have read *The Antiquary,* Jonathan Oldbuck is slightly different every time. We notice different things; our observation of face and voice differs; and thus Scott's characters, like Shakespeare's and Jane Austen's, have the seed of life in them. They change as we change. But though this gift is an essential element in what we call immortality, it does not by any means prove that the character lives as profoundly, as fully, as Falstaff lives or Hamlet. Scott's characters, indeed, suffer from a serious disability; it is only when they speak that they are alive; they never think; as for prying into their minds himself, or drawing inferences from their behaviour, Scott never attempted it. "Miss Wardour, as if she felt that she had said too much, turned and got into the carriage"—he will penetrate no further into the privacy of Miss Wardour than that; and it is not far. But this matters the less because the characters he cared for were by temperament chatterboxes; Edie Ochiltree, Oldbuck, Mrs. Mucklebackit talk incessantly. They reveal their characters in talk. If they stop talking it is to act. By their talk and by their acts—that is how we know them.

But how far then can we know people, the hostile critic may ask, if we only know that they say this and do that, if they never talk about themselves, and if their creator lets them go their ways, provided they forward his plot, in complete independence of his supervision or interference? Are they not all of them, Ochiltrees, Antiquaries, Dandy Dinmonts, and the rest, merely bundles of humours, and innocent childish humours at that, who serve to beguile our dull hours and charm our sick ones, and are packed off to the nursery when the working day returns and our normal faculties crave something tough to set their teeth into? Compare the Waverley Novels with the novels of Tolstoy, of Stendhal, of Proust! These comparisons of course lead to questions that lie at the root of fiction, but without discussing them, they reveal unmistakably what Scott is not. He is not among the great observers of the intricacies of the heart. He is not going to break seals or loose fountains. But he has the power of the artist who can create a scene and leave us to analyse it for ourselves. When we read the scene in the cottage where Steenie Mucklebackit lies dead, the different emotions—the father's grief, the mother's irritability, the minister's consolations—all rise spontaneously, as if Scott had merely to record, and we have merely to observe. What we lose in intricacy we gain perhaps in spontaneity and the stimulus given to our own creative powers. It is true that Scott creates carelessly, as if the parts came together without his willing it; it is true also that his scene breaks into ruin without his caring.

For who taps at the door and destroys that memorable scene? The cadaverous Earl of Glenallan; the unhappy nobleman who had married his sister in the belief that she was his cousin; and had stalked the world in sables ever after. Falsity breaks in; the peerage breaks in; all the trappings of the undertaker and heralds' office press upon us their unwholesome claims. The emotions then in which Scott excels are not those of human beings pitted against other human beings, but of man pitted against Nature, of man in relation to fate. His romance is the romance of hunted men hiding in woods at night; of brigs standing out to sea; of waves breaking in the moonlight; of solitary sands and distant horsemen; of violence and suspense. And he is perhaps the last novelist to practise the great, the Shakespearean art, of making people reveal themselves in speech.

AMERICAN FICTION

Written in 1925

Excursions into the literature of a foreign country much resemble our travels abroad. Sights that are taken for
granted by the inhabitants seem to us astonishing; however well we seemed to know the language at home, it sounds differently on the lips of those who have spoken it from birth; and above all, in our desire to get at the heart of the country we seek out whatever it may be that is most unlike what we are used to, and declaring this to be the very essence of the French or American genius proceed to lavish upon it a credulous devotion, to build up upon it a structure of theory which may well amuse, annoy, or even momentarily enlighten those who are French or American by birth.

The English tourist' in American literature wants above all things something different from what he has at home. For this reason the one American writer whom the English wholeheartedly admire is Walt Whitman. There, you will hear them say, is the real American undisguised. In the whole of English literature there is no figure which resembles his—among all our poetry none in the least comparable to *Leaves of Grass*. This very unlikeness becomes a merit, and leads us, as we steep ourselves in the refreshing unfamiliarity, to become less and less able to appreciate Emerson, Lowell, Hawthorne, who have had their counterparts among us and drew their culture from our books. The obsession, whether well or ill founded, fair or unfair in its results, persists at the present moment. To dismiss such distinguished names as those of Henry James,

Mr. Hergesheimer, and Mrs. Wharton would be impossible; but their praises are qualified with the reservation—they are not Americans; they do not give us anything that we have not got already.

Thus having qualified the tourist's attitude, in its crudity and one-sidedness, let us begin our excursion into modern American fiction by asking what are the sights we ought to see. Here our bewilderment begins; for the names of so many authors, the titles of so many books, rise at once to the lips. Mr. Dreiser, Mr. Cabell, Miss Canfield, Mr. Sherwood Anderson, Miss Hurst, Mr. Sinclair Lewis, Miss Willa Cather, Mr. Ring Lardner—all have done work which, if time allowed, we should do well to examine carefully, and, if we must concentrate upon two or three at most, it is because, travellers and tourists as we are, it seems best to sketch a theory of the tendency of American fiction from the inspection of a few important books rather than to examine each writer separately by himself. Of all American novelists the most discussed and read in England at the present moment are probably Mr. Sherwood Anderson and Mr. Sinclair Lewis. And among all their fiction we find one volume, *A Story Teller's Story*, which, being fact rather than fiction, may serve as interpreter, may help us to guess the nature of American writers' problems before we see them tussled with or solved. Peering over Mr. Sherwood Anderson's shoulder, we may get a preliminary view of the world as it looks to the novelist before it is disguised and arranged for the reception of his characters. Indeed, if we look over Mr. Anderson's shoulder, America appears a very strange place. What is it that we see here? A vast continent, scattered here and there with brand new villages which nature has not absorbed into herself with ivy and moss, summer and winter, as in England, but man has built recently, hastily, economically, so that the village is like the suburb of a town. The slow English wagons are turned into Ford cars; the primrose banks have become heaps of old tins; the barns sheds of corrugated iron. It is cheap, it is new, it is ugly, it is made of odds and ends, hurriedly flung together, loosely tied in temporary cohesion—that is the burden of Mr. Anderson's complaint. And, he proceeds to ask, how can the imagination of an artist take root here, where the soil is stony and the imagination stubs itself upon the rocks? There is one solution and one only—by being resolutely and defiantly American. Explicitly and implicitly that is the conclusion he reaches; that is the note which turns the discord to harmony. Mr. Anderson is for ever repeating over and over like a patient hypnotising himself, "I am the American man". The words rise in his mind with the persistency of a submerged but fundamental desire. Yes, he is the American man; it is a terrible misfortune; it is an enormous opportunity; but for good or for bad, he is the American man. "Behold in me the American man striving to become an artist, to become conscious of himself, filled with wonder concerning himself and others, trying to have a good time and not fake a good time. I am not English, Italian, Jew, German, Frenchman, Russian. What am I?" Yes, we may be excused for repeating, what is he? One thing is certain— whatever the American man may be, he is not English; whatever he may become, he will not become an Englishman.

For that is the first step in the process of being American—to be not English. The first step in the education of an American writer is to dismiss the whole army of English words which have marched so long under the command of dead English generals. He must tame and compel to his service the "little American words"; he must forget all that he learnt in the school of Fielding and Thackeray; he must learn to write as he talks to men in Chicago bar-rooms, to men in the factories of Indiana. That is the first step; but the next step is far more difficult. For having decided what he is not, he must proceed to discover what he is. This is the beginning of a stage of acute self-consciousness which manifests itself in writers otherwise poles asunder. Nothing, indeed, surprises the English tourist more than the prevalence of this self-consciousness and the bitterness, for the most part against England, with which it is accompanied. One is reminded constantly of the attitude of another race, till lately subject and still galled by the memory of its chains. Women writers have to meet many of the same problems that beset Americans. They too are conscious of their own peculiarities as a sex; apt to suspect insolence, quick to avenge grievances, eager to shape an art of their own. In both cases all kinds of consciousness— consciousness of self, of race, of sex, of civilisation—which have nothing to do with art, have got between them and the paper, with results that are, on the surface at least, unfortunate. It is easy enough to see that Mr. Anderson, for example, would be a much more perfect artist if he could forget that he is an American; he would write better prose if he could use all words impartially, new or old, English or American, classical or slang.

Nevertheless as we turn from his autobiography to his fiction we are forced to own (as some women writers also make us own) that to come fresh to the world, to turn a new angle to the light, is so great an achievement that for its sake we can pardon the bitterness, the self-consciousness, the angularity which inevitably go with it. In *The Triumph of the Egg* there is some rearrangement of the old elements of art which makes us rub our eyes. The feeling recalls that with which we read Chekhov for the first time. There are no familiar handles to lay hold of in *The Triumph of the Egg*. The stories baffle our efforts, slip through our fingers and leave us feeling, not that it is Mr. Anderson who has failed us, but that we as readers have muffed our work and must go back, like chastened schoolchildren, and spell the lesson over again in the attempt to lay hold of the meaning.

Mr. Anderson has bored into that deeper and warmer layer of human nature which it would be frivolous to ticket new or old, American or European. In his determination to be "true to the essence of things" he has fumbled his way into something genuine, persistent, of universal significance, in proof of which he has done what, after all, very few writers succeed in doing— he has made a world of his own. It is a world in which the senses flourish; it is dominated by instincts rather than by ideas;

racehorses make the hearts of little boys beat high; cornfields flow around the cheap towns like golden seas, illimitable and profound; everywhere boys and girls are dreaming of voyages and adventures, and this world of sensuality and instinctive desire is clothed in a warm cloudy atmosphere, wrapped about in a soft caressing envelope, which always seems a little too loose to fit the shape. Pointing to the formlessness of Mr. Anderson's work, the vagueness of his language, his tendency to land his stories softly in a bog, the English tourist would say that all this confirms him in his theory of what is to be expected of an American writer of insight and sincerity. The softness, the shellessness of Mr. Anderson are inevitable since he has scooped out from the heart of America matter which has never been confined in a shell before. He is too much enamoured of this precious stuff to squeeze it into any of those old and intricate poems which the art and industry of Europe have secreted. Rather he will leave what he has found exposed, defenceless, naked to scorn and laughter.

But if this theory holds good of the work of American novelists, how then are we to account for the novels of Mr. Sinclair Lewis? Does it not explode at the first touch of *Babbitt* and *Main Street* and *Our Mr. Wrenn* like a soap bubble dashed against the edge of a hard mahogany wardrobe? For it is precisely by its hardness, its efficiency, its compactness that Mr. Lewis's work excels. Yet he also is an American; he also has devoted book after book to the description and elucidation of America. Far from being shelless, however, his books, one is inclined to say, are all shell; the only doubt is whether he has left any room for the snail. At any rate *Babbitt* completely refutes the theory that an American writer, writing about America, must necessarily lack the finish, the technique, the power to model and control his material which one might suppose to be the bequest of an old civilisation to its artists. In all these respects, *Babbitt is* the equal of any novel written in English in the present century. The tourist therefore must make his choice between two alternatives. Either there is no profound difference between English and American writers, and their experience is so similar that it can be housed in the same form; or Mr. Lewis has modelled himself so closely upon the English—H. G. Wells is a very obvious master—that he has sacrificed his American characteristics in the process. But the art of reading would be simpler and less adventurous than it is if writers could be parcelled out in strips of green and blue. Study of Mr. Lewis more and more convinces us that the surface appearance of downright decision is deceptive; the outer composure hardly holds together the warring elements within; the colours have run.

For though *Babbitt* would appear as solid and authentic a portrait of the American business man as can well be painted, certain doubts run across us and shake our conviction. But, we may ask, where all is so masterly, self-assured, and confident, what foothold can there be for doubt to lodge upon? To begin with we doubt Mr. Lewis himself: we doubt, that is to say, that he is nearly as sure of himself or of his subject as he would have us believe. For he, too, though in a way very different from Mr. Anderson's way, is writing with one eye on Europe, a division of attention which the reader is quick to feel and resent. He too has the American self-consciousness, though it is masterfully suppressed and allowed only to utter itself once or twice in a sharp cry of bitterness ("Babbitt was as much amused by the antiquated provincialism as any proper Englishman by any American"). But the uneasiness is there. He has not identified himself with America; rather he has constituted himself the guide and interpreter between the Americans and the English, and, as he conducts his party of Europeans over the typical American city (of which he is a native) and shows them the typical American citizen (to whom he is related) he is equally divided between shame at what he has to show and anger at the Europeans for laughing at it. Zenith is a despicable place, but the English are even more despicable for despising it.

In such an atmosphere intimacy is impossible. All that a

writer of Mr. Lewis's powers can do is to be unflinchingly accurate and more and more on his guard against giving himself away. Accordingly, never was so complete a model of a city made before. We turn on the taps and the water runs; we press a button and cigars are lit and beds warmed. But this glorification of machinery, this lust for "toothpastes, socks, tires, cameras, instantaneous hot water bottles . . . at first the signs, then the substitutes for joy and passion and wisdom" is only a device for putting off the evil day which Mr. Lewis sees looming ahead. However he may dread what people will think of him, he must give himself away. Babbitt must be proved to possess some share in truth and beauty, some character, some emotion of his own, or Babbitt will be nothing but an improved device for running motor cars, a convenient surface for the display of mechanical ingenuity. To make us care for Babbitt—that was his problem. With this end in view Mr. Lewis shamefacedly assures us that Babbitt has his dreams. Stout though he is, this elderly business man dreams of a fairy child waiting at a gate. "Her dear and tranquil hand caressed his cheek. He was gallant and wise and well-beloved; warm ivory were her arms; and beyond perilous moors the brave sea glittered." But that is not a dream; that is simply the protest of a man who has never dreamed in his life, but is determined to prove that dreaming is as easy as shelling peas. What are dreams made of—the most expensive dreams? Seas, fairies, moors? Well, he will have a little of each, and if that is not a dream, he seems to demand, jumping out of bed in a fury, what then is it? With sex relations and family affection he is much more at ease. Indeed it would be impossible to deny that if we put our ears to his shell, the foremost citizen in Zenith can be heard moving cumbrously but unmistakably within. One has moments of affection for him, moments of sympathy and even of desire that some miracle may happen, the rock be cleft asunder, and the living creature, with his capacity for fun, suffering, and happiness, be set at liberty. But no; his movements are too sluggish; Babbitt will never escape; he will die in his prison, bequeathing only the chance of escape to his son.

In some such way as this, then, the English tourist makes his theory embrace both Mr. Anderson and Mr. Sinclair Lewis. Both suffer as novelists from being American; Mr. Anderson, because he must protest his pride; Mr. Lewis, because he must conceal his bitterness. Mr. Anderson's way is the less injurious to him as an artist, and his imagination is the more vigorous of the two. He has gained more than he has lost by being the spokesman of a new country, the worker in fresh clay. Mr. Lewis it would seem was meant by nature to take his place with Mr. Wells and Mr. Bennett, and had he been born in England would undoubtedly have proved himself the equal of these two famous men. Denied, however, the richness of an old civilisation—the swarm of ideas upon which the art of Mr. Wells has battened, the solidity of custom which has nourished the art of Mr. Bennett—he has been forced to criticise rather than to explore, and the object of his criticism—the civilisation of Zenith—was unfortunately too meagre to sustain him. Yet a little reflection, and a comparison between Mr. Anderson and Mr. Lewis, put a different colour on our conclusion. Look at Americans as an American, see Mrs. Opal Emerson Mudge as she is herself, not as a type and symbol of America displayed for the amusement of the condescending Britisher, and then, we dimly suspect, Mrs. Mudge is no type, no scarecrow, no abstraction. Mrs. Mudge is—but it is not for an English writer to say what. He can only peep and peer between the chinks of the barrier and hazard the opinion that Mrs. Mudge and the Americans generally are, somehow, human beings into the bargain.

That suspicion suddenly becomes a certainty as we read the first pages of Mr. Ring Lardner's *You Know Me, Al,* and the change is bewildering. Hitherto we have been kept at arm's length, reminded constantly of our superiority, of our inferiority, of the fact, anyhow, that we are alien blood and bone. But Mr. Lardner is not merely unaware that we differ; he is unaware that we exist. When a crack player is in the middle of an exciting game of baseball he does not stop to wonder whether the audience likes the colour of his hair. All his mind is on the game. So Mr. Lardner does not waste a moment when he writes in thinking whether he is using American slang or Shakespeare's English; whether he is remembering Fielding or forgetting Fielding; whether he is proud of being American or ashamed of not being Japanese; all his mind is on the story. Hence all our minds are on the story. Hence, incidentally, he writes the best prose that has come our way. Hence we feel at last freely admitted to the society of our fellows.

That this should be true of *You Know Me, Al,* a story about baseball, a game which is not played in England, a story written often in a language which is not English, gives us pause. To what does he owe his success? Besides his unconsciousness and the additional power which he is thus free to devote to his art, Mr. Lardner has talents of a remarkable order. With extraordinary ease and aptitude, with the quickest strokes, the surest touch, the sharpest insight, he lets Jack Keefe the baseball player cut out his own outline, fill in his own depths, until the figure of the foolish, boastful, innocent athlete lives before us. As he babbles out his mind on paper there rise up friends, sweethearts, the scenery, town, and country—all surround him and make him up in his completeness. We gaze into the depths of a society which goes its ways intent on its own concerns. There, perhaps, is one of the elements of Mr. Lardner's success. He is not merely himself intent on his own game, but his characters are equally intent on theirs. It is no coincidence that the best of Mr. Lardner's stories are about games, for one may guess that Mr. Lardner's interest in games has solved one of the most difficult problems of the American writer; it has given him a clue, a centre, a meeting place for the divers activities of people whom a vast continent isolates, whom no tradition controls. Games give him what society gives his English brother. Whatever the precise reason, Mr. Lardner at any rate provides something unique in its kind, something indigenous to the soil, which the traveller may carry off as a trophy to prove to the incredulous that he has actually been to America and found it a foreign land. But the time has come when the tourist must reckon up his expenses and experiences, and attempt to cast up his account of the tour as a whole.

At the outset let us admit that our impressions are highly mixed and the opinions we have come to, if anything, less definite, less assured than those with which we started. For when we consider the mixed origin of the literature we are trying to understand, its youth, its age, and all those currents which are blowing across the stream of its natural development, we may well exclaim that French is simpler, English is simpler, all modern literatures are simpler to sum up and understand than this new American literature. A discord lies at the root of it; the natural bent of the American is twisted at the start. For the more sensitive he is, the more he must read English literature; the more he reads English literature, the more alive he must become to the puzzle and perplexity of this great art which uses the language on his own lips to express an experience which is not his and to mirror a civilisation which he has never known. The choice has to be made—whether to yield or to rebel. The more sensitive, or at least the more sophisticated, the Henry Jameses, the Hergesheimers, the Edith Whartons, decide in favour of England 'and pay the penalty by exaggerating the English culture, the traditional English good manners, and stressing too heavily or in the wrong places those social differences which, though the first to strike the foreigner, are by no means the most profound. What their work gains in refinement it loses in that perpetual distortion of values, that obsession with surface distinctions—the age of old houses, the glamour of great names—which makes it necessary to remember that Henry James was a foreigner if we are not to call him a snob.

On the other hand, the simpler and cruder writers, like Walt Whitman, Mr. Anderson, Mr. Masters—decide in favour of America, but truculently, self-consciously, protestingly, "showing off" as the nurses would say, their newness, their independence, their individuality. Both influences are unfortunate and serve to obscure and delay the development of the real American literature itself. But, some critics would interpose, are we not making mountains out of molehills, conjuring up distinctions where none exist? The "real American literature" in the time of Hawthorne, Emerson, and Lowell was much of a piece with contemporary English literature, and the present movement towards a national literature is confined to a few enthusiasts and extremists who will grow older and wiser and see the folly of their ways.

But the tourist can no longer accept this comfortable doctrine, flattering though it be to his pride of birth. Obviously there are American writers who do not care a straw for English opinion or for English culture, and write very vigorously none the less—witness Mr. Lardner; there are Americans who have all the accomplishments of culture without a trace of its excess—witness Miss Willa Cather; there are Americans whose aim it is to write a book off their own bat and no one else's—witness Miss Fannie Hurst. But the shortest tour, the most superficial inspection, must impress him with what is of far greater importance—the fact that where the land itself is so different, and the society so different, the literature must needs differ, and differ more and more widely as time goes by, from those of other countries.

American literature will be influenced, no doubt, like all others, and the English influence may well predominate But clearly the English tradition is already unable to cope with this vast land, these prairies, these cornfields, these lonely little groups of men and women scattered at immense distances from each other, these vast industrial cities with their skyscrapers and their night signs and their perfect organisation of machinery. It cannot extract their meaning and interpret their beauty. How could it be otherwise? The English tradition is formed upon a little country; its centre is an old house with many rooms each crammed with objects and crowded with people who know each other intimately, whose manners, thoughts, and speech are ruled all the time, if unconsciously, by the spirit of the past. But in America there is baseball instead of society; instead of the old landscape which has moved men to emotion for endless summers and springs, a new land, its tin cans, its prairies, its cornfields flung disorderly about like a mosaic of incongruous pieces waiting order at the artist's hands; while the people are equally diversified into fragments of many nationalities.

To describe, to unify, to make order out of all these severed parts, a new art is needed and the control of a new tradition. That both are in process of birth the language itself gives us proof. For the Americans are doing what the Elizabethans did— they are coining new words. They are instinctively making the language adapt itself to their needs. In England, save for the impetus given by the war, the word-coining power has lapsed; our writers vary the metres of their poetry, remodel the rhythms of prose, but one may search English fiction in vain for a single new word. It is significant that when we want to freshen our speech we borrow from America—poppycock, rambunctious, flipflop, booster, good-mixer—all the expressive ugly vigorous slang which creeps into use among us first in talk, later in writing, comes from across the Atlantic. Nor does it need much foresight to predict that when words are being made, a literature will be made out of them. Already we hear the first jars and dissonances, the strangled difficult music of the prelude. As we shut our books and look out again upon the English fields a strident note rings in our ears. We hear the first lovemaking and the first laughter of the child who was exposed by its parents three hundred years ago upon a rocky shore and survived solely by its own exertions and is a little sore and proud and diffident and self-assertive in consequence and is now on the threshold of man's estate.

JANE AUSTEN

First published in 1925

It is probable that if Miss Cassandra Austen had had her way we should have had nothing of Jane Austen's except her novels. To her elder sister alone did she write freely; to her alone she confided her hopes and, if rumour is true, the one great disappointment of her life; but when Miss Cassandra Austen grew old, and the growth of her sister's fame made her suspect that a time might come when strangers would pry and scholars speculate, she burnt, at great cost to herself, every letter that could gratify their curiosity, and spared only what she judged too trivial to be of interest.

Hence our knowledge of Jane Austen is derived from a little gossip, a few letters, and her books. As for the gossip, gossip which has survived its day is never despicable; with a little rearrangement it suits our purpose admirably. For example, Jane "is not at all pretty and very prim, unlike a girl of twelve . . . Jane is whimsical and affected," says little Philadelphia Austen of her cousin. Then we have Mrs. Mitford, who knew the Austens as girls and thought Jane "the prettiest, silliest, most affected husband-hunting butterfly she ever remembers ". Next, there is Miss Mitford's anonymous friend "who visits her now [and] says that she has stiffened into the most perpendicular, precise, taciturn piece of 'single blessedness' that ever existed, and that, until *Pride and Prejudice* showed what a precious gem was hidden in that unbending case, she was no more regarded in society than a poker or firescreen. . . . The case is very different now", the good lady goes on; "she is still a poker—but a poker of whom everybody is afraid. . . . A wit, a delineator of character, who does not talk is terrific indeed!" On the other side, of course, there are the Austens, a race little given to panegyric of themselves, but nevertheless, they say, her brothers "were very fond and very proud of her. They were attached to her by her talents, her virtues, and her engaging manners, and each loved afterwards to fancy a resemblance in some niece or daughter of his own to the dear sister Jane, whose perfect equal they yet never expected to see." Charming but perpendicular, loved at home but feared by strangers, biting of tongue but tender of heart—these contrasts are by no means incompatible, and when we turn to the novels we shall find ourselves stumbling there too over the same complexities in the writer.

To begin with, that prim little girl whom Philadelphia found so unlike a child of twelve, whimsical and affected, was soon to be the authoress of an astonishing and unchildish story, *Love and Freindship*[5], which, incredible though it appears, was written at the age of fifteen. It was written, apparently, to amuse the schoolroom; one of the stories in the same book is dedicated with mock solemnity to her brother; another is neatly illustrated with water-colour heads by her sister. These are jokes which, one feels, were family property; thrusts of satire, which went home because all little Austens made mock in common of fine ladies who "sighed and fainted on the sofa".

Brothers and sisters must have laughed when Jane read out loud her last hit at the vices which they all abhorred. "I die a martyr to my grief for the loss of Augustus. One fatal swoon has cost me my life. Beware of Swoons, Dear Laura. . . . Run mad as often as you chuse, but do not faint. . . ." And on she rushed, as fast as she could write and quicker than she could spell, to tell the incredible adventures of Laura and Sophia, of Philander and Gustavus, of the gentleman who drove a coach between Edinburgh and Stirling every other day, of the theft

5   *Love and Freindship,* Chatto and Windus.

of the fortune that was kept in the table drawer, of the starving mothers and the sons who acted Macbeth. Undoubtedly, the story must have roused the schoolroom to uproarious laughter. And yet, nothing is more obvious than that this girl of fifteen, sitting in her private corner of the common parlour, was writing not to draw a laugh from brother and sisters, and not for home consumption. She was writing for everybody, for nobody, for our age, for her own; in other words, even at that early age Jane Austen was writing. One hears it in the rhythm and shapeliness and severity of the sentences. "She was nothing more than a mere good-tempered, civil, and obliging young woman; as such we could scarcely dislike her—she was only an object of contempt." Such a sentence is meant to outlast the Christmas holidays. Spirited, easy, full of fun, verging with freedom upon sheer nonsense,—*Love and Freindship* is all that; but what is this note which never merges in the rest, which sounds distinctly and penetratingly all through the volume? It is the sound of laughter. The girl of fifteen is laughing, in her corner, at the world.

Girls of fifteen are always laughing. They laugh when Mr. Binney helps himself to salt instead of sugar. They almost die of laughing when old Mrs. Tomkins sits down upon the cat. But they are crying the moment after. They have no fixed abode from which they see that there is something eternally laughable in human nature, some quality in men and women that for ever excites our satire. They do not know that Lady Greville who snubs, and poor Maria who is snubbed, are permanent features of every ballroom. But Jane Austen knew it from her birth upwards. One of those fairies who perch upon cradles must have taken her a flight through the world directly she was born. When she was laid in the cradle again she knew not only what the world looked like, but had already chosen her kingdom. She had agreed that if she might rule over that territory, she would covet no other. Thus at fifteen she had few illusions about other people and none about herself. Whatever she writes is finished and turned and set in its relation, not to the parsonage, but to the universe. She is impersonal; she is inscrutable. When the writer, Jane Austen, wrote down in the most remarkable sketch in the book a little of Lady Greville's conversation, there is no trace of anger at the snub which the clergyman's daughter, Jane Austen, once received. Her gaze passes straight to the mark, and we know precisely where, upon the map of human nature, that mark is. We know because Jane Austen kept to her compact; she never trespassed beyond her boundaries. Never, even at the emotional age of fifteen, did she round upon herself in shame, obliterate a sarcasm in a spasm of compassion, or blur an outline in a mist of rhapsody. Spasms and rhapsodies, she seems to have said, pointing with her stick, end *there*; and the boundary line is perfectly distinct. But she does not deny that moons and mountains and castles exist—on the other side. She has even one romance of her own. It is for the Queen of Scots. She really admired her very much. "One of the first characters in the world", she called her, "a bewitching Princess whose only friend was then the Duke of Norfolk, and whose only ones now Mr. Whitaker, Mrs. Lefroy, Mrs. Knight and myself." With these words her passion is neatly circumscribed, and rounded with a laugh. It is amusing to remember in what terms the young Brontë's wrote, not very much later, in their northern parsonage, about the Duke of Wellington.

The prim little girl grew up. She became "the prettiest, silliest, most affected husband-hunting butterfly" Mrs. Mitford ever remembered, and, incidentally, the authoress of a novel called *Pride and Prejudice,* which, written stealthily under cover of a creaking door, lay for many years unpublished. A little later, it is thought, she began another story, *The Watsons,* and being for some reason dissatisfied with it, left it unfinished. The second-rate works of a great writer are worth reading because they offer the best criticism of his masterpieces. Here her difficulties are more apparent, and the method she took to overcome them less artfully concealed. To begin with, the stiffness and the bareness of the first chapters prove that she was one of those writers who lay their facts out rather baldly in the first version and then go back and back and back and cover them with flesh and atmosphere. How it would have been done we cannot say—by what suppressions and insertions and artful devices. But the miracle would have been accomplished; the dull history of fourteen years of family life would have been converted into another of those exquisite and apparently effortless introductions; and we should never have guessed what pages of preliminary drudgery Jane Austen forced her pen to go through. Here we perceive that she was no conjuror after all. Like other writers, she had to create the atmosphere in which her own peculiar genius could bear fruit. Here she fumbles; here she keeps us waiting. Suddenly she has done it; now things can happen as she likes things to happen. The Edwardses are going to the ball. The Tomlinsons' carriage is passing; she can tell us that Charles is "being provided with his gloves and told to keep them on"; Tom Musgrave retreats to a remote corner with a barrel of oysters and is famously snug. Her genius is freed and active. At once our senses quicken; we are possessed with the peculiar intensity which she alone can impart. But of what is it all composed? Of a ball in a country town; a few couples meeting and taking hands in an assembly room; a little eating and drinking; and for catastrophe, a boy being snubbed by one young lady and kindly treated by another. There is no tragedy and no heroism. Yet for some reason the little scene is moving out of all proportion to its surface solemnity. We have been made to see that if Emma acted so in the ball-room, how considerate, how tender, inspired by what sincerity of feeling she would have shown herself in those graver crises of life which, as we watch her, come inevitably before our eyes. Jane Austen is thus a mistress of much deeper emotion than appears upon the surface. She stimulates us to supply what is not there. What she offers is, apparently, a trifle, yet is composed of something that expands in the reader's mind and endows with the most enduring form of life scenes which are outwardly trivial. Always the stress is laid upon character. How, we are made to wonder, will Emma behave when Lord Osborne and Tom Musgrave make their call at five minutes before three, just as Mary is bringing in the tray and the knife-case? It is an extremely awkward situation. The young men are accustomed to much greater refinement. Emma may prove herself ill-bred, vulgar, a nonentity. The turns and twists of the dialogue keep us on the tenterhooks of suspense. Our attention is half upon the present moment, half upon the future. And when, in the end, Emma behaves in such a way as to vindicate our highest hopes of her, we are moved as if we had been made witnesses of a matter of the highest importance. Here, indeed, in this unfinished and in the main inferior story, are all the elements of Jane Austen's greatness. It has the permanent quality of literature. Think away the surface animation, the likeness to life, and there remains, to provide a deeper pleasure, an exquisite discrimination of human values. Dismiss this too from the mind and one can dwell with extreme satisfaction upon the more abstract art which, in the ball-room scene, so varies the emotions and proportions the parts that it is possible to enjoy it, as one enjoys poetry, for itself, and not as a link which carries the story this way and that.

But the gossip says of Jane Austen that she was perpendicular, precise, and taciturn—"a poker of whom everybody is afraid". Of this too there are traces; she could be merciless enough; she is one of the most consistent satirists in the whole of literature. Those first angular chapters of *The Watsons* prove that hers was not a prolific genius; she had not, like Emily Brontë, merely to open the door to make herself felt. Humbly and gaily she collected the twigs and straws out of which the nest was to be made and placed them neatly together. The twigs and straws were a little dry and a little dusty in themselves. There was the big house and the little house; a tea party, a dinner party, and an occasional picnic; life was hedged in by valuable connections and adequate incomes; by muddy roads, wet feet, and a tendency on the part of the ladies to get tired; a little principle supported it, a little consequence, and the education commonly enjoyed by upper middle-class families living in the country. Vice, adventure, passion were left outside. But of all this prosiness, of all this littleness, she evades nothing, and nothing is slurred over. Patiently and precisely she tells us how they "made no stop anywhere till they reached Newbury, where a comfortable meal, uniting dinner and supper, wound up the enjoyments and fatigues of the day". Nor does she pay to conventions merely the tribute of lip homage; she believes in them besides accepting them. When she is describing a clergyman, like Edmund Bertram, or a sailor, in particular, she appears debarred by the sanctity of his office from the free use of her chief tool, the comic genius, and is apt therefore to lapse into decorous panegyric or matter-of-fact description. But these are exceptions; for the most part her attitude recalls the anonymous lady's ejaculation—"A wit, a delineator of character, who does not talk is terrific indeed!" She wishes neither to reform nor to annihilate; she is silent; and that is terrific indeed. One after another she creates her fools, her prigs, her worldlings, her Mr. Collinses, her Sir Walter Elliotts, her Mrs. Bennets. She encircles them with the lash of a whip-like phrase which, as it runs round them, cuts out their silhouettes for ever. But there they remain; no excuse is found for them and no mercy shown them. Nothing remains of Julia and Maria Bertram when she has done with them; Lady Bertram is left "sitting and calling to Pug and trying to keep him from the flower-beds" eternally. A divine justice is meted out; Dr. Grant, who begins by liking his goose tender, ends by bringing on "apoplexy and death, by three great institutionary dinners in one week". Sometimes it seems as if her creatures were born merely to give Jane Austen the supreme delight of slicing their heads off. She is satisfied; she is content; she would not alter a hair on anybody's head, or move one brick or one blade of grass in a world which provides her with such exquisite delight.

Nor, indeed, would we. For even if the pangs of outraged vanity, or the heat of moral wrath, urged us to improve away a world so full of spite, pettiness, and folly, the task is beyond our powers. People are like that—the girl of fifteen knew it; the mature woman proves it. At this very moment some Lady Bertram is trying to keep Pug from the flower beds; she sends Chapman to help Miss Fanny a little late. The discrimination is so perfect, the satire so just, that, consistent though it is, it almost escapes our notice. No touch of pettiness, no hint of spite, rouse us from our contemplation. Delight strangely mingles with our amusement. Beauty illumines these fools.

That elusive quality is, indeed, often made up of very different parts, which it needs a peculiar genius to bring together. The wit of Jane Austen has for partner the perfection of her taste. Her fool is a fool, her snob is a snob, because he departs from the model of sanity and sense which she has in mind, and conveys to us unmistakably even while she makes us laugh. Never did any novelist make more use of an impeccable sense of human values. It is against the disc of an unerring heart, an unfailing good taste, an almost stern morality, that she shows up those deviations from kindness, truth, and sincerity which are among the most delightful things in English literature. She depicts a Mary Crawford in her mixture of good and bad entirely by this means. She lets her rattle on against the clergy, or in favour of a baronetage and ten thousand a year, with all the ease and spirit possible; but now and again she strikes one note of her own, very quietly, but in perfect tune, and at once all Mary Crawford's chatter, though it continues to amuse, rings flat. Hence the depth, the beauty, the complexity of her scenes. From such contrasts there comes a beauty, a solemnity even, which are not only as remarkable as her wit, but an inseparable part of it. In *The Watsons* she gives us a foretaste of this power; she makes us wonder why an ordinary act of kindness, as she describes it, becomes so full of meaning. In her masterpieces, the same gift is brought to perfection. Here is nothing out of the way; it is midday in Northamptonshire; a dull young man is talking to rather a weakly young woman on the stairs as they go up to dress for dinner, with housemaids passing. But, from triviality, from commonplace, their words become suddenly full of meaning, and the moment for both one of the most memorable in their lives. It fills itself; it shines; it glows; it hangs before us, deep, trembling, serene for a second; next, the housemaid passes, and this drop, in which all the happiness of life has collected, gently subsides again to become part of the ebb and flow of ordinary existence.

What more natural, then, with this insight into their profundity, than that Jane Austen should have chosen to write of the trivialities of day-to-day existence, of parties, picnics, and country dances? No "suggestions to alter her style of writing" from the Prince Regent or Mr. Clarke could tempt her; no romance, no adventure, no politics or intrigue could hold a candle to life on a country-house staircase as she saw it. Indeed, the Prince Regent and his librarian had run their heads against a very formidable obstacle; they were trying to tamper with an incorruptible conscience, to disturb an infallible discretion. The child who formed her sentences so finely when she was fifteen never ceased to form them, and never wrote for the Prince Regent or his Librarian, but for the world at large. She knew exactly what her powers were, and what material they were fitted to deal with as material should be dealt with by a writer whose standard of finality was high. There were impressions that lay outside her province; emotions that by no stretch or artifice could be properly coated and covered by her own resources. For example, she could not make a girl talk enthusiastically of banners and chapels. She could not throw herself whole-heartedly into a romantic moment. She had all sorts of devices for evading scenes of passion. Nature and its beauties she approached in a sidelong way of her own. She describes a beautiful night without once mentioning the moon. Nevertheless, as we read the few formal phrases about "the brilliancy of an unclouded night and the contrast of the deep shade of the woods", the night is at once as "solemn, and soothing, and lovely" as she tells us, quite simply, that it was.

The balance of her gifts was singularly perfect. Among her finished novels there are no failures, and among her many chapters few that sink markedly below the level of the others. But, after all, she died at the age of forty-two. She died at the height of her powers. She was still subject to those changes which often make the final period of a writer's career the most interesting of all. Vivacious, irrepressible, gifted with an invention of great vitality, there can be no doubt that she would have written more, had she lived, and it is tempting to consider whether she would not have written differently. The boundaries were marked; moons, mountains, and castles lay on the other side. But was she not sometimes tempted to trespass for a minute? Was she not beginning, in her own gay and brilliant manner, to contemplate a little voyage of discovery?

Let us take *Persuasion,* the last completed novel, and look by its light at the books she might have written had she lived. There is a peculiar beauty and a peculiar dullness in *Persuasion.* The dullness is that which so often marks the transition stage between two different periods. The writer is a little bored. She has grown too familiar with the ways of her world; she no longer notes them freshly. There is an asperity in her comedy which suggests that she has almost ceased to be amused by the vanities of a Sir Walter or the snobbery of a Miss Elliott. The satire is harsh, and the comedy crude. She is no longer so freshly aware of the amusements of daily life. Her mind is not altogether on her object. But, while we feel that Jane Austen has done this before, and done it better, we also feel that she is trying to do something which she has never yet attempted. There is a new element in *Persuasion,* the quality, perhaps, that made Dr. Whewell fire up and insist that it was "the most beautiful of her works". She is beginning to discover that the world is larger, more mysterious, and more romantic than she had supposed. We feel it to be true of herself when she says of Anne: "She had been forced into prudence in her youth, she learned romance as she grew older—the natural sequel of an unnatural beginning". She dwells frequently upon the beauty and the melancholy of nature, upon the autumn where she had been wont to dwell upon the spring. She talks of the "influence so sweet and so sad of autumnal months in the country". She marks "the tawny leaves and withered hedges". "One does not love a place the less because one has suffered in it", she observes. But it is not only in a new sensibility to nature that we detect the change. Her attitude to life itself is altered. She is seeing it, for the greater part of the book, through the eyes of a woman who, unhappy herself, has a special sympathy for the happiness and unhappiness of others, which, until the very end, she is forced to comment upon in silence. Therefore the observation is less of facts and more of feelings than is usual. There is an expressed emotion in the scene at the concert and in the famous talk about woman's constancy which proves not merely the biographical fact that Jane Austen had loved, but the aesthetic fact that she was no longer afraid to say so. Experience, when it was of a serious kind, had to sink very deep, and to be thoroughly disinfected by the passage of time, before she allowed herself to deal with it in fiction. But now, in 1817, she was ready. Outwardly, too, in her circumstances, a change was imminent. Her fame had grown very slowly. "I doubt ", wrote Mr. Austen Leigh, "whether it would be possible to mention any other author of note whose personal obscurity was so complete." Had she lived a few more years only, all that would have been altered. She would have stayed in London, dined out, lunched out, met famous people, made new friends, read, travelled, and carried back to the quiet country cottage a hoard of observations to feast upon at leisure.

And what effect would all this have had upon the six novels that Jane Austen did not write? She would not have written of crime, of passion, or of adventure. She would not have been rushed by the importunity of publishers or the flattery of friends into slovenliness or insincerity. But she would have known more. Her sense of security would have been shaken. Her comedy would have suffered. She would have trusted less (this is already perceptible in *Persuasion*) to dialogue and more to reflection to give us a knowledge of her characters. Those marvellous little speeches which sum up, in a few minutes' chatter, all that we need in order to know an Admiral Croft or a Mrs. Musgrove for ever, that shorthand, hit-or-miss method which contains chapters of analysis and psychology, would have become too crude to hold all that she now perceived of the complexity of human nature. She would have devised a method, clear and composed as ever, but deeper and more suggestive, for conveying not only what people say, but what they leave unsaid; not only what they are, but what life is. She would have stood farther away from her characters, and seen them more as a group, less as individuals. Her satire, while it played less incessantly, would have been more stringent and severe. She would have been the forerunner of Henry James and of Proust—but enough. Vain are these speculations: the most perfect artist among women, the writer whose books are immortal, died "just as she was beginning to feel confidence in her own success".

GEORGE ELIOT

First published in 1925

To read George Eliot attentively is to become aware how little one knows about her. It is also to become aware of the credulity, not very creditable to one's insight, with which, half consciously and partly maliciously, one had accepted the late Victorian version of a deluded woman who held phantom sway over subjects even more deluded than herself. At what moment and by what means her spell was broken it is difficult to ascertain. Some people attribute it to the publication of her *Life*. Perhaps George Meredith, with his phrase about the "mercurial little showman" and the "errant woman" on the daïs, gave point and poison to the arrows of thousands incapable of aiming them so accurately, but delighted to let fly. She became one of the butts for youth to laugh at, the convenient symbol of a group of serious people who were all guilty of the same idolatry and could be dismissed with the same scorn. Lord Acton had said that she was greater than Dante; Herbert Spencer exempted her novels, as if they were not novels, when he banned all fiction from the London Library. She was the pride and paragon of her sex. Moreover, her private record was not more alluring than her public. Asked to describe an afternoon at the Priory, the story-teller always intimated that the memory of those serious Sunday afternoons had come to tickle his sense of humour. He had been so much alarmed by the grave lady in her low chair; he had been so anxious to say the intelligent thing. Certainly, the talk had been very serious, as a note in the fine clear hand of the great novelist bore witness. It was dated on the Monday morning, and she accused herself of having spoken without due forethought of Marivaux when she meant another; but no doubt, she said, her listener had already supplied the correction. Still, the memory of talking about Marivaux to George Eliot on a Sunday afternoon was not a romantic memory. It had faded with the passage of the years. It had not become picturesque.

Indeed, one cannot escape the conviction that the long, heavy face with its expression of serious and sullen and almost equine power has stamped itself depressingly upon the minds of people who remember George Eliot, so that it looks out upon them from her pages. Mr. Gosse has lately described her as he saw her driving through London in a victoria:

> a large, thick-set sybil, dreamy and immobile, whose
> massive features, somewhat grim when seen in profile,
> were incongruously bordered by a hat, always in the height
> of Paris fashion, which in those days commonly included
> an immense ostrich feather.

Lady Ritchie, with equal skill, has left a more intimate indoor portrait:

> She sat by the fire in a beautiful black satin gown, with a
> green shaded lamp on the table beside her, where I saw
> German books lying and pamphlets and ivory paper-
> cutters. She was very quiet and noble, with two steady little
> eyes and a sweet voice. As I looked I felt her to be a friend,
> not exactly a personal friend, but a good and benevolent
> impulse.

A scrap of her talk is preserved. "We ought to respect our influence," she said. "We know by our own experience how very much others affect our lives, and we must remember that we in turn must have the same effect upon others." Jealously treasured, committed to memory, one can imagine recalling the scene, repeating the words, thirty years later and suddenly, for the first time, bursting into laughter.

In all these records one feels that the recorder, even when he was in the actual presence, kept his distance and kept his head, and never read the novels in later years with the light of a vivid, or puzzling, or beautiful personality dazzling in his eyes. In fiction, where so much of personality is revealed, the absence of charm is a great lack; and her critics, who have been, of course, mostly of the opposite sex, have resented, half consciously perhaps, her deficiency in a quality which is held to be supremely desirable in women. George Eliot was not charming; she was not strongly feminine; she had none of those eccentricities and inequalities of temper which give to so many artists the endearing simplicity of children. One feels that to most people, as to Lady Ritchie, she was "not exactly a personal friend, but a good and benevolent impulse". But if we consider these portraits more closely we shall find that they are all the portraits of an elderly celebrated woman, dressed in black satin, driving in her victoria, a woman who has been through her struggle and issued from it with a profound desire to be of use to others, but with no wish for intimacy, save with the little circle who had known her in the days of her youth. We know very little about the days of her youth; but we do know that the culture, the philosophy, the fame, and the influence were all built upon a very humble foundation—she was the grand-daughter of a carpenter.

The first volume of her life is a singularly depressing record. In it we see her raising herself with groans and struggles from the intolerable boredom of petty provincial society (her father had risen in the world and become more middle class, but less picturesque) to be the assistant editor of a highly intellectual London review, and the esteemed companion of Herbert Spencer. The stages are painful as she reveals them in the sad soliloquy in which Mr. Cross condemned her to tell the story of her life. Marked in early youth as one "sure to get something up very soon in the way of a clothing club", she proceeded to raise funds for restoring a church by making a chart of ecclesiastical history; and that was followed by a loss of faith which so disturbed her father that he refused to live with her. Next came the struggle with the translation of Strauss, which, dismal and "soul-stupefying" in itself, can scarcely have been made less so by the usual feminine tasks of ordering a household and nursing a dying father, and the distressing conviction, to one so dependent upon affection, that by becoming a blue-stocking she was forfeiting her brother's respect. "I used to go about like an owl," she said, "to the great disgust of my brother." "Poor thing," wrote a friend who saw her toiling through Strauss with a statue of the risen Christ in front of her, "I do pity her sometimes, with her pale sickly face and dreadful headaches, and anxiety, too, about her father." Yet, though we cannot read the story without a strong desire that the stages of her pilgrimage might have been made, if not more easy, at least more beautiful, there is a dogged determination in her advance upon the citadel of culture which raises it above our pity. Her development was very slow and very awkward, but it had the irresistible impetus behind it of a deep-seated and noble ambition. Every obstacle at length was thrust from her path. She knew every one. She read everything. Her astonishing intellectual vitality had triumphed. Youth was over, but youth had been full of suffering. Then, at the age of thirty-five, at the height of her powers, and in the fulness of her freedom, she made the decision which was of such profound moment to her and still matters even to us, and went to Weimar, alone with George Henry Lewes.

The books which followed so soon after her union testify in the fullest manner to the great liberation which had come to her with personal happiness. In themselves they provide us with a plentiful feast. Yet at the threshold of her literary career one may find in some of the circumstances of her life influences that turned her mind to the past, to the country village, to the quiet and beauty and simplicity of childish memories and away from herself and the present. We understand how it was that her first book was *Scenes of Clerical Life,* and not *Middlemarch.* Her union with Lewes had surrounded her with affection, but in view of the circumstances and of the conventions it had also isolated her. "I wish it to be understood", she wrote in 1857, "that I should never invite any one to come and see me who did not ask for the invitation." She had been "cut off from what is called the world", she said later, but she did not regret it. By becoming thus marked, first by circumstances and later, inevitably, by her fame, she lost the power to move on equal terms unnoted among her kind; and the loss for a novelist was serious. Still, basking in the light and sunshine of *Scenes of Clerical Life,* feeling the large mature mind spreading itself with a luxurious sense of freedom in the world of her "remotest past", to speak of loss seems inappropriate. Everything to such a mind was gain. All experience filtered down through layer after layer of perception and reflection, enriching and nourishing. The utmost we can say, in qualifying her attitude towards fiction by what little we know of her life, is that she had taken to heart certain lessons not usually learnt early, if learnt at all, among which, perhaps, the most branded upon her was the melancholy virtue of tolerance; her sympathies are with the everyday lot, and play most happily in dwelling upon the homespun of ordinary joys and sorrows. She has none of that romantic intensity which is connected with a sense of one's own individuality, unsated and unsubdued, cutting its shape sharply upon the background of the world. What were the loves and sorrows of a snuffy old clergyman, dreaming over his whisky, to the fiery egotism of Jane Eyre? The beauty of those first books, *Scenes of Clerical Life, Adam Bede, The Mill on the Floss,* is very great. It is impossible to estimate the merit of the Poysers, the Dodsons, the Gilfils, the Bartons, and the rest with all their surroundings and dependencies, because they have put on flesh and blood and we move among them, now bored, now sympathetic, but always with that unquestioning acceptance of all that they say and do, which we accord to the great originals only. The flood of memory and humour which she pours so spontaneously into one figure, one scene after another, until the whole fabric of ancient rural England is revived, has so much in common with a natural process that it leaves us with little consciousness that there is anything to criticise. We accept; we feel the delicious warmth and release of spirit which the great creative writers alone procure for us. As one comes back to the books after years of absence they pour out, even against our expectation, the same store of energy and heat, so that we want more than anything to idle in the warmth as in the sun beating down from the red orchard wall. If there is an element of unthinking abandonment in thus submitting to the humours of Midland farmers and their wives, that, too, is right in the circumstances. We scarcely wish to analyse what we feel to be so large and deeply human. And when we consider how distant in time the world of Shepperton and Hayslope is, and how remote the minds of farmer and agricultural labourers from those of most of George Eliot's readers, we can only attribute the ease and pleasure with which we ramble from house to smithy, from cottage parlour to rectory garden, to the fact that George Eliot makes us share their lives, not in a spirit of condescension or of curiosity, but in a spirit of sympathy. She is no satirist. The movement of her mind was too slow and cumbersome to lend itself to comedy. But she gathers in her large grasp a great bunch of the main elements of human nature and groups them loosely together with a tolerant and wholesome understanding which, as one finds upon re-reading, has not only kept her figures fresh and free, but has given them an unexpected hold upon our laughter and tears. There is the famous Mrs. Poyser. It would have been easy to work her idiosyncrasies to death, and, as it is, perhaps, George Eliot gets her laugh in the same place a little too often. But memory, after the book is shut, brings out, as sometimes in real life, the details and subtleties which some more salient characteristic has prevented us from noticing at the time. We recollect that her health was not good. There were occasions upon which she said nothing at all. She was patience itself with a sick child. She doted upon Totty. Thus one can muse and speculate about the greater number of George Eliot's characters and find, even in the least important, a roominess and margin where those qualities lurk which she has no call to bring from their obscurity.

But in the midst of all this tolerance and sympathy there are, even in the early books, moments of greater stress. Her humour has shown itself broad enough to cover a wide range of fools and failures, mothers and children, dogs and flourishing midland fields, farmers, sagacious or fuddled over their ale, horse-dealers, inn-keepers, curates, and carpenters. Over them all broods a certain romance, the only romance that George Eliot allowed herself—the romance of the past. The books are astonishingly readable and have no trace of pomposity or pretence. But to the reader who holds a large stretch of her early work in view it will become obvious that the mist of recollection gradually withdraws. It is not that her power diminishes, for, to our thinking, it is at its highest in the mature *Middlemarch*, the magnificent book which with all its imperfections is one of the few English novels written for grown-up people. But the world of fields and farms no longer contents her. In real life she had sought her fortunes elsewhere; and though to look back into the past was calming and consoling, there are, even in the early works, traces of that troubled spirit, that exacting and questioning and baffled presence who was George Eliot herself. In *Adam Bede* there is a hint of her in Dinah. She shows herself far more openly and completely in Maggie in *The Mill on the Floss*. She is Janet in *Janet's Repentance*, and Romola, and Dorothea seeking wisdom and finding one scarcely knows what in marriage with Ladislaw. Those who fall foul of George Eliot do so, we incline to think, on account of her heroines; and with good reason; for there is no doubt that they bring out the worst of her, lead her into difficult places, make her self-conscious, didactic, and occasionally vulgar. Yet if you could delete the whole sisterhood you would leave a much smaller and a much inferior world, albeit a world of greater artistic perfection and far superior jollity and comfort. In accounting for her failure, in so far as it was a failure, one recollects that she never wrote a story until she was thirty-seven, and that by the time she was thirty-seven she had come to think of herself with a mixture of pain and something like resentment. For long she preferred not to think of herself at all. Then, when the first flush of creative energy was exhausted and self-confidence had come to her, she wrote more and more from the personal standpoint, but she did so without the unhesitating abandonment of the young. Her self-consciousness is always marked when her heroines say what she herself would have said. She disguised them in every possible way. She granted them beauty and wealth into the bargain; she invented, more improbably, a taste for brandy. But the disconcerting and stimulating fact remained that she was compelled by the very power of her genius to step forth in person upon the quiet bucolic scene.

The noble and beautiful girl who insisted upon being born into the Mill on the Floss is the most obvious example of the ruin which a heroine can strew about her. Humour controls her and keeps her lovable so long as she is small and can be satisfied by eloping with the gipsies or hammering nails into her doll; but she develops; and before George Eliot knows what has happened she has a full-grown woman on her hands demanding what neither gipsies, nor dolls, nor St. Ogg's itself is capable of giving her. First Philip Wakem is produced, and later Stephen Guest. The weakness of the one and the coarseness of the other have often been pointed out; but both, in their weakness and coarseness, illustrate not so much George Eliot's inability to draw the portrait of a man, as the uncertainty, the infirmity, and the fumbling which shook her hand when she had to conceive a fit mate for a heroine. She is in the first place driven beyond the home world she knew and loved, and forced to set foot in middle-class drawing-rooms where young men sing all the summer morning and young women sit embroidering smoking-caps for bazaars. She feels herself out of her element, as her clumsy satire of what she calls "good society" proves.

> Good society has its claret and its velvet carpets, its dinner engagements six weeks deep, its opera, and its faery ball rooms . . . gets its science done by Faraday and its religion by the superior clergy who are to be met in the best houses; how should it have need of belief and emphasis?

There is no trace of humour or insight there, but only the vindictiveness of a grudge which we feel to be personal in its origin. But terrible as the complexity of our social system is in its demands upon the sympathy and discernment of a novelist straying across the boundaries, Maggie Tulliver did worse than drag George Eliot from her natural surroundings. She insisted upon the introduction of the great emotional scene. She must love; she must despair; she must be drowned clasping her brother in her arms. The more one examines the great emotional scenes the more nervously one anticipates the brewing and gathering and thickening of the cloud which will burst upon our heads at the moment of crisis in a shower of disillusionment and verbosity. It is partly that her hold upon dialogue, when it is not dialect, is slack; and partly that she seems to shrink with an elderly dread of fatigue from the effort of emotional concentration. She allows her heroines to talk too much. She has little verbal felicity. She lacks the unerring taste which chooses one sentence and compresses the heart of the scene within that. "Whom are you going to dance with?" asked Mr. Knightley, at the Westons' ball. "With you, if you will ask me," said Emma; and she has said enough. Mrs. Casaubon would have talked for an hour and we should have looked out of the window.

Yet, dismiss the heroines without sympathy, confine George Eliot to the agricultural world of her "remotest past", and you not only diminish her greatness but lose her true flavour. That greatness is here we can have no doubt. The width of the prospect, the large strong outlines of the principal features, the ruddy light of the early books, the searching power and reflective richness of the later tempt us to linger and expatiate beyond our limits. But it is upon the heroines that we would cast a final glance. "I have always been finding out my religion since I was a little girl," says Dorothea Casaubon. "I used to pray so much—now I hardly ever pray. I try not to have desires merely for myself. . . ." She is speaking for them all. That is their problem. They cannot live without religion, and they start out on the search for one when they are little girls. Each has the deep feminine passion for goodness, which makes the place where she stands in aspiration and agony the heart of the book—still and cloistered like a place of worship, but that she no longer knows to whom to pray. In learning they seek their goal; in the ordinary tasks of womanhood; in the wider service of their kind. They do not find what they seek, and we cannot wonder. The ancient consciousness of woman, charged with suffering and sensibility, and for so many ages dumb, seems in them to have brimmed and overflowed and uttered a demand for something—they scarcely know what—for something that is perhaps incompatible with the facts of human existence. George Eliot had far too strong an intelligence to tamper with those facts, and too broad a humour to mitigate the truth because it was a stern one. Save for the supreme courage of their endeavour, the struggle ends, for her heroines, in tragedy, or in a compromise that is even more melancholy. But their story is the incomplete version of the story of George Eliot herself. For her, too, the burden and the complexity of womanhood were not enough; she must reach beyond the sanctuary and pluck for herself the strange bright fruits of art and knowledge. Clasping them as few women have ever clasped them, she would not renounce her own inheritance—the difference of view, the difference of standard—nor accept an inappropriate reward. Thus we behold her, a memorable figure, inordinately praised and shrinking from her fame, despondent, reserved, shuddering

122

back into the arms of love as if there alone were satisfaction and, it might be, justification, at the same time reaching out with "a fastidious yet hungry ambition" for all that life could offer the free and inquiring mind and confronting her feminine aspirations with the real world of men. Triumphant was the issue for her, whatever it may have been for her creations, and as we recollect all that she dared and achieved, how with every obstacle against her—sex and health and convention— she sought more knowledge and more freedom till the body, weighted with its double burden, sank worn out, we must lay upon her grave whatever we have it in our power to bestow of laurel and rose.

THE RUSSIAN
POINT OF VIEW

First published in 1925

Doubtful as we frequently are whether either the French or the Americans, who have so much in common with us, can yet understand English literature, we must admit graver doubts whether, for all their enthusiasm, the English can understand Russian literature. Debate might protract itself indefinitely as to what we mean by "understand". Instances will occur to everybody of American writers in particular who have written with the highest discrimination of our literature and of ourselves; who have lived a lifetime among us, and finally have taken legal steps to become subjects of King George. For all that, have they understood us, have they not remained to the end of their days foreigners? Could any one believe that the novels of Henry James were written by a man who had grown up in the society which he describes, or that his criticism of English writers was written by a man who had read Shakespeare without any sense of the Atlantic Ocean and two or three hundred years on the far side of it separating his civilisation from ours? A special acuteness and detachment, a sharp angle of vision the foreigner will often achieve; but not that absence of self-consciousness, that ease and fellowship and sense of common values which make for intimacy, and sanity, and the quick give and take of familiar intercourse.

Not only have we all this to separate us from Russian literature, but a much more serious barrier—the difference of language. Of all those who feasted upon Tolstoi, Dostoevsky, and Tchekov during the past twenty years, not more than one or two perhaps have been able to read them in Russian. Our estimate of their qualities has been formed by critics who have never read a word of Russian, or seen Russia, or even heard the language spoken by natives; who have had to depend, blindly and implicitly, upon the work of translators.

What we are saying amounts to this, then, that we have judged a whole literature stripped of its style. When you have changed every word in a sentence from Russian to English, have thereby altered the sense a little, the sound, weight, and accent of the words in relation to each other completely, nothing remains except a crude and coarsened version of the sense. Thus treated, the great Russian writers are like men deprived by an earthquake or a railway accident not only of all their clothes, but also of something subtler and more important—their manners, the idiosyncrasies of their characters. What remains is, as the English have proved by the fanaticism of their admiration, something very powerful and very impressive, but it is difficult to feel sure, in view of these mutilations, how far we can trust ourselves not to impute, to distort, to read into them an emphasis which is false.

They have lost their clothes, we say, in some terrible catastrophe, for some such figure as that describes the simplicity, the humanity, startled out of all effort to hide and disguise its instincts, which Russian literature, whether it is due to translation or to some more profound cause, makes upon us. We find these qualities steeping it through, as obvious in the lesser writers as in the greater. "Learn to make yourselves akin to people. I would even like to add: make yourself indispensable to them. But let this sympathy be not with the mind—for it is easy with the mind—but with the heart, with love towards them." "From the Russian", one would say instantly, wherever one chanced on that quotation. The simplicity, the absence of effort, the assumption that in a world bursting with misery the chief call upon us is to understand our fellow-sufferers, "and not with the mind—for it is easy with the mind—but with the heart"—this is the cloud which broods above the whole of Russian literature, which lures us from our own parched brilliancy and scorched thoroughfares to expand in its shade— and of course with disastrous results. We become awkward and self-conscious; denying our own qualities, we write with an affectation of goodness and simplicity which is nauseating in the extreme. We cannot say "Brother" with simple conviction. There is a story by Mr. Galsworthy in which one of the characters so addresses another (they are both in the depths of misfortune). Immediately everything becomes strained and affected. The English equivalent for "Brother" is "Mate"—a very different word, with something sardonic in it, an indefinable suggestion of humour. Met though they are in the depths of misfortune the two Englishmen who thus accost each other will, we are sure, find a job, make their fortunes, spend the last years of their lives in luxury, and leave a sum of money to prevent poor devils from calling each other "Brother" on the Embankment. But it is common suffering, rather than common happiness, effort, or desire that produces the sense of brotherhood. It is the "deep sadness" which Dr. Hagberg Wright finds typical of the Russian people that creates their literature.

A generalisation of this kind will, of course, even if it has some degree of truth when applied to the body of literature, be changed profoundly when a writer of genius sets to work on it. At once other questions arise. It is seen that an "attitude" is not simple; it is highly complex. Men reft of their coats and their manners, stunned by a railway accident, say hard things, harsh things, unpleasant things, difficult things, even if they say them with the abandonment and simplicity which catastrophe has bred in them. Our first impressions of Tchekov are not of simplicity but of bewilderment. What is the point of it, and why does he make a story out of this? we ask as we read story after story. A man falls in love with a married woman, and they part and meet, and in the end are left talking about their position and

127

by what means they can be free from "this intolerable bondage".

"'How? How?' he asked, clutching his head. . . . And it seemed as though in a little while the solution would be found and then a new and splendid life would begin." That is the end. A postman drives a student to the station and all the way the student tries to make the postman talk, but he remains silent. Suddenly the postman says unexpectedly, "It's against the regulations to take any one with the post". And he walks up and down the platform with a look of anger on his face. "With whom was he angry? Was it with people, with poverty, with the autumn nights?" Again, that story ends.

But is it the end, we ask? We have rather the feeling that we have overrun our signals; or it is as if a tune had stopped short without the expected chords to close it. These stories are inconclusive, we say, and proceed to frame a criticism based upon the assumption that stories ought to conclude in a way that we recognise. In so doing, we raise the question of our own fitness as readers. Where the tune is familiar and the end emphatic— lovers united, villains discomfited, intrigues exposed—as it is in most Victorian fiction, we can scarcely go wrong, but where the tune is unfamiliar and the end a note of interrogation or merely the information that they went on talking, as it is in Tchekov, we need a very daring and alert sense of literature to make us hear the tune, and in particular those last notes which complete the harmony. Probably we have to read a great many stories before we feel, and the feeling is essential to our satisfaction, that we hold the parts together, and that Tchekov was not merely rambling disconnectedly, but struck now this note, now that with intention, in order to complete his meaning.

We have to cast about in order to discover where the emphasis in these strange stories rightly comes. Tchekov's own words give us a lead in the right direction. ". . . such a conversation as this between us", he says, "would have been unthinkable for our parents. At night they did not talk, but slept sound; we, our generation, sleep badly, are restless, but talk a great deal, and are always trying to settle whether we are right or not." Our literature of social satire and psychological finesse both sprang from that restless sleep, that incessant talking; but after all, there is an enormous difference between Tchekov and Henry James, between Tchekov and Bernard Shaw. Obviously—but where does it arise? Tchekov, too, is aware of the evils and injustices of the social state; the condition of the peasants appals him, but the reformer's zeal is not his—that is not the signal for us to stop. The mind interests him enormously; he is a most subtle and delicate analyst of human relations. But again, no; the end is not there. Is it that he is primarily interested not in the soul's relation with other souls, but with the soul's relation to health—with the soul's relation to goodness? These stories are always showing us some affectation, pose, insincerity. Some woman has got into a false relation; some man has been perverted by the inhumanity of his circumstances. The soul is ill; the soul is cured; the soul is not cured. Those are the emphatic points in his stories.

Once the eye is used to these shades, half the "conclusions" of fiction fade into thin air; they show like transparences with a light behind them—gaudy, glaring, superficial. The general tidying up of the last chapter, the marriage, the death, the statement of values so sonorously trumpeted forth, so heavily underlined, become of the most rudimentary kind. Nothing is solved, we feel; nothing is rightly held together. On the other hand, the method which at first seemed so casual, inconclusive, and occupied with trifles, now appears the result of an exquisitely original and fastidious taste, choosing boldly, arranging infallibly, and controlled by an honesty for which we can find no match save among the Russians themselves. There may be no answer to these questions, but at the same time let us never manipulate the evidence so as to produce something fitting, decorous, agreeable to our vanity. This may not be the way to catch the ear of the public; after all, they are used to louder music, fiercer measures; but as the tune sounded so he has written it. In consequence, as we read these little stories about nothing at all, the horizon widens; the soul gains an astonishing sense of freedom.

In reading Tchekov we find ourselves repeating the word "soul" again and again. It sprinkles his pages. Old drunkards use it freely; ". . . you are high up in the service, beyond all reach, but haven't real soul, my dear boy . . . there's no strength in it". Indeed, it is the soul that is the chief character in Russian fiction. Delicate and subtle in Tchekov, subject to an infinite number of humours and distempers, it is of greater depth and volume in Dostoevsky; it is liable to violent diseases and raging fevers, but still the predominant concern. Perhaps that is why it needs so great an effort on the part of an English reader to read *The Brothers Karamazov* or *The Possessed* a second time. The "soul" is alien to him. It is even antipathetic. It has little sense of humour and no sense of comedy. It is formless. It has slight connection with the intellect. It is confused, diffuse, tumultuous, incapable, it seems, of submitting to the control of logic or the discipline of poetry. The novels of Dostoevsky are seething whirlpools, gyrating sandstorms, waterspouts which hiss and boil and suck us in. They are composed purely and wholly of the stuff of the soul. Against our wills we are drawn in, whirled round, blinded, suffocated, and at the same time filled with a giddy rapture. Out of Shakespeare there is no more exciting reading. We open the door and find ourselves in a room full of Russian generals, the tutors of Russian generals, their step-daughters and cousins, and crowds of miscellaneous people who are all talking at the tops of their voices about their most private affairs. But where are we? Surely it is the part of a novelist to inform us whether we are in an hotel, a flat, or hired lodging. Nobody thinks of explaining. We are souls, tortured, unhappy souls, whose only business it is to talk, to reveal, to confess, to draw up at whatever rending of flesh and nerve those crabbed sins which crawl on the sand at the bottom of us. But, as we listen, our confusion slowly settles. A rope is flung to us; we catch hold of a soliloquy; holding on by the skin of our teeth, we are rushed through the water; feverishly, wildly, we rush on and on, now submerged, now in a moment of vision understanding more than we have ever understood before, and receiving such revelations as we are wont to get only from the press of life at its fullest. As we fly we pick it all up—the names of the people, their relationships, that they are staying in an hotel at Roulettenburg, that Polina is involved in an intrigue with the Marquis de Grieux—but what unimportant matters these are compared with the soul! It is the soul that matters, its passion, its tumult, its astonishing medley of beauty and vileness. And if our voices suddenly rise into shrieks of laughter, or if we are shaken by the most violent sobbing, what more natural?—it hardly calls for remark. The pace at which we are living is so tremendous that sparks must rush off our wheels as we fly. Moreover, when the speed is thus increased and the elements of the soul are seen, not separately in scenes of humour or scenes of passion as our slower English minds conceive them, but streaked, involved, inextricably confused, a new panorama of the human mind is revealed. The old divisions melt into each other. Men are at the same time villains and saints; their acts are at once beautiful and despicable. We love and we hate at the same time. There is none of that precise division between good and bad to which we are used. Often those for whom we feel most affection are the greatest criminals, and the most abject sinners move us to the strongest admiration as well as love.

Dashed to the crest of the waves, bumped and battered on the stones at the bottom, it is difficult for an English reader to feel at ease. The process to which he is accustomed in his own literature is reversed. If we wished to tell the story of a General's love affair (and we should find it very difficult in the first place not to laugh at a General), we should begin with his house; we should solidify his surroundings. Only when all was ready should we attempt to deal with the General himself. Moreover, it is not the samovar but the teapot that rules in England; time is limited; space crowded; the influence of other points of view, of other books, even of other ages, makes itself felt. Society is sorted out into lower, middle, and upper classes, each with its own traditions, its own manners, and, to some extent, its own language. Whether he wishes it or not, there is a constant pressure upon an English novelist to recognise these barriers, and, in consequence, order is imposed on him and some kind of form; he is inclined to satire rather than to compassion, to scrutiny of society rather than understanding of individuals themselves.

No such restraints were laid on Dostoevsky. It is all the same to him whether you are noble or simple, a tramp or a great lady. Whoever you are, you are the vessel of this perplexed liquid, this cloudy, yeasty, precious stuff, the soul. The soul is not restrained by barriers. It overflows, it floods, it mingles with the souls of others. The simple story of a bank clerk who could not pay for a bottle of wine spreads, before we know what is happening, into the lives of his father-in-law and the five mistresses whom his father-in-law treated abominably, and the postman's life, and the charwoman's, and the Princesses' who lodged in the same block of flats; for nothing is outside Dostoevsky's province; and when he is tired, he does not stop, he goes on. He cannot restrain himself. Out it tumbles upon us, hot, scalding, mixed, marvellous, terrible, oppressive—the human soul.

There remains the greatest of all novelists—for what else can we call the author of *War and Peace?* Shall we find Tolstoi, too, alien, difficult, a foreigner? Is there some oddity in his angle of vision which, at any rate until we have become disciples and so lost our bearings, keeps us at arm's length in suspicion and bewilderment? From his first words we can be sure of one thing at any rate—here is a man who sees what we see, who proceeds, too, as we are accustomed to proceed, not from the inside outwards, but from the outside inwards. Here is a world in which the postman's knock is heard at eight o'clock, and people go to bed between ten and eleven. Here is a man, too, who is no savage, no child of nature; he is educated; he has had every sort of experience. He is one of those born aristocrats who have used their privileges to the full. He is metropolitan, not suburban. His senses, his intellect, are acute, powerful, and well nourished. There is something proud and superb in the attack of such a mind and such a body upon life. Nothing seems to escape him. Nothing glances off him unrecorded. Nobody, therefore, can so convey the excitement of sport, the beauty of horses, and all the fierce desirability of the world to the senses of a strong young man. Every twig, every feather sticks to his magnet. He notices the blue or red of a child's frock; the way a horse shifts its tail; the sound of a cough; the action of a man trying to put his hands into pockets that have been sewn up. And what his infallible eye reports of a cough or a trick of the hands his infallible brain refers to something hidden in the character, so that we know his people, not only by the way they love and their views on politics and the immortality of the soul, but also by the way they sneeze and choke. Even in a translation we feel that we have been set on a mountain-top and had a telescope put into our hands. Everything is astonishingly clear and absolutely sharp. Then, suddenly, just as we are exulting, breathing deep, feeling at once braced and purified, some detail—perhaps the head of a man—comes at us out of the picture in an alarming way, as if extruded by the very intensity of its life. "Suddenly a strange thing happened to me: first I ceased to see what was around me; then his face seemed to vanish till only the eyes were left, shining over against mine; next the eyes seemed to be in my own head, and then all became confused—I could see nothing and was forced to shut my eyes, in order to break loose from the feeling of pleasure and fear which his gaze was producing in me. . . ." Again and again we share Masha's feelings in *Family Happiness*. One shuts one's eyes to escape the feeling of pleasure and fear. Often it is pleasure that is uppermost. In this very story there are two descriptions, one of a girl walking in a garden at night with her lover, one of a newly married couple prancing down their drawing-room, which so convey the feeling of intense happiness that we shut the book to feel it better. But always there is an element of fear which makes us, like Masha, wish to escape from the gaze which Tolstoi fixes on us. Is it the sense, which in real life might harass us, that such happiness as he describes is too intense to last, that we are on the edge of disaster? Or is it not that the very intensity of our pleasure is somehow questionable and forces us to ask, with Pozdnyshev in the *Kreutzer Sonata*, "But why live?" Life dominates Tolstoi as the soul dominates Dostoevsky. There is always at the centre of all the brilliant and flashing petals of the flower this scorpion, "Why live?" There is always at the centre of the book some Olenin, or Pierre, or Levin who gathers into himself all experience, turns the world round between his fingers, and never ceases to ask, even as he enjoys it, what is the meaning of it, and what should be our aims. It is not the priest who shatters our desires most effectively; it is the man who has known them, and loved them himself. When he derides them, the world indeed turns to dust and ashes beneath our feet. Thus fear mingles with our pleasure, and of the three great Russian writers, it is Tolstoi who most enthralls us and most repels.

But the mind takes its bias from the place of its birth, and no doubt, when it strikes upon a literature so alien as the Russian, flies off at a tangent far from the truth.

DAVID COPPERFIELD

Written in 1925

Like the ripening of strawberries, the swelling of apples, and all other natural processes, new editions of Dickens—cheap, pleasant-looking, well printed—are born into the world and call for no more notice than the season's plums and strawberries, save when by some chance the emergence of one of these masterpieces in its fresh green binding suggests an odd and overwhelming enterprise—that one should read *David Copperfield* for the second time. There is perhaps no person living who can remember reading *David Copperfield* for the first time. Like *Robinson Crusoe* and *Grimm's Fairy Tales* and the Waverley Novels, *Pickwick* and *David Copperfield* are not books, but stories communicated by word of mouth in those tender years when fact and fiction merge, and thus belong to the memories and myths of life, and not to its aesthetic experience. When we lift it from this hazy atmosphere, when we consider it as a book, bound and printed and ordered by the rules of art, what impression does *David Copperfield* make upon us? As Peggotty and Barkis, the rooks and the workbox with the picture of St. Paul's, Traddles who drew skeletons, the donkeys who would cross the green, Mr. Dick and the Memorial, Betsey Trotwood and Jip and Dora and Agnes and the Heeps and the Micawbers once more come to life with all their appurtenances and peculiarities, are they still possessed of the old 'fascination or have they in the interval been attacked by that parching wind which blows about books and, without our reading them, remodels them and changes their features while we sleep? The rumour about Dickens is to the effect that his sentiment is disgusting and his style commonplace; that in reading him every refinement must be hidden and every sensibility kept under glass; but that with these precautions and reservations he is of course Shakespearean; like Scott, a born creator; like Balzac, prodigious in his fecundity; but, rumour adds, it is strange that while one reads Shakespeare and one reads Scott, the precise moment for reading Dickens seldom comes our way.

This last charge may be resolved into this—that he lacks charm and idiosyncrasy, is everybody's writer and no one's in particular, is an institution, a monument, a public thoroughfare trodden dusty by a million feet. It is based largely upon the fact that of all great writers Dickens is both the least personally charming and the least personally present in his books. No one has ever loved Dickens as he loves Shakespeare and Scott. Both in his life and in his work the impression that he makes is the same. He has to perfection the virtues conventionally ascribed to the male; he is self-assertive, self-reliant, self-assured; energetic in the extreme. His message, when he parts the veil of the story and steps forward in person, is plain and forcible; he preaches the value of "plain hardworking qualities", of punctuality, order, diligence, of doing what lies before one with all one's might. Agitated as he was by the most violent passions, ablaze with indignation, teeming with queer characters, unable to keep the dreams out of his head at night, nobody appears, as we read him, more free from the foibles and eccentricities and charms of genius. He comes before us, as one of his biographers described him, "like a prosperous sea captain", stalwart, weather-beaten, self-reliant, with a great contempt for the finicky, the inefficient, or the effeminate. His sympathies indeed have strict limitations. Speaking roughly, they fail him whenever a man or woman has more than two thousand a year, has been to the university, or can count his ancestors back to the third generation. They fail him when he has to treat of the mature emotions—the seduction of Emily, for example, or the death of Dora; whenever it is no longer possible to keep moving and creating, but it is necessary to stand still and search into things and penetrate to the depths of what is there. Then, indeed, he fails grotesquely, and the pages in which he describes what in our convention are the peaks and pinnacles of human life, the explanation of Mrs. Strong, the despair of Mrs. Steerforth, or the anguish of Ham, are of an indescribable unreality—of that uncomfortable complexion which, if we heard Dickens talking so in real life, would either make us blush to the roots of our hair or dash out of the room to conceal our laughter. " . . . Tell him then," says Emily, "that when I hear the wind blowing at night I feel as if it was passing angrily from seeing him and uncle, and was going up to God against me." Miss Dartle raves—about carrion and pollution and earthworms, and worthless spangles and broken toys, and how she will have Emily "proclaimed on the common stair". The failure is akin to that other failure to think deeply, to describe beautifully. Of the men who go to make up the perfect novelist and should live in amity under his hat, two—the poet and the philosopher—failed to come when Dickens called them.

But the greater the creator the more derelict the regions where his powers fail him; all about their fertile lands are deserts where not a blade of grass grows, swamps where the foot sinks deep in mud. Nevertheless, while we are under their spell these great geniuses make us see the world any shape they choose. We remodel our psychological geography when we read Dickens; we forget that we have ever felt the delights of solitude or observed with wonder the intricate emotions of our friends, or luxuriated in the beauty of nature. What we remember is the ardour, the excitement, the humour, the oddity of people's characters; the smell and savour and soot of London; the incredible coincidences which hook the most remote lives together; the city, the law courts; this man's nose, that man's limp; some scene under an archway or on the high road; and above all some gigantic and dominating figure, so stuffed and swollen with life that he does not exist singly and solitarily, but seems to need for his own realisation a host of others, to call into existence the severed parts that complete him, so that wherever he goes he is the centre of conviviality and merriment and punch-making; the room is full, the lights are bright; there are Mrs. Micawber, the twins, Traddles, Betsey Trotwood—all in full swing.

This is the power which cannot fade or fail in its effect— the power not to analyse or to interpret, but to produce, apparently without thought or effort or calculation of the effect upon the story, characters who exist not in detail, not accurately or exactly, but abundantly in a cluster of wild and yet extraordinarily revealing remarks, bubble climbing on the top of bubble as the breath of the creator fills them. And the fecundity and apparent irreflectiveness have a strange effect. They make creators of us, and not merely readers and spectators. As we listen to Micawber pouring himself forth and venturing perpetually some new flight of astonishing imagination, we see, unknown to Mr. Micawber, into the depths of his soul. We say, as Dickens himself says while Micawber holds forth: "How wonderfully like Mr. Micawber that is!" Why trouble, then, if the scenes where emotion and psychology are to be expected fail us completely? Subtlety and complexity are all there if we know where to look for them, if we can get over the surprise of finding them—as it seems to us, who have another convention in these matters—in the wrong places. As a creator of character his peculiarity is that he creates wherever his eyes rest—he has the visualising power in the extreme. His people are branded upon our eyeballs before we hear them speak, by what he sees them doing, and it seems as if it were the sight that sets his thought in action. He saw Uriah Heep "breathing into the pony's nostrils and immediately covering them with his hand"; he saw David Copperfield looking in the glass to see how red his eyes were after his mother's death; he saw oddities and blemishes, gestures and incidents, scars, eyebrows, everything that was in the room, in a second. His eye brings in almost too rich a harvest for him to deal with, and gives him an aloofness and a hardness which freeze his sentimentalism and make it seem a concession to the public, a veil thrown over the penetrating glance which left to itself pierced to the bone. With such a power at his command Dickens made his books blaze up, not by tightening the plot or sharpening the wit, but by throwing another handful of people upon the fire. The interest flags and he creates Miss Mowcher, completely alive, equipped in every detail as if she were to play a great part in the story, whereas once the dull stretch of road is passed by her help, she disappears; she is needed no longer. Hence a Dickens novel is apt to become a bunch of separate characters loosely held together, often by the most arbitrary conventions, who tend to fly asunder and split our attention into so many different parts that we drop the book in despair. But that danger is surmounted in *David Copperfield*. There, though characters swarm and life flows into every creek and cranny, some common feeling—youth, gaiety, hope—envelops the tumult, brings the scattered parts together, and invests the most perfect of all the Dickens novels with an atmosphere of beauty.

NOTE:

The following letter by Virginia Woolf appears in *The Nation* of September 12, 1925.

SIR,

Fear of a sudden death very naturally distracted Kappa's mind from my article on *David Copperfield* or he would, I think, have taken my meaning. That nobody can remember reading *David Copperfield* for the first time is a proof not, as he infers, that the reading makes so little impression that it slips off the mind unremembered, but that *David Copperfield* takes such rank among our classics and is a book of such astonishing vividness that parents will read it aloud to their children before they can quite distinguish fact from fiction, and they will never in later life be able to recall the first time they read it. *Grimm's Fairy Tales* and *Robinson Crusoe* are for many people in the same case. Questions of affection are of course always disputable. I can only reiterate that while I would cheerfully become Shakespeare's cat, Scott's pig, or Keats's canary, if by so doing I could share the society of these great men, I would not cross the road (reasons of curiosity apart) to dine with Wordsworth, Byron, or Dickens. Yet I venerate their genius; and my tears would certainly help to swell the "unparalleled flow of popular grief" at their deaths. It only means that writers have characters apart from their books, which are sympathetic to some, antipathetic to others. And I maintain that if it could be put to the vote, Which do you prefer as man, Shakespeare, Scott, or Dickens? Shakespeare would be first, Scott second, and Dickens nowhere at all

Yours, etc.,
VIRGINIA WOOLF

THE ART
OF FICTION

Written in 1927

That fiction is a lady, and a lady who has somehow got herself into trouble, is a thought that must often have struck her admirers. Many gallant gentlemen have ridden to her rescue, chief among them Sir Walter Raleigh and Mr. Percy Lubbock. But both were a little ceremonious in their approach; both, one felt, had a great deal of knowledge of her, but not much intimacy with her. Now comes Mr. Forster,[6] who disclaims knowledge but cannot deny that he knows the lady well. If he lacks something of the others' authority, he enjoys the privileges which are allowed the lover. He knocks at the bedroom door and is admitted when the lady is in slippers and dressing-gown. Drawing up their chairs to the fire they talk easily, wittily, subtly, like old friends who have no illusions, although in fact the bedroom is a lecture-room and the place the highly austere city of Cambridge.

This informal attitude on Mr. Forster's part is of course deliberate. He is not a scholar; he refuses to be a pseudo-scholar. There remains a point of view which the lecturer can adopt usefully, if modestly. He can, as Mr. Forster puts it, "visualise the English novelists not as floating down that stream which bears all its sons away unless they are careful, but as seated together in a room, a circular room—a sort of British Museum reading-room—all writing their novels simultaneously". So

6   *Aspects of the Novel*, by E. M. Forster.

simultaneous are they, indeed, that they persist in writing out of their turn. Richardson insists that he is contemporary with Henry James. Wells will write a passage which might be written by Dickens. Being a novelist himself, Mr. Forster is not annoyed at this discovery. He knows from experience what a muddled and illogical machine the brain of a writer is. He knows how little they think about methods; how completely they forget their grandfathers; how absorbed they tend to become in some vision of their own. Thus, though the scholars have all his respect, his sympathies are with the untidy and harassed people who are scribbling away at their books. And looking down on them, not from any great height, but, as he says, over their shoulders, he makes out, as he passes, that certain shapes and ideas tend to recur in their minds whatever their period. Since story-telling began stories have always been made of much the same elements; and these, which he calls The Story, People, Plot, Fantasy, Prophecy, Pattern, and Rhythm, he now proceeds to examine.

Many are the judgments that we would willingly argue, many are the points over which we would willingly linger, as Mr. Forster passes lightly on his way. That Scott is a storyteller and nothing more; that a story is the lowest of literary organisms; that the novelist's unnatural preoccupation with love is largely a reflection of his own state of mind while he composes—every page has a hint or a suggestion which makes us stop to think or wish to contradict. Never raising his voice above the speaking level, Mr. Forster has the art of saying things which sink airily enough into the mind to stay there and unfurl like those Japanese flowers which open up in the depths of the water. But greatly though these sayings intrigue us, we want to call a halt at some definite stopping place; we want to make Mr. Forster stand and deliver. For possibly, if fiction is, as we suggest, in difficulties, it may be because nobody grasps her firmly and defines her severely. She has had no rules drawn up for her, very little thinking done on her behalf. And though rules may be wrong and must be broken, they have this advantage—they confer dignity and order upon their subject; they admit her to a place in civilised society; they prove that she is worthy of consideration. But this part of his duty, if it is his duty, Mr. Forster expressly disowns. He is not going to theorise about fiction except incidentally; he doubts even whether she is to be approached by a critic, and if so, with what critical equipment. All we can do is to edge him into a position which is definite enough for us to see where he stands. And perhaps the best way to do this is to quote, much summarised, his estimates of three great figures—Meredith, Hardy, and Henry James. Meredith is an exploded philosopher. His vision of nature is "fluffy and lush". When he gets serious and noble he becomes a bully. "And his novels; most of the social values are faked. The tailors are not tailors, the cricket matches are not cricket." Hardy is a far greater writer. But he is not so successful as a novelist because his characters are "required to contribute too much to the plot; except in their rustic humours their vitality has been impoverished, they have gone thin and dry—he has emphasised causality more strongly than his medium permits". Henry James pursued the narrow path of aesthetic duty and was successful. But at what a sacrifice? "Most of human life has to disappear before he can do us a novel Maimed creatures can alone breathe in his novels. His characters are few in number and constructed on stingy lines."

Now if we look at these judgments, and place beside them certain admissions and omissions, we shall see that if we cannot pin Mr. Forster to a creed we can commit him to a point of view. There is something—we hesitate to be more precise—which he calls "life". It is to this that he brings the books of Meredith, Hardy, or James for comparison. Always their failure is some failure in relation to life. It is the humane as opposed to the aesthetic view of fiction. It maintains that the novel is "sogged with humanity"; that "human beings have their great chance in the novel"; triumph won at the expense of life is in fact a defeat. Thus we arrive at the notably harsh judgment of Henry James.

For Henry James brought into the novel something besides human beings. He created patterns which, though beautiful in themselves, are hostile to humanity. And for his neglect of life, says Mr. Forster, he will perish.

But at this point the pertinacious pupil may demand: "What is this 'Life' that keeps on cropping up so mysteriously and so complacently in books about fiction? Why is it absent in a pattern and present in a tea party? Why is the pleasure that we get from the pattern in *The Golden Bowl* less valuable than the emotion which Trollope gives us when he describes a lady drinking tea in a parsonage? Surely the definition of life is too arbitrary, and requires to be expanded." To all of this Mr. Forster would reply, presumably, that he lays down no laws; the novel somehow seems to him too soft a substance to be carved like the other arts; he is merely telling us what moves him and what leaves him cold. Indeed, there is no other criterion. So then we are back in the old bog; nobody knows anything about the laws of fiction; or what its relation is to life; or to what effects it can lend itself. We can only trust our instincts. If instinct leads one reader to call Scott a story-teller, another to call him a master of romance; if one reader is moved by art, another by life, each is right, and each can pile a card-house of theory on top of his opinion as high as he can go. But the assumption that fiction is more intimately and humbly attached to the service of human beings than the other arts leads to a further position which Mr. Forster's book again illustrates. It is unnecessary to dwell upon her aesthetic functions because they are so feeble that they can safely be ignored. Thus, though it is impossible to imagine a book on painting in which not a word should be said about the medium in which a painter works, a wise and brilliant book, like Mr. Forster's, can be written about fiction without saying more than a sentence or two about the medium in which a novelist works. Almost nothing is said about words. One might suppose, unless one had read them, that a sentence means the same thing and is used for the same purposes by Sterne and by Wells.

One might conclude that *Tristram Shandy* gains nothing from the language in which it is written. So with the other aesthetic qualities. Pattern, as we have seen, is recognised, but savagely censured for her tendency to obscure the human features. Beauty occurs but she is suspect. She makes one furtive appearance— "beauty at which a novelist should never aim, though he fails if he does not achieve it"—and the possibility that she may emerge again as rhythm is briefly discussed in a few interesting pages at the end. But for the rest fiction is treated as a parasite which draws sustenance from life and must in gratitude resemble life or perish. In poetry, in drama, words may excite and stimulate and deepen without this allegiance; but in fiction they must first and foremost hold themselves at the service of the teapot and the pug dog, and to be found wanting is to be found lacking.

Strange though this unaesthetic attitude would be in the critic of any other art, it does not surprise us in the critic of fiction. For one thing, the problem is extremely difficult. A book fades like a mist, like a dream. How are we to take a stick and point to that tone, that relation, in the vanishing pages, as Mr. Roger Fry points with his wand at a line or a colour in the picture displayed before him? Moreover, a novel in particular has roused a thousand ordinary human feelings in its progress. To drag in art in such a connection seems priggish and cold-hearted. It may well compromise the critic as a man of feeling and domestic ties. And so while the painter, the musician, and the poet come in for their share of criticism, the novelist goes unscathed. His character will be discussed; his morality, it may be his genealogy, will be examined; but his writing will go scot-free. There is not a critic alive now who will say that a novel is a work of art and that as such he will judge it.

And perhaps, as Mr. Forster insinuates, the critics are right. In England at any rate the novel is not a work of art. There are none to be stood beside *War and Peace, The Brothers Karamazov,* or *A la Recherche du Temps Perdu.* But while we accept the fact, we cannot suppress one last conjecture. In France and Russia they take fiction seriously. Flaubert spends a month seeking a phrase to describe a cabbage. Tolstoy writes *War and Peace* seven times over. Something of their pre-eminence may be due to the pains they take, something to the severity with which they are judged. If the English critic were less domestic, less assiduous to protect the rights of what it pleases him to call life, the novelist might be holder too. He might cut adrift from the eternal tea-table and the plausible and preposterous formulas which are supposed to represent the whole of our human adventure. But then the story might wobble; the plot might crumble; ruin might seize upon the characters. The novel, in short, might become a work of art.

Such are the dreams that Mr. Forster leads us to cherish. For his is a book to encourage dreaming. None more suggestive has been written about the poor lady whom, with perhaps mistaken chivalry, we still persist in calling the art of fiction.

THE NOVELS
OF THOMAS HARDY

Written in January, 1928

When we say that the death of Thomas Hardy leaves English
fiction without a leader, we mean that there is no other writer
whose supremacy would be generally accepted, none to whom
it seems so fitting and natural to pay homage. Nobody of course
claimed it less. The unworldly and simple old man would have
been painfully embarrassed by the rhetoric that flourishes on
such occasions as this. Yet it is no less than the truth to say that
while he lived there was one novelist at all events who made the
art of fiction seem an honourable calling; while Hardy lived
there was no excuse for thinking meanly of the art he practised.
Nor was this solely the result of his peculiar genius. Something
of it sprang from his character in its modesty and integrity, from
his life, lived simply down in Dorsetshire without self-seeking
or self-advertisement. For both reasons, because of his genius
and because of the dignity with which his gift was used, it was
impossible not to honour him as an artist and to feel respect and
affection for the man. But it is of the work that we must speak,
of the novels that were written so long ago that they seem as
detached from the fiction of the moment as Hardy himself was
remote from the stir of the present and its littleness.

We have to go back more than a generation if we are to trace
the career of Hardy as a novelist. In the year 1871 he was a man
of thirty-one; he had written a novel, *Desperate Remedies,* but
he was by no means an assured craftsman. He "was feeling his
way to a method", he said himself; as if he were conscious that

he possessed all sorts of gifts, yet did not know their nature, or how to use them to advantage. To read that first novel is to share in the perplexity of its author. The imagination of the writer is powerful and sardonic; he is book-learned in a home-made way; he can create characters but he cannot control them; he is obviously hampered by the difficulties of his technique and, what is more singular, he is driven by some sense that human beings are the sport of forces outside themselves, to make use of an extreme and even melodramatic use of coincidence. He is already possessed of the conviction that a novel is not a toy, nor an argument; it is a means of giving truthful if harsh and violent impressions of the lives of men and women. But perhaps the most remarkable quality in the book is the sound of a waterfall that echoes and booms through its pages. It is the first manifestation of the power that was to assume such vast proportions in the later books. He already proves himself a minute and skilled observer of Nature; the rain, he knows, falls differently as it falls upon roots or arable; he knows that the wind sounds differently as it passes through the branches of different trees. But he is aware in a larger sense of Nature as a force; he feels in it a spirit that can sympathize or mock or remain the indifferent spectator of human fortunes. Already that sense was his; and the crude story of Miss Aldclyffe and Cytherea is memorable because it is watched by the eyes of the gods, and worked out in the presence of Nature.

That he was a poet should have been obvious; that he was a novelist might still have been held uncertain. But the year after, when *Under the Greenwood Tree* appeared, it was clear that much of the effort of "feeling for a method" had been overcome. Something of the stubborn originality of the earlier book was lost. The second is accomplished, charming, idyllic compared with the first. The writer, it seems, may well develop into one of our English landscape painters, whose pictures are all of cottage gardens and old peasant women, who lingers to collect and preserve from oblivion the old-fashioned ways and words which are rapidly falling into disuse. And yet what kindly lover of antiquity, what naturalist with a microscope in his pocket, what scholar solicitous for the changing shapes of language, ever heard the cry of a small bird killed in the next wood by an owl with such intensity? The cry "passed into the silence without mingling with it". Again we hear, very far away, like the sound of a gun out at sea on a calm summer's morning, a strange and ominous echo. But as we read these early books there is a sense of waste. There is a feeling that Hardy's genius was obstinate and perverse; first one gift would have its way with him and then another. They would not consent to run together easily in harness. Such indeed was likely to be the fate of a writer who was at once poet and realist, a faithful son of field and down, yet tormented by the doubts and despondencies bred of book-learning; a lover of old ways and plain countrymen, yet doomed to see the faith and flesh of his forefathers turn to thin and spectral transparencies before his eyes.

To this contradiction Nature had added another element likely to disorder a symmetrical development. Some writers are born conscious of everything; others are unconscious of many things. Some, like Henry James and Flaubert, are able not merely to make the best use of the spoil their gifts bring in, but control their genius in the act of creation; they are aware of all the possibilities of every situation, and are never taken by surprise. The unconscious writers, on the other hand, like Dickens and Scott, seem suddenly and without their own consent to be lifted up and swept onwards. The wave sinks and they cannot say what has happened or why. Among them—it is the source of his strength and of his weakness—we must place Hardy. His own word, "moments of vision", exactly describes those passages of astonishing beauty and force which are to be found in every book that he wrote. With a sudden quickening of power which we cannot foretell, nor he, it seems, control, a single scene breaks off from the rest. We see, as if it existed alone and for all time, the wagon with Fanny's dead body inside travelling along the road under the dripping trees; we see the bloated sheep struggling among the clover; we see Troy flashing his sword round Bathsheba where she stands motionless, cutting the lock off her head and spitting the caterpillar on her breast. Vivid to the eye, but not to the eye alone, for every sense participates, such scenes dawn upon us and their splendour remains. But the power goes as it comes. The moment of vision is succeeded by long stretches of plain daylight, nor can we believe that any craft or skill could have caught the wild power and turned it to a better use. The novels therefore are full of inequalities; they are lumpish and dull and inexpressive; but they are never arid; there is always about them a little blur of unconsciousness, that halo of freshness and margin of the unexpressed which often produce the most profound sense of satisfaction. It is as if Hardy himself were not quite aware of what he did, as if his consciousness held more than he could produce, and he left it for his readers to make out his full meaning and to supplement it from their own experience.

For these reasons Hardy's genius was uncertain in development, uneven in accomplishment, but, when the moment came, magnificent in achievement. The moment came, completely and fully, in *Far from the Madding Crowd*. The subject was right; the method was right; the poet and the countryman, the sensual man, the sombre reflective man, the man of learning, all enlisted to produce a book which, however fashions may chop and change, must hold its place among the great English novels. There is, in the first place, that sense of the physical world which Hardy more than any novelist can bring before us; the sense that the little prospect of man's existence is ringed by a landscape which, while it exists apart, yet confers a deep and solemn beauty upon his drama. The dark downland, marked by the barrows of the dead and the huts of shepherds, rises against the sky, smooth as a wave of the sea, but solid and eternal; rolling away to the infinite distance, but sheltering in its folds quiet villages whose smoke rises in frail columns by day, whose lamps burn in the immense darkness by night. Gabriel Oak tending his sheep up there on the back of the world is the eternal shepherd; the stars are ancient beacons; and for ages he has watched beside his sheep.

But down in the valley the earth is full of warmth and life; the farms are busy, the barns stored, the fields loud with the lowing of cattle and the bleating of sheep. Nature is prolific, splendid, and lustful; not yet malignant and still the Great Mother of labouring men. And now for the first time Hardy gives full play to his humour, where it is freest and most rich, upon the lips of country men. Jan Coggan and Henry Fray and Joseph Poorgrass gather in the malthouse when the day's work is over and give vent to that half-shrewd, half-poetic humour which has been brewing in their brains and finding expression over their beer since the pilgrims tramped the Pilgrims' Way; which Shakespeare and Scott and George Eliot all loved to overhear, but none loved better or heard with greater understanding than Hardy. But it is not the part of the peasants in the Wessex novels to stand out as individuals. They compose a pool of common wisdom, of common humour, a fund of perpetual life. They comment upon the actions of the hero and heroine, but while Troy or Oak or Fanny or Bathsheba come in and out and pass away, Jan Coggan and Henry Fray and Joseph Poorgrass remain. They drink by night and they plough the fields by day. They are eternal. We meet them over and over again in the novels, and they always have something typical about them, more of the character that marks a race than of the features which belong to an individual. The peasants are the great sanctuary of sanity, the country the last stronghold of happiness. When they disappear, there is no hope for the race.

With Oak and Troy and Bathsheba and Fanny Robin we come to the men and women of the novels at their full stature. In every book three or four figures predominate, and stand up like lightning conductors to attract the force of the elements. Oak and Troy and Bathsheba; Eustacia, Wildeve, and Venn; Henchard,

Lucetta, and Farfrae; Jude, Sue Bridehead, and Phillotson. There is even a certain likeness between the different groups. They live as individuals and they differ as individuals; but they also live as types and have a likeness as types. Bathsheba is Bathsheba, but she is woman and sister to Eustacia and Lucetta and Sue; Gabriel is Gabriel Oak, but he is man and brother to Henchard, Venn, and Jude. However lovable and charming Bathsheba may be, still she is weak; however stubborn and ill-guided Henchard may be, still he is strong. This is a fundamental part of Hardy's vision; the staple of many of his books. The woman is the weaker and the fleshlier, and she clings to the stronger and obscures his vision. How freely, nevertheless, in his greater books life is poured over the unalterable framework! When Bathsheba sits in the wagon among her plants, smiling at her own loveliness in the little looking-glass, we may know, and it is proof of Hardy's power that we do know, how severely she will suffer and cause others to suffer before the end. But the moment has all the bloom and beauty of life. And so it is, time and time again. His characters, both men and women, were creatures to him of an infinite attraction. For the women he shows a more tender solicitude than for the men, and in them, perhaps, he takes a keener interest. Vain might their beauty be and terrible their fate, but while the glow of life is in them their step is free, their laughter sweet, and theirs is the power to sink into the breast of Nature and become part of her silence and solemnity, or to rise and put on them the movement of the clouds and the wildness of the flowering woodlands. The men who suffer, not like the women through dependence upon other human beings, but through conflict with fate, enlist our sterner sympathies. For such a man as Gabriel Oak we need have no passing fears. Honour him we must, though it is not granted us to love him quite so freely. He is firmly set upon his feet and can give as shrewd a blow, to men at least, as any he is likely to receive. He has a prevision of what is to be expected that springs from character rather than from education. He is stable in his temperament, steadfast in his affections, and capable of open-eyed endurance without flinching. But he, too, is no puppet. He is a homely, humdrum fellow on ordinary occasions. He can walk the street without making people turn to stare at him. In short, nobody can deny Hardy's power—the true novelist's power—to make us believe that his characters are fellow-beings driven by their own passions and idiosyncrasies, while they have—and this is the poet's gift—something symbolical about them which is common to us all.

And it is when we are considering Hardy's power of creating men and women that we become most conscious of the profound differences that distinguish him from his peers. We look back at a number of these characters and ask ourselves what it is that we remember them for. We recall their passions. We remember how deeply they have loved each other and often with what tragic results. We remember the faithful love of Oak for Bathsheba; the tumultuous but fleeting passions of men like Wildeve, Troy, and Fitzpiers; we remember the filial love of Clym for his mother, the jealous paternal passion of Henchard for Elizabeth Jane. But we do not remember how they have loved. We do not remember how they talked and changed and got to know each other, finely, gradually, from step to step and from stage to stage. Their relationship is not composed of those intellectual apprehensions and subtleties of perception which seem so slight yet are so profound. In all the books love is one of the great facts that mould human life. But it is a catastrophe; it happens suddenly and overwhelmingly, and there is little to be said about it. The talk between the lovers when it is not passionate is practical or philosophic, as though the discharge of their daily duties left them with more desire to question life and its purpose than to investigate each other's sensibilities. Even if it were in their power to analyse their emotions, life is too stirring to give them time. They need all their strength to deal with the downright blows, the freakish ingenuity, the gradually increasing malignity of fate. They have none to spend upon the subtleties and delicacies of the human comedy.

Thus there comes a time when we can say with certainty that we shall not find in Hardy some of the qualities that have given us most delight in the works of other novelists. He has not the perfection of Jane Austen, or the wit of Meredith, or the range of Thackeray, or Tolstoy's amazing intellectual power. There is in the work of the great classical writers a finality of effect which places certain of their scenes, apart from the story, beyond the reach of change. We do not ask what bearing they have upon the narrative, nor do we make use of them to interpret problems which lie on the outskirts of the scene. A laugh, a blush, half a dozen words of dialogue, and it is enough; the source of our delight is perennial. But Hardy has none of this concentration and completeness. His light does not fall directly upon the human heart. It passes over it and out on to the darkness of the heath and upon the trees swaying in the storm. When we look back into the room the group by the fireside is dispersed. Each man or woman is battling with the storm, alone, revealing himself most when he is least under the observation of other human beings. We do not know them as we know Pierre or Natasha or Becky Sharp. We do not know them in and out and all round as they are revealed to the casual caller, to the Government official, to the great lady, to the general on the battlefield. We do not know the complication and involvement and turmoil of their thoughts. Geographically, too, they remain fixed to the same stretch of the English countryside. It is seldom, and always with unhappy results, that Hardy leaves the yeoman or farmer to describe the class above theirs in the social scale. In the drawing-room and clubroom and ballroom, where people of leisure and education come together, where comedy is bred and shades of character revealed, he is awkward and ill at ease. But the opposite is equally true. If we do not know his men and women in their relations to each other, we know them in their relations to time, death, and fate. If we do not see them in quick agitation against the lights and crowds of cities, we see them against the earth, the storm, and the seasons. We know their attitude towards some of the most tremendous problems that can confront mankind. They take on a more than mortal size in memory. We see them, not in detail but enlarged and dignified. We see Tess reading the baptismal service in her nightgown "with an impress of dignity that was almost regal". We see Marty South, "like a being who had rejected with indifference the attribute of sex for the loftier quality of abstract humanism", laying the flowers on Winterbourne's grave. Their speech has a Biblical dignity and poetry. They have a force in them which cannot be defined, a force of love or of hate, a force which in the men is the cause of rebellion against life, and in the women implies an illimitable capacity for suffering, and it is this which dominates the character and makes it unnecessary that we should see the finer features that lie hid. This is the tragic power; and, if we are to place Hardy among his fellows, we must call him the greatest tragic writer among English novelists.

But let us, as we approach the danger-zone of Hardy's philosophy, be on our guard. Nothing is more necessary, in reading an imaginative writer, than to keep at the right distance above his page. Nothing is easier, especially with a writer of marked idiosyncrasy, than to fasten on opinions, convict him of a creed, tether him to a consistent point of view. Nor was Hardy any exception to the rule that the mind which is most capable of receiving impressions is very often the least capable of drawing conclusions. It is for the reader, steeped in the impression, to supply the comment. It is his part to know when to put aside the writer's conscious intention in favour of some deeper intention of which perhaps he may be unconscious. Hardy himself was aware of this. A novel "is an impression, not an argument", he has warned us, and, again

Unadjusted impressions have their value, and the road to a true philosophy of life seems to lie in humbly recording diverse readings of its phenomena as they are forced upon us by chance and change.

Certainly it is true to say of him that, at his greatest, he gives us impressions; at his weakest, arguments. In *The Woodlanders*, *The Return of the Native*, *Far from the Madding Crowd*, and above all, in *The Mayor of Casterbridge*, we have Hardy's impression of life as it came to him without conscious ordering. Let him once begin to tamper with his direct intuitions and his power is gone. "Did you say the stars were worlds, Tess?" asks little Abraham as they drive to market with their beehives. Tess replies that they are like "the apples on our stubbard-tree, most of them splendid and sound—a few blighted". "Which do we live on—a splendid or a blighted one?" "A blighted one," she replies, or rather the mournful thinker who has assumed her mask speaks for her. The words protrude, cold and raw, like the springs of a machine where we had seen only flesh and blood. We are crudely jolted out of that mood of sympathy which is renewed a moment later when the little cart is run down and we have a concrete instance of the ironical methods which rule our planet.

That is the reason why *Jude the Obscure* is the most painful of all Hardy's books, and the only one against which we can fairly bring the charge of pessimism. In *Jude the Obscure* argument is allowed to dominate impression, with the result that though the misery of the book is overwhelming it is not tragic. As calamity succeeds calamity we feel that the case against society is not being argued fairly or with profound understanding of the facts. Here is nothing of that width and force and knowledge of mankind which, when Tolstoy criticizes society, makes his indictment formidable. Here we have revealed to us the petty cruelty of men, not the large injustice of the gods. It is only necessary to compare *Jude the Obscure* with *The Mayor of Casterbridge* to see where Hardy's true power lay. Jude carries on his miserable contest against the deans of colleges and the conventions of sophisticated society. Henchard is pitted, not against another man, but against something outside himself which is opposed to men of his ambition and power. No human being wishes him ill. Even Farfrae and Newson and Elizabeth Jane whom he has wronged all come to pity him, and even to admire his strength of character. He is standing up to fate, and in backing the old Mayor whose ruin has been largely his own fault, Hardy makes us feel that we are backing human nature in an unequal contest. There is no pessimism here. Throughout the book we are aware of the sublimity of the issue, and yet it is presented to us in the most concrete form. From the opening scene in which Henchard sells his wife to the sailor at the fair to his death on Egdon Heath the vigour of the story is superb, its humour rich and racy, its movement large-limbed and free. The skimmity ride, the fight between Farfrae and Henchard in the loft, Mrs. Cuxsom's speech upon the death of Mrs. Henchard, the talk of the ruffians at Peter's Finger with Nature present in the background or mysteriously dominating the foreground, are among the glories of English fiction. Brief and scanty, it may be, is the measure of happiness allowed to each, but so long as the struggle is, as Henchard's was, with the decrees of fate and not with the laws of man, so long as it is in the open air and calls for activity of the body rather than of the brain, there is greatness in the contest, there is pride and pleasure in it, and the death of the broken corn merchant in his cottage on Egdon Heath is comparable to the death of Ajax, lord of Salamis. The true tragic emotion is ours.

Before such power as this we are made to feel that the ordinary tests which we apply to fiction are futile enough. Do we insist that a great novelist shall be a master of melodious prose? Hardy was no such thing. He feels his way by dint of sagacity and uncompromising sincerity to the phrase he wants, and it is often of unforgettable pungency. Failing it, he will make do with any homely or clumsy or old-fashioned turn of speech, now of the utmost angularity, now of a bookish elaboration. No style in literature, save Scott's, is so difficult to analyse; it is on the face of it so bad, yet it achieves its aim so unmistakably. As well might one attempt to rationalize the charm of a muddy country road, or of a plain field of roots in winter. And then, like Dorsetshire itself, out of these very elements of stiffness and angularity his prose will put on greatness; will roll with a Latin sonority; will shape itself in a massive and monumental symmetry like that of his own bare downs. Then again, do we require that a novelist shall observe the probabilities, and keep close to reality? To find anything approaching the violence and convolution of Hardy's plots one must go back to the Elizabethan drama. Yet we accept his story completely as we read it; more than that, it becomes obvious that his violence and his melodrama, when they are not due to a curious peasant-like love of the monstrous for its own sake, are part of that wild spirit of poetry which saw with intense irony and grimness that no reading of life can possibly outdo the strangeness of life itself, no symbol of caprice and unreason be too extreme to represent the astonishing circumstances of our existence.

But as we consider the great structure of the Wessex Novels it seems irrelevant to fasten on little points—this character, that scene, this phrase of deep and poetic beauty. It is something larger that Hardy has bequeathed to us. The Wessex Novels are not one book, but many. They cover an immense stretch; inevitably they are full of imperfections—some are failures, and others exhibit only the wrong side of their maker's genius. But undoubtedly, when we have submitted ourselves fully to them, when we come to take stock of our impression of the whole, the effect is commanding and satisfactory. We have been freed from the cramp and pettiness imposed by life. Our imaginations have been stretched and heightened; our humour has been made to laugh out; we have drunk deep of the beauty of the earth. Also we have been made to enter the shade of a sorrowful and brooding spirit which, even in its saddest mood, bore itself with a grave uprightness and never, even when most moved to anger, lost its deep compassion for the sufferings of men and women. Thus it is no mere transcript of life at a certain time and place that Hardy has given us. It is a vision of the world and of man's lot as they revealed themselves to a powerful imagination, a profound and poetic genius, a gentle and humane soul.

THE NOVELS OF
GEORGE MEREDITH

Written in January, 1928

Twenty years ago the reputation of George Meredith was at its height. His novels had won their way to celebrity through all sorts of difficulties, and their fame was all the brighter and the more singular for what it had subdued. Then, too, it was generally discovered that the maker of these splendid books was himself a splendid old man. Visitors who went down to Box Hill reported that they were thrilled as they walked up the drive of the little suburban house by the sound of a voice booming and reverberating within. The novelist, seated among the usual knick-knacks of the drawing-room, was like the bust of Euripides to look at. Age had worn and sharpened the fine features, but the nose was still acute, the blue eyes still keen and ironical. Though he had sunk immobile into an arm-chair, his aspect was still vigorous and alert. It was true that he was almost stone-deaf, but this was the least of afflictions to one who was scarcely able to keep pace with the rapidity of his own ideas. Since he could not hear what was said to him, he could give himself wholeheartedly to the delights of soliloquy. It did not much matter, perhaps, whether his audience was cultivated or simple. Compliments that would have flattered a duchess were presented with equal ceremony to a child. To neither could he speak the simple language of daily life. But all the time this highly wrought, artificial conversation, with its crystallized phrases and its high-piled metaphors, moved and tossed on a current of laughter. His laugh curled round his sentences as if he himself enjoyed their humorous exaggeration. The master of language was splashing and diving in his element of words. So the legend grew; and the fame of George Meredith, who sat with the head of a Greek poet on his shoulders in a suburban villa beneath Box Hill, pouring out poetry and sarcasm and wisdom in a voice that could be heard almost on the high road, made his fascinating and brilliant books seem more fascinating and brilliant still.

But that is twenty years ago. His fame as a talker is necessarily dimmed, and his fame as a writer seems also under a cloud. On none of his successors is his influence now marked. When one of them whose own work has given him the right to be heard with respect chances to speak his mind on the subject, it is not flattering.

> Meredith [writes Mr. Forster in his *Aspects of the Novel*]
> is not the great name he was twenty years ago. . . . His
> philosophy has not worn well. His heavy attacks on
> sentimentality—they bore the present generation. . . .
> When he gets serious and noble-minded there is a strident
> overtone, a bullying that becomes distressing. . . . What
> with the faking, what with the preaching, which was never
> agreeable and is now said to be hollow, and what with
> the home counties posing as the universe, it is no wonder
> Meredith now lies in the trough.

The criticism is not, of course, intended to be a finished estimate; but in its conversational sincerity it condenses accurately enough what is in the air when Meredith is mentioned. No, the general conclusion would seem to be, Meredith has not worn well. But the value of centenaries lies in the occasion they offer us for solidifying such airy impressions. Talk, mixed with half-rubbed-out memories, forms a mist by degrees through which we scarcely see plain. To open the books again, to try to read them as if for the first time, to try

162

to free them from the rubbish of reputation and accident—that, perhaps, is the most acceptable present we can offer to a writer on his hundredth birthday.

And since the first novel is always apt to be an unguarded one, where the author displays his gifts without knowing how to dispose of them to the best advantage, we may do well to open *Richard Feverel* first. It needs no great sagacity to see that the writer is a novice at his task. The style is extremely uneven. Now he twists himself into iron knots; now he lies flat as a pancake. He seems to be of two minds as to his intention. Ironic comment alternates with long-winded narrative. He vacillates from one attitude to another. Indeed, the whole fabric seems to rock a little insecurely. The baronet wrapped in a cloak; the county family; the ancestral home; the uncles mouthing epigrams in the dining-room; the great ladies flaunting and swimming; the jolly farmers slapping their thighs: all liberally if spasmodically sprinkled with dried aphorisms from a pepper-pot called the Pilgrim's Scrip—what an odd conglomeration it is! But the oddity is not on the surface; it is not merely that whiskers and bonnets have gone out of fashion: it lies deeper, in Meredith's intention, in what he wishes to bring to pass. He has been, it is plain, at great pains to destroy the conventional form of the novel. He makes no attempt to preserve the sober reality of Trollope and Jane Austen; he has destroyed all the usual staircases by which we have learnt to climb. And what is done so deliberately is done with a purpose. This defiance of the ordinary, these airs and graces, the formality of the dialogue with its Sirs and Madams are all there to create an atmosphere that is unlike that of daily life, to prepare the way for a new and an original sense of the human scene. Peacock, from whom Meredith learnt so much, is equally arbitrary, but the virtue of the assumptions he asks us to make is proved by the fact that we accept Mr. Skionar and the rest with natural delight. Meredith's characters in *Richard Feverel,* on the other hand, are at odds with their surroundings. We at once exclaim how unreal they are, how artificial, how impossible. The baronet and the butler, the hero and the heroine, the good woman and the bad woman are mere types of baronets and butlers, good women and bad. For what reason, then, has he sacrificed the substantial advantages of realistic common sense—the staircase and the stucco? Because, it becomes clear as we read, he possessed a keen sense not of the complexity of character, but of the splendour of a scene. One after another in this first book he creates a scene to which we can attach abstract names—Youth, The Birth of Love, The Power of Nature. We are galloped to them over every obstacle on the pounding hoofs of rhapsodical prose.

> Away with Systems! Away with a corrupt World! Let us breathe the air of the Enchanted Island! Golden lie the meadows; golden run the streams; red gold is on the pine stems.

We forget that Richard is Richard and that Lucy is Lucy; they are youth; the world runs molten gold. The writer is a rhapsodist, a poet then; but we have not yet exhausted all the elements in this first novel. We have to reckon with the author himself. He has a mind stuffed with ideas, hungry for argument. His boys and girls may spend their time picking daisies in the meadows, but they breathe, however unconsciously, an air bristling with intellectual question and comment. On a dozen occasions these incongruous elements strain and threaten to break apart. The book is cracked through and through with those fissures which come when the author seems to be of twenty minds at the same time. Yet it succeeds in holding miraculously together, not certainly by the depths and originality of its character drawing but by the vigour of its intellectual power and by its lyrical intensity.

We are left, then, with our curiosity aroused. Let him write another book or two; get into his stride; control his crudities: and we will open *Harry Richmond* and see what has happened now. Of all the things that might have happened this surely is the strangest. All trace of immaturity is gone; but with it every trace of the uneasy adventurous mind has gone too. The story bowls smoothly along the road which Dickens has already trodden of autobiographical narrative. It is a boy speaking, a boy thinking, a boy adventuring. For that reason, no doubt, the author has curbed his redundance and pruned his speech. The style is the most rapid possible. It runs smooth, without a kink in it. Stevenson, one feels, must have learnt much from this supple narrative, with its precise adroit phrases, its exact quick glance at visible things.

> Plunged among dark green leaves, smelling wood-smoke,
> at night; at morning waking up, and the world alight,
> and you standing high, and marking the hills where you
> will see the next morning and the next, morning after
> morning, and one morning the dearest person in the
> world surprising you just before you wake: I thought this a
> heavenly pleasure.

It goes gallantly, but a little self-consciously. He hears himself talking. Doubts begin to rise and hover and settle at last (as in *Richard Feverel*) upon the human figures. These boys are no more real boys than the sample apple which is laid on top of the basket is a real apple. They are too simple, too gallant, too adventurous to be of the same unequal breed as David Copperfield, for example. They are sample boys, novelist's specimens; and again we encounter the extreme conventionality of Meredith's mind where we found it, to our surprise, before. With all his boldness (and there is no risk that he will not run with probability) there are a dozen occasions on which a reach-me-down character will satisfy him well enough. But just as we are thinking that the young gentlemen are altogether too pat, and the adventures which befall them altogether too slick, the shallow bath of illusion closes over our heads and we sink with Richmond Roy and the Princess Ottilia into the world of fantasy and romance, where all holds together and we are able to put our imagination at the writer's service without reserve. That such surrender is above all things delightful: that it adds spring-heels to our boots: that it fires the cold scepticism out of us and makes the world glow in lucid transparency before our eyes, needs no showing, as it certainly submits to no analysis. That Meredith can induce such moments proves him possessed of an extraordinary power. Yet it is a capricious power and highly intermittent. For pages all is effort and agony; phrase after phrase is struck and no light comes. Then, just as we are about to drop the book, the rocket roars into the air; the whole scene flashes into light; and the book, years after, is recalled by that sudden splendour.

If, then, this intermittent brilliancy is Meredith's characteristic excellence, it is worth while to look into it more closely. And perhaps the first thing that we shall discover is that the scenes which catch the eye and remain in memory are static; they are illuminations, not discoveries; they do not improve our knowledge of the characters. It is significant that Richard and Lucy, Harry and Ottilia, Clara and Vernon, Beauchamp and Renée are presented in carefully appropriate surroundings—on board a yacht, under a flowering cherry tree, upon some river-bank, so that the landscape always makes part of the emotion. The sea or the sky or the wood is brought forward to symbolize what the human beings are feeling or looking.

> The sky was bronze, a vast furnace dome. The folds of light
> and shadow everywhere were satin rich. That afternoon
> the bee hummed of thunder and refreshed the ear.

That is a description of a state of mind.

> These winter mornings are divine. They move on
> noiselessly. The earth is still as if waiting. A wren warbles,

and flits through the lank, drenched branches; hillside opens green; everywhere is mist, everywhere expectancy.

That is a description of a woman's face. But only some states of mind and some expressions of face can be described in imagery—only those which are so highly wrought as to be simple and, for that reason, will not submit to analysis. This is a limitation; for though we may be able to see these people, very brilliantly, in a moment of illumination, they do not change or grow; the light sinks and leaves us in darkness. We have no such intuitive knowledge of Meredith's characters as we have of Stendhal's, Tchekov's, Jane Austen's. Indeed, our knowledge of such characters is so intimate that we can almost dispense with "great scenes" altogether. Some of the most emotional scenes in fiction are the quietest. We have been wrought upon by nine hundred and ninety-nine little touches; the thousandth, when it comes, is as slight as the others, but the effect is prodigious. But with Meredith there are no touches; there are hammer-strokes only, so that our knowledge of his characters is partial, spasmodic, and intermittent.

Meredith, then, is not among the great psychologists who feel their way, anonymously and patiently, in and out of the fibres of the mind and make one character differ minutely and completely from another. He is among the poets who identify the character with the passion or with the idea; who symbolize and make abstract. And yet—here lay his difficulty perhaps—he was not a poet-novelist wholly and completely as Emily Brontë was a poet-novelist. He did not steep the world in one mood. His mind was too self-conscious, and too sophisticated to remain lyrical for long. He does not sing only; he dissects. Even in his most lyrical scenes a sneer curls its lash round the phrases and laughs at their extravagance. And as we read on, we shall find that the comic spirit, when it is allowed to dominate the scene, licked the world to a very different shape. *The Egoist* at once modifies our theory that Meredith is pre-eminently the master of great

167

scenes. Here there is none of that precipitate hurry that has rushed us over obstacles to the summit of one emotional peak after another. The case is one that needs argument; argument needs logic; Sir Willoughby, "our original male in giant form", is turned slowly round before a steady fire of scrutiny and criticism which allows no twitch on the victim's part to escape it. That the victim is a wax model and not entirely living flesh and blood is perhaps true. At the same time Meredith pays us a supreme compliment to which as novel-readers we are little accustomed. We are civilized people, he seems to say, watching the comedy of human relations together. Human relations are of profound interest. Men and women are not cats and monkeys, but beings of a larger growth and of a greater range. He imagines us capable of disinterested curiosity in the behaviour of our kind. This is so rare a compliment from a novelist to his reader that we are at first bewildered and then delighted. Indeed his comic spirit is a far more penetrating goddess than his lyrical. It is she who cuts a clear path through the brambles of his manner; she who surprises us again and again by the depth of her observations; she who creates the dignity, the seriousness, and the vitality of Meredith's world. Had Meredith, one is tempted to reflect, lived in an age or in a country where comedy was the rule, he might never have contracted those airs of intellectual superiority, that manner of oracular solemnity which it is, as he points out, the use of the comic spirit to correct.

But in many ways the age—if we can judge so amorphous a shape—was hostile to Meredith, or, to speak more accurately, was hostile to his success with the age we now live in—the year 1928. His teaching seems now too strident and too optimistic and too shallow. It obtrudes; and when philosophy is not consumed in a novel, when we can underline this phrase with a pencil, and cut out that exhortation with a pair of scissors and paste the whole into a system, it is safe to say that there is something wrong with the philosophy or with the novel or with both. Above all, his teaching is too insistent. He cannot, even to hear the profoundest secret, suppress his own opinion. And there is nothing that characters in fiction resent more. If, they seem to argue, we have been called into existence merely to express Mr. Meredith's views upon the universe, we would rather not exist at all. Thereupon they die; and a novel that is full of dead characters, even though it is also full of profound wisdom and exalted teaching, is not achieving its aim as a novel. But here we reach another point upon which the present age may be inclined to have more sympathy with Meredith. When he wrote, in the seventies and eighties of the last century, the novel had reached a stage where it could only exist by moving onward. It is a possible contention that after those two perfect novels, *Pride and Prejudice* and *The Small House at Allington,* English fiction had to escape from the dominion of that perfection, as English poetry had to escape from the perfection of Tennyson. George Eliot, Meredith, and Hardy were all imperfect novelists largely because they insisted upon introducing qualities, of thought and of poetry, that are perhaps incompatible with fiction at its most perfect. On the other hand, if fiction had remained what it was to Jane Austen and Trollope, fiction would by this time be dead. Thus Meredith deserves our gratitude and excites our interest as a great innovator. Many of our doubts about him and much of our inability to frame any definite opinion of his work comes from the fact that it is experimental and thus contains elements that do not fuse harmoniously—the qualities are at odds: the one quality which binds and concentrates has been omitted. To read Meredith, then, to our greatest advantage we must make certain allowances and relax certain standards. We must not expect the perfect quietude of a traditional style nor the triumphs of a patient and pedestrian psychology. On the other hand, his claim, "My method has been to prepare my readers for a crucial exhibition of the personae, and then to give the scene in the fullest of their blood and brain under stress of a fierce situation", is frequently justified. Scene after scene rises on the mind's eye with a flare of fiery intensity. If we are irritated by the dancing-

169

master dandyism which made him write "gave his lungs full play" instead of laughed, or "tasted the swift intricacies of the needle" instead of sewed, we must remember that such phrases prepare the way for the "fierce situations". Meredith is creating the atmosphere from which we shall pass naturally into a highly pitched state of emotion. Where the realistic novelist, like Trollope, lapses into flatness and dullness, the lyrical novelist, like Meredith, becomes meretricious and false; and such falsity is, of course, not only much more glaring than flatness, but it is a greater crime against the phlegmatic nature of prose fiction. Perhaps Meredith had been well advised if he had abjured the novel altogether and kept himself wholly to poetry. Yet we have to remind ourselves that the fault may be ours. Our prolonged diet upon Russian fiction, rendered neutral and negative in translation, our absorption in the convolutions of psychological Frenchmen, may have led us to forget that the English language is naturally exuberant, and the English character full of humours and eccentricities. Meredith's flamboyancy has a great ancestry behind it; we cannot avoid all memory of Shakespeare.

When such questions and qualifications crowd upon us as we read, the fact may be taken to prove that we are neither near enough to be under his spell nor far enough to see him in proportion. Thus the attempt to pronounce a finished estimate is even more illusive than usual. But we can testify even now that to read Meredith is to be conscious of a packed and muscular mind; of a voice booming and reverberating with its own unmistakable accent even though the partition between us is too thick for us to hear what he says distinctly. Still, as we read we feel that we are in the presence of a Greek god though he is surrounded by the innumerable ornaments of a suburban drawing-room; who talks brilliantly, even if he is deaf to the lower tones of the human voice; who, if he is rigid and immobile, is yet marvellously alive and on the alert. This brilliant and uneasy figure has his place with the great eccentrics rather than with the great masters. He will be read, one may guess, by fits and starts; he will be forgotten and discovered and again discovered and forgotten like Donne, and Peacock, and Gerard Hopkins. But if English fiction continues to be read, the novels of Meredith must inevitably rise from time to time into view; his work must inevitably be disputed and discussed.

"TWELFTH NIGHT"
AT THE OLD VIC

Written in 1933

Shakespeareans are divided, it is well known, into three classes; those who prefer to read Shakespeare in the book; those who prefer to see him acted on the stage; and those who run perpetually from book to stage gathering plunder. Certainly there is a good deal to be said for reading Twelfth Night in the book if the book can be read in a garden, with no sound but the thud of an apple falling to the earth, or of the wind ruffling the branches of the trees. For one thing there is time—time not only to hear "the sweet sound that breathes upon a bank of violets" but to unfold the implications of that very subtle speech as the Duke winds into the nature of love. There is time, too, to make a note in the margin; time to wonder at queer jingles like "that live in her; when liver, brain, and heart" . . . "and of a foolish knight that you brought in one night" and to ask oneself whether it was from them that was born the lovely, "And what should I do in Illyria? My brother he is in Elysium." For Shakespeare is writing, it seems, not with the whole of his mind mobilized and under control but with feelers left flying that sort and play with words so that the trail of a chance word is caught and followed recklessly. From the echo of one word is born another word, for which reason, perhaps, the play seems as we read it to tremble perpetually on the brink of music. They are always calling for songs in Twelfth Night, "0 fellow come, the song we had last night." Yet Shakespeare was not so deeply in love with words but that he could turn and laugh at them. "They that do dally with

173

words do quickly make them wanton." There is a roar of laughter and out burst Sir Toby, Sir Andrew, Maria. Words on their lips are things that have meaning; that rush and leap out with a whole character packed in a little phrase. When Sir Andrew says "I was adored once," we feel that we hold him in the hollow of our hands; a novelist would have taken three volumes to bring us to that pitch of intimacy. And Viola, Malvolio, Olivia, the Duke—the mind so brims and spills over with all that we know and guess about them as they move in and out among the lights and shadows of the mind's stage that we ask why should we imprison them within the bodies of real men and women? Why exchange this garden for the theatre? The answer is that Shakespeare wrote for the stage and presumably with reason. Since they are acting *Twelfth Night* at the Old Vic, let us compare the two versions.

Many apples might fall without being heard in the Waterloo Road, and as for the shadows, the electric light has consumed them all. The first impression upon entering the Old Vic is overwhelmingly positive and definite. We seem to have issued out from the shadows of the garden upon the bridge of the Parthenon. The metaphor is mixed, but then so is the scenery. The columns of the bridge somehow suggest an Atlantic liner and the austere splendours of a classical temple in combination. But the body is almost as upsetting as the scenery. The actual persons of Malvolio, Sir Toby, Olivia and the rest expand our visionary characters out of all recognition. At first we are inclined to resent it. You are not Malvolio; or Sir Toby either, we want to tell them; but merely impostors. We sit gaping at the ruins of the play, at the travesty of the play. And then by degrees this same body or rather all these bodies together, take our play and remodel it between them. The play gains immensely in robustness, in solidity. The printed word is changed out of all recognition when it is heard by other people. We watch it strike upon this man or woman; we see them laugh or shrug their shoulders, or tum aside to hide their faces. The word is given a body as well as a soul. Then again as the actors pause, or topple over a barrel, or stretch their hands out, the flatness of the print is broken up as by crevasses or precipices; all the proportions are changed. Perhaps the most impressive effect in the play is achieved by the long pause which Sebastian and Viola make as they stand looking at each other in a silent ecstasy of recognition. The reader's eye may have slipped over that moment entirely. Here we are made to pause and think about it; and are reminded that Shakespeare wrote for the body and for the mind simultaneously.

But now that the actors have done their proper work of solidifying and intensifying our impressions, we begin to criticize them more minutely and to compare their version with our own. We make Mr. Quartermaine's Malvolio stand beside our Malvolio. And to tell the truth, wherever the fault may lie, they have very little in common. Mr. Quartermaine's Malvolio is a splendid gentleman, courteous, considerate, well bred; a man of parts and humour who has no quarrel with the world. He has never felt a twinge of vanity or a moment's envy in his life. If Sir Toby and Maria fool him he sees through it, we may be sure, and only suffers it as a fine gentleman puts up with the games of foolish children. Our Malvolio, on the other hand, was a fantastic complex creature, twitching with vanity, tortured by ambition. There was cruelty in his teasing, and a hint of tragedy in his defeat; his final threat had a momentary terror in it. But when Mr. Quartermaine says "I'll be revenged on the whole pack of you," we feel merely that the powers of the law will be soon and effectively invoked. What, then, becomes of Olivia's "He hath been most notoriously abused"? Then there is Olivia. Madame Lopokova has by nature that rare quality which is neither to be had for the asking nor to be subdued by the will—the genius of personality. She has only to float on to the stage and everything round her suffers, not a sea change, but a change into light, into gaiety; the birds sing, the sheep are garlanded, the air rings with melody and human beings dance towards each other on the tips of their toes possessed of an exquisite friendliness, sympathy and delight. But our Olivia was a stately lady; of sombre complexion, slow moving, and of few sympathies. She could not love the Duke nor change her feeling. Madame Lopokova loves everybody. She is always changing. Her hands, her face, her feet, the whole of her body, are always quivering in sympathy with the moment. She could make the moment, as she proved when she walked down the stairs with Sebastian, one of intense and moving beauty; but she was not our Olivia. Compared with her the comic group, Sir Toby, Sir Andrew, Maria, the fool were more than ordinarily English. Coarse, humorous, robust, they trolled out their words, they rolled over their barrels; they acted magnificently. No reader, one may make bold to say, could outpace Miss Seyler's Maria, with its quickness, its inventiveness, its merriment; nor add anything to the humours of Mr. Livesey's Sir Toby. And Miss jeans as Viola was satisfactory; and Mr. Hare as Antonio was admirable; and Mr. Morland's clown was a good clown. What, then, was lacking in the play as a whole? Perhaps that it was not a whole. The fault may lie partly with Shakespeare. It is easier to act his comedy than his poetry, one may suppose, for when he wrote as a poet he was apt to write too quick for the human tongue. The prodigality of his metaphors can be flashed over by the eye, but the speaking voice falters in the middle. Hence the comedy was out of proportion to the rest. Then, perhaps, the actors were too highly charged with individuality or too incongruously cast. They broke the play up into separate pieces—now we were in the groves of Arcady, now in some inn at Blackfriars. The mind in reading spins a web from scene to scene, compounds a background from apples falling, and the toll of a church bell, and an owl's fantastic flight which keeps the play together. Here that continuity was sacrificed. We left the theatre possessed of many brilliant fragments but without the sense of all things conspiring and combining together which may be the satisfying culmination of a less brilliant performance. Nevertheless, the play has served its purpose. It has made us compare our Malvolio with Mr. Quartermaine's; our Olivia with Madame Lopokova's; our reading of the whole play with Mr. Guthrie's; and since they all differ back we must go to Shakespeare. We must read Twelfth Night again. Mr. Guthrie has made that necessary and whetted our appetite for The Cherry Orchard, Measure for Measure, and Henry the Eighth that are still to come.

"ROBINSON CRUSOE"

First published in 1935

There are many ways of approaching this classical volume; but which shall we choose? Shall we begin by saying that, since Sidney died at Zutphen leaving the *Arcadia* unfinished, great changes had come over English life, and the novel had chosen, or had been forced to choose, its direction? A middle class had come into existence, able to read and anxious to read not only about the loves of princes and princesses, but about themselves and the details of their humdrum lives. Stretched upon a thousand pens, prose had accommodated itself to the demand; it had fitted itself to express the facts of life rather than the poetry. That is certainly one way of approaching *Robinson Crusoe*— through the development of the novel; but another immediately suggests itself—through the life of the author. Here too, in the heavenly pastures of biography, we may spend many more hours than are needed to read the book itself from cover to cover. The date of Defoe's birth, to begin with, is doubtful—was it 1660 or 1661? Then again, did he spell his name in one word or in two? And who were his ancestors? He is said to have been a hosier; but what, after all, was a hosier in the seventeenth century? He became a pamphleteer, and enjoyed the confidence of William the Third; one of his pamphlets caused him to be stood in the pillory and imprisoned at Newgate; he was employed by Harley and later by Godolphin; he was the first of the hireling journalists; he wrote innumerable pamphlets and articles; also *Moll Flanders* and *Robinson Crusoe*; he had a wife and six children; was spare in figure, with a hooked nose, a sharp chin,

179

grey eyes, and a large mole near his mouth. Nobody who has any slight acquaintance with English literature needs to be told how many hours can be spent and how many lives have been spent in tracing the development of the novel and in examining the chins of the novelists. Only now and then, as we turn from theory to biography and from biography to theory, a doubt insinuates itself—if we knew the very moment of Defoe's birth and whom he loved and why, if we had by heart the history of the origin, rise, growth, decline, and fall of the English novel from its conception (say) in Egypt to its decease in the wilds (perhaps) of Paraguay, should we suck an ounce of additional pleasure from *Robinson Crusoe* or read it one whit more intelligently?

For the book itself remains. However we may wind and wriggle, loiter and dally in our approach to books, a lonely battle waits us at the end. There is a piece of business to be transacted between writer and reader before any further dealings are possible, and to be reminded in the middle of this private interview that Defoe sold stockings, had brown hair, and was stood in the pillory is a distraction and a worry. Our first task, and it is often formidable enough, is to master his perspective. Until we know how the novelist orders his world, the ornaments of that world, which the critics press upon us, the adventures of the writer, to which biographers draw attention, are superfluous possessions of which we can make no use. All alone we must climb upon the novelist's shoulders and gaze through his eyes until we, too, understand in what order he ranges the large common objects upon which novelists are fated to gaze: man and men; behind them Nature; and above them that power which for convenience and brevity we may call God. And at once confusion, misjudgement, and difficulty begin. Simple as they appear to us, these objects can be made monstrous and indeed unrecognizable by the manner in which the novelist relates them to each other. It would seem to be true that people who live cheek by jowl and breathe the same air vary enormously in their sense of proportion; to one the human being is vast, the tree minute; to the other, trees are huge and human beings insignificant little objects in the background. So, in spite of the text-books, writers may live at the same time and see nothing the same size. Here is Scott, for example, with his mountains looming huge and his men therefore drawn to scale; Jane Austen picking out the roses on her teacups to match the wit of her dialogues; while Peacock bends over heaven and earth one fantastic distorting mirror in which a tea-cup may be Vesuvius or Vesuvius a tea-cup. Nevertheless Scott, Jane Austen, and Peacock lived through the same years; they saw the same world; they are covered in the text-books by the same stretch of literary history. It is in their perspective that they are different. If, then, it were granted us to grasp this firmly, for ourselves, the battle would end in victory; and we could turn, secure in our intimacy, to enjoy the various delights with which the critics and biographers so generously supply us.

But here many difficulties arise. For we have our own vision of the world; we have made it from our own experience and prejudices, and it is therefore bound up with our own vanities and loves. It is impossible not to feel injured and insulted if tricks are played and our private harmony is upset. Thus when *Jude the Obscure* appears or a new volume of Proust, the newspapers are flooded with protests. Major Gibbs of Cheltenham would put a bullet through his head tomorrow if life were as Hardy paints it; Miss Wiggs of Hampstead must protest that though Proust's art is wonderful, the real world, she thanks God, has nothing in common with the distortions of a perverted Frenchman. Both the gentleman and the lady are trying to control the novelist's perspective so that it shall resemble and reinforce their own. But the great writer—the Hardy or the Proust—goes on his way regardless of the rights of private property; by the sweat of his brow he brings order from chaos; he plants his tree there, and his man here; he makes the figure of his deity remote or present as he wills. In masterpieces—books, that is, where the vision is clear and order has been achieved—he inflicts his own perspective upon us so severely that as often as not we suffer agonies—our vanity is injured because our own order is upset; we are afraid because the old supports are being wrenched from us; and we are bored—for what pleasure or amusement can be plucked from a brand new idea? Yet from anger, fear, and boredom a rare and lasting delight is sometimes born.

Robinson Crusoe, it may be, is a case in point. It is a masterpiece, and it is a masterpiece largely because Defoe has throughout kept consistently to his own sense of perspective. For this reason he thwarts us and flouts us at every turn. Let us look at the theme largely and loosely, comparing it with our preconceptions. It is, we know, the story of a man who is thrown, after many perils and adventures, alone upon a desert island. The mere suggestion—peril and solitude and a desert island—is enough to rouse in us the expectation of some far land on the limits of the world; of the sun rising and the sun setting; of man, isolated from his kind, brooding alone upon the nature of society and the strange ways of men. Before we open the book we have perhaps vaguely sketched out the kind of pleasure we expect it to give us. We read; and we are rudely contradicted on every page. There are no sunsets and no sunrises; there is no solitude and no soul. There is, on the contrary, staring us full in the face nothing but a large earthenware pot. We are told, that is to say, that it was the 1st of September 1651; that the hero's name is Robinson Crusoe; and that his father has the gout. Obviously, then, we must alter our attitude. Reality, fact, substance is going to dominate all that follows. We must hastily alter our proportions throughout; Nature must furl her splendid purples; she is only the giver of drought and water; man must be reduced to a struggling, life-preserving animal; and God shrivel into a magistrate whose seat, substantial and somewhat hard, is only a little way above the horizon. Each sortie of ours in pursuit of information upon these cardinal points of perspective— God, man, Nature—is snubbed back with ruthless common sense. Robinson Crusoe thinks of God: "sometimes I would expostulate with myself, why providence should thus completely ruin its creatures. . . . But something always return'd swift upon me to check these thoughts." God does not exist. He thinks of Nature, the fields "adorn'd with flowers and grass, and full of very fine woods", but the important thing about a wood is that it harbours an abundance of parrots who may be tamed and taught to speak. Nature does not exist. He considers the dead, whom he has killed himself. It is of the utmost importance that they should be buried at once, for "they lay open to the sun and would presently be offensive". Death does not exist. Nothing exists except an earthenware pot. Finally, that is to say, we are forced to drop our own preconceptions and to accept what Defoe himself wishes to give us.

Let us then go back to the beginning and repeat again, "I was born in the year 1632 in the city of York of a good family". Nothing could be plainer, more matter of fact, than that beginning. We are drawn on soberly to consider all the blessings of orderly, industrious middle-class life. There is no greater good fortune we are assured than to be born of the British middle class. The great are to be pitied and so are the poor; both are exposed to distempers and uneasiness; the middle station between the mean and the great is the best; and its virtues— temperance, moderation, quietness, and health—are the most desirable. It was a sorry thing, then, when by some evil fate a middle-class youth was bitten with the foolish love of adventure. So he proses on, drawing, little by little, his own portrait, so that we never forget it—imprinting upon us indelibly, for he never forgets it either, his shrewdness, his caution, his love of order and comfort and respectability; until by whatever means, we find ourselves at sea, in a storm; and, peering out, everything is seen precisely as it appears to Robinson Crusoe. The waves, the seamen, the sky, the ship—all are seen through those shrewd, middle-class, unimaginative eyes. There is no escaping him. Everything appears as it would appear to that naturally cautious, apprehensive, conventional, and solidly matter-of-fact intelligence. He is incapable of enthusiasm. He has a natural slight distaste for the sublimities of Nature. He suspects even Providence of exaggeration. He is so busy and has such an eye to the main chance that he notices only a tenth part of what is going on round him. Everything is capable of a rational explanation, he is sure, if only he had time to attend to it. We are much more alarmed by the "vast great creatures" that swim out in the night and surround his boat than he is. He at once takes his gun and fires at them, and off they swim—whether they are lions or not he really cannot say. Thus before we know it we are opening our mouths wider and wider. We are swallowing monsters that we should have jibbed at if they had been offered us by an imaginative and flamboyant traveller. But anything that this sturdy middle-class man notices can be taken for a fact. He is for ever counting his barrels, and making sensible provisions for his water supply; nor do we ever find him tripping even in a matter of detail. Has he forgotten, we wonder, that he has a great lump of beeswax on board? Not at all. But as he had already made candles out of it, it is not nearly as great on page thirty-eight as it was on page twenty-three. When for a wonder he leaves some inconsistency hanging loose—why if the wild cats are so very tame are the goats so very shy?—we are not seriously perturbed, for we are sure that there was a reason, and a very good one, had he time to give it us. But the pressure of life when one is fending entirely for oneself alone on a desert island is really no laughing matter. It is no crying one either. A man must have an eye to everything; it is no time for raptures about Nature when the lightning may explode one's gunpowder—it is imperative to seek a safer lodging for it. And so by means of telling the truth undeviatingly as it appears to him—by being a great artist and forgoing this and daring that in order to give effect to his prime quality, a sense of reality—he comes in the end to make common actions dignified and common objects beautiful. To dig, to bake, to plant, to build—how serious these simple occupations are; hatchets, scissors, logs, axes—how beautiful these simple objects become. Unimpeded by comment, the story marches on with magnificent downright simplicity. Yet how could comment have made it more impressive? It is true that he takes the opposite way from the psychologist's—he describes the effect of emotion on the body, not on the mind. But when he says how, in a moment of anguish, he clinched his hands so that any soft thing would have been crushed; how "my teeth in my head would strike together, and set against one another so strong that for the time I could not part them again", the effect is as deep as pages of analysis could have made it. His own instinct in the matter is right. "Let the naturalists", he says, "explain these things, and the reason and manner of them; all I can say to them is, to describe the fact. . . ." If you are Defoe, certainly to describe the fact is enough; for the fact is the right fact. By means of this genius for fact Defoe achieves effects that are beyond any but the great masters of descriptive prose. He has only to say a word or two about "the grey of the morning" to paint vividly a windy dawn. A sense of desolation and of the deaths of many men is conveyed by remarking in the most prosaic way in the world, "I never saw them afterwards, or any sign of them except three of their hats, one cap, and two shoes that were not fellows". When at last he exclaims, "Then to see how like a king I din'd too all alone, attended by my servants"—his parrot and his dog and his two cats, we cannot help but feel that all humanity is on a desert island alone—though Defoe at once informs us, for he has a way of snubbing off our enthusiasms, that the cats were not the same cats that had come in the ship. Both of those were dead; these cats were new cats, and as a matter of fact cats became very troublesome before long from their fecundity, whereas dogs, oddly enough, did not breed at all.

Thus Defoe, by reiterating that nothing but a plain earthenware pot stands in the foreground, persuades us to see remote islands and the solitudes of the human soul. By believing fixedly in the solidity of the pot and its earthiness, he has subdued every other element to his design; he has roped

185

the whole universe into harmony. And is there any reason, we ask as we shut the book, why the perspective that a plain earthenware pot exacts should not satisfy us as completely, once we grasp it, as man himself in all his sublimity standing against a background of broken mountains and tumbling oceans with stars flaming in the sky?

DE QUINCEY'S
AUTOBIOGRAPHY

First published in 1935

It must often strike the reader that very little criticism worthy of being called so has been written in English of prose—our great critics have given the best of their minds to poetry. And the reason perhaps why prose so seldom calls out the higher faculties of the critic, but invites him to argue a case or to discuss the personality of the writer—to take a theme from the book and make his criticism an air played in variation on it—is to be sought in the prose-writer's attitude to his own work. Even if he writes as an artist, without a practical end in view, still he treats prose as a humble beast of burden which must accommodate all sorts of odds and ends; as an impure substance in which dust and twigs and flies find lodgment. But more often than not the prose-writer has a practical aim in view, a theory to argue, or a cause to plead, and with it adopts the moralist's view that the remote, the difficult, and the complex are to be abjured. His duty is to the present and the living. He is proud to call himself a journalist. He must use the simplest words and express himself as clearly as possible in order to reach the greatest number in the plainest way. Therefore he cannot complain of the critics if his writing, like the irritation in the oyster, serves only to breed other art; nor be surprised if his pages, once they have delivered their message, are thrown on the rubbish heap like other objects that have served their turn.

But sometimes we meet even in prose with writing that seems inspired by other aims. It does not wish to argue or to convert

187

or even to tell a story. We can draw all our pleasure from the words themselves; we have not to enhance it by reading between the lines or by making a voyage of discovery into the psychology of the writer. De Quincey, of course, is one of these rare beings. When we bring his work to mind we recall it by some passage of stillness and completeness, like the following:

> *"Life is Finished!"* was the secret misgiving of my heart; for the heart of infancy is as apprehensive as that of maturest wisdom in relation to any capital wound inflicted on the happiness. *"Life is Finished! Finished it is!"* was the hidden meaning that, half-unconsciously to myself, lurked within my sighs; and, as bells heard from a distance on a summer evening seem charged at times with an articulate form of words, some monitory message, that rolls round unceasingly, even so for me some noiseless and subterraneous voice seemed to chant continually a secret word, made audible only to my own heart—that "now is the blossoming of life withered for ever".

Such passages occur naturally, for they consist of visions and dreams, not of actions or of dramatic scenes, in his autobiographic sketches. And yet we are not made to think of him, De Quincey, as we read. If we try to analyse our sensations we shall find that we are worked upon as if by music—the senses are stirred rather than the brain. The rise and fall of the sentence immediately soothes us to a mood and removes us to a distance in which the near fades and detail is extinguished. Our minds, thus widened and lulled to a width of apprehension, stand open to receive one by one in slow and stately procession the ideas which De Quincey wishes us to receive; the golden fullness of life; the pomps of the heaven above; the glory of the flowers below, as he stands "between an open window and a dead body on a summer's day". The theme is supported and amplified and varied. The idea of hurry and trepidation, of reaching towards something that for ever flies, intensifies the impression of stillness and eternity. Bells heard on summer evenings, palm-trees waving, sad winds that blow for ever, keep us by successive waves of emotion in the same mood. The emotion is never stated; it is suggested and brought slowly by repeated images before us until it stays, in all its complexity, complete.

The effect is one that is very rarely attempted in prose and is rarely appropriate to it because of this very quality of finality. It does not lead anywhere. We do not add to our sense of high summer and death and immortality any consciousness of who is hearing, seeing, and feeling. De Quincey wished to shut out from us everything save the picture "of a solitary infant, and its solitary combat with grief—a mighty darkness, and a sorrow without a voice", to make us fathom and explore the depths of that single emotion. It is a state which is general and not particular. Therefore De Quincey was at odds with the aims of the prose-writer and his morality. His reader was to be put in possession of a meaning of that complex kind which is largely a sensation. He had to become fully aware not merely of the fact that a child was standing by a bed, but of stillness, sunlight, flowers, the passage of time and the presence of death. None of this could be conveyed by simple words in their logical order; clarity and simplicity would merely travesty and deform such a meaning. De Quincey, of course, was fully aware of the gulf that lay between him as a writer who wished to convey such ideas and his contemporaries. He turned from the neat, precise speech of his time to Milton and Jeremy Taylor and Sir Thomas Browne; from them he learnt the roll of the long sentence that sweeps its coils in and out, that piles its summit higher and higher. Then followed a discipline exacted, most drastically, by the fineness of his own ear—the weighing of cadences, the consideration of pauses; the effect of repetitions and consonances and assonances—all this was part of the duty of a writer who wishes to put a complex meaning fully and completely before his reader.

When, therefore, we come to consider critically one of the

passages that has made so deep an impression we find that it has been produced much as a poet like Tennyson would produce it. There is the same care in the use of sound; the same variety of measure; the length of the sentence is varied and its weight shifted. But all these measures are diluted to a lower degree of strength and their force is spread over a much greater space, so that the transition from the lowest compass to the highest is by a gradation of shallow steps and we reach the utmost heights without violence. Hence the difficulty of stressing the particular quality of any single line as in a poem and the futility of taking one passage apart from the context, since its effect is compound of suggestions that have been received sometimes several pages earlier. Moreover, De Quincey, unlike some of his masters, was not at his best in sudden majesty of phrase; his power lay in suggesting large and generalised visions; landscapes in which nothing is seen in detail; faces without features; the stillness of midnight or summer; the tumult and trepidation of flying multitudes; anguish that for ever falls and rises and casts its arms upwards in despair.

But De Quincey was not merely the master of separate passages of beautiful prose; if that had been so his achievement would have been far less than it is. He was also a writer of narrative, an autobiographer, and one, if we consider that he wrote in the year 1833, with very peculiar views of the art of autobiography. In the first place he was convinced of the enormous value of candour.

If he were really able to pierce the haze which so often envelops, even to himself, his own secret springs of action and reserve, there cannot be a life moving at all under intellectual impulses that would not, through that single force of absolute frankness, fall within the reach of a deep, solemn, and sometimes even of a thrilling interest.

He understood by autobiography the history not only of the external life but of the deeper and more hidden emotions. And he realised the difficulty of making such a confession: ". . . vast numbers of people, though liberated from all reasonable motives of self-restraint, *cannot* be confidential—have it not in their power to lay aside reserve". Aerial chains, invisible spells, bind and freeze the free spirit of communication. "It is because a man cannot see and measure these mystical forces which palsy him that he cannot deal with them effectually." With such perceptions and intentions it is strange that De Quincey failed to be among the great autobiographers of our literature. Certainly he was not tongue-tied or spellbound. Perhaps one of the reasons that led him to fail in his task of self-delineation was not the lack of expressive power, but the superfluity. He was profusely and indiscriminately loquacious. Discursiveness—the disease that attacked so many of the nineteenth-century English writers—had him in her coils. But while it is easy to see why the works of Ruskin or Carlyle are huge and formless—every kind of heterogeneous object had to be found room for somehow, somewhere—De Quincey had not their excuse. The burden of the prophet was not laid upon him. He was, moreover, the most careful of artists. Nobody tunes the sound and modulates the cadence of a sentence more carefully and more exquisitely. But strangely enough, the sensibility which was on the alert to warn him instantly if a sound clashed or a rhythm flagged failed him completely when it came to the architecture of the whole. Then he could tolerate a disproportion and profusion that make his book as dropsical and shapeless as each sentence is symmetrical and smooth. He is indeed, to use the expressive word coined by his brother to describe De Quincey's tendency as a small boy "to plead some distinction or verbal demur", the prince of Pettifogulisers. Not only did he find "in everybody's words an unintentional opening left for double interpretations"; he could not tell the simplest story without qualifying and illustrating and introducing additional information until the point that was to be cleared up has long since become extinct in the dim mists of the distance.

Together with this fatal verbosity and weakness of architectural power, De Quincey suffered too as an autobiographer from a tendency to meditative abstraction. "It was my disease", he said, "to meditate too much and to observe too little." A curious formality diffuses his vision to a general vagueness, lapsing into a colourless monotony. He shed over everything the lustre and the amenity of his own dreaming, pondering absent-mindedness. He approached even the two disgusting idiots with their red eyes with the elaboration of a great gentleman who has by mistake wandered into a slum. So too he slipped mellifluously across all the fissures of the social scale—talking on equal terms with the young aristocrats at Eton or with the working-class family as they chose a joint of meat for their Sunday dinner. De Quincey indeed prided himself upon the ease with which he passed from one sphere to another: ". . . from my very earliest youth", he observed, "it has been my pride to converse familiarly, *more Socratico,* with all human beings, man, woman, and child, that chance might fling in my way". But as we read his descriptions of these men, women, and children we are led to think that he talked to them so easily because to him they differed so little. The same manner served equally for them all. His relations even with those with whom he was most intimate, whether it was Lord Altamont, his schoolboy friend, or Ann the prostitute, were equally ceremonial and gracious. His portraits have the flowing contours, the statuesque poses, the undifferentiated features of Scott's heroes and heroines. Nor is his own face exempted from the general ambiguity. When it came to telling the truth about himself he shrank from the task with all the horror of a well-bred English gentleman. The candour which fascinates us in the confessions of Rousseau— the determination to reveal the ridiculous, the mean, the sordid in himself—was abhorrent to him. "Nothing indeed is more revolting to English feelings", he wrote, "than the spectacle of a human being obtruding on our notice his moral ulcers and scars."

Clearly, therefore, De Quincey as an autobiographer labours under great defects. He is diffuse and redundant; he is aloof and dreamy and in bondage to the old pruderies and conventions. At the same time he was capable of being transfixed by the mysterious solemnity of certain emotions; of realising how one moment may transcend in value fifty years. He was able to devote to their analysis a skill which the professed analysts of the human heart—the Scotts, the Jane Austens, the Byrons—did not then possess. We find him writing passages which, in their self-consciousness, are scarcely to be matched in the fiction of the nineteenth century:

> And, recollecting it, I am struck with the truth, that far more of our deepest thoughts and feelings pass to us through perplexed combinations of *concrete* objects, pass to us as *involutes* (if I may coin that word) in compound experiences incapable of being disentangled, than ever reach us *directly* and in their own abstract shapes. . . . Man is doubtless *one* by some subtle *nexus*, some system of links, that we cannot perceive, extending from the new-born infant to the superannuated dotard: but, as regards many affections and passions incident to his nature at different stages, he is *not* one, but an intermitting creature, ending and beginning anew; the unity of man, in this respect, is co-extensive only with the particular stage to which the passion belongs. Some passions, as that of sexual love, are celestial by one-half of their origin, animal and earthly by the other half. These will not survive their own appropriate stage. But love which is *altogether* holy, like that between two children, is privileged to revisit by glimpses the silence and the darkness of declining years. . .

When we read such passages of analysis, when such states of

193

mind seem in retrospect to be an important element in life and so to deserve scrutiny and record, the art of autobiography as the eighteenth century knew it is changing its character. The art of biography also is being transformed. Nobody after that could maintain that the whole truth of life can be told without "piercing the haze"; without revealing "his own secret springs of action and reserve". Yet external events also have their importance. To tell the whole story of a life the autobiographer must devise some means by which the two levels of existence can be recorded— the rapid passage of events and actions; the slow opening up of single and solemn moments of concentrated emotion. It is the fascination of De Quincey's pages that the two levels are beautifully, if unequally, combined. For page after page we are in company with a cultivated gentleman who describes with charm and eloquence what he has seen and known—the stage coaches, the Irish rebellion, the appearance and conversation of George the Third. Then suddenly the smooth narrative parts asunder, arch opens beyond arch, the vision of something for ever flying, for ever escaping, is revealed, and time stands still.

FOUR FIGURES

First published in 1935

I
COWPER AND LADY AUSTEN

It happened, of course, many years ago, but there must have been something remarkable about the meeting, since people still like to bring it before their eyes. An elderly gentleman was looking out of his window in a village street in the summer of 1781 when he saw two ladies go into a draper's shop opposite. The look of one of them interested him very much, and he seems to have said so, for soon a meeting was arranged.

A quiet and solitary life that must have been, in which a gentleman stood in the morning looking out of the window, in which the sight of an attractive face was an event. Yet perhaps it was an event partly because it revived some half-forgotten but still pungent memories. For Cowper had not always looked at the world from the windows of a house in a village street. Time was when the sight of ladies of fashion had been familiar enough. In his younger days he had been very foolish. He had flirted and giggled; he had gone smartly dressed to Vauxhall and Marylebone Gardens. He had taken his work at the Law Courts with a levity that alarmed his friends—for he had nothing whatever to live upon. He had fallen in love with his cousin Theodora Cowper. Indeed, he had been a thoughtless, wild young man. But suddenly in the heyday of his youth, in the midst of his gaiety, something terrible had happened. There lurked beneath that levity and perhaps inspired it a morbidity

195

that sprang from some defect of person, a dread which made action, which made marriage, which made any public exhibition of himself insupportable. If goaded to it, and he was now committed to a public career in the House of Lords, he must fly, even into the jaws of death. Rather than take up his appointment he would drown himself. But a man sat on the quay when he came to the water's edge; some invisible hand mysteriously forced the laudanum from his lips when he tried to drink it; the knife which he pressed to his heart broke; and the garter with which he tried to hang himself from the bed-post let him fall. Cowper was condemned to live.

When, therefore, that July morning he looked out of the window at the ladies shopping, he had come through gulfs of despair, but he had reached at last not only the haven of a quiet country town, but a settled state of mind, a settled way of life. He was domesticated with Mrs. Unwin, a widow six years his elder. By letting him talk, and listening to his terrors and understanding them, she had brought him very wisely, like a mother, to something like peace of mind. They had lived side by side for many years in methodical monotony. They began the day by reading the Scriptures together; they then went to church; they parted to read or walk; they met after dinner to converse on religious topics or to sing hymns together; then again they walked if it were fine, or read and talked if it were wet, and at last the day ended with more hymns and more prayers. Such for many years had been the routine of Cowper's life with Mary Unwin. When his fingers found their way to a pen they traced the lines of a hymn, or if they wrote a letter it was to urge some misguided mortal, his brother John, for instance, at Cambridge, to seek salvation before it was too late. Yet this urgency was akin perhaps to the old levity; it, too, was an attempt to ward off some terror, to propitiate some deep unrest that lurked at the bottom of his soul. Suddenly the peace was broken. One night in February 1773 the enemy rose; it smote once and for ever. An awful voice called out to Cowper in a dream. It proclaimed that he was damned, that he was outcast, and he fell prostrate before it. After that he could not pray. When the others said grace at table, he took up his knife and fork as a sign that he had no right to join their prayers. Nobody, not even Mrs. Unwin, understood the terrific import of the dream. Nobody realised why he was unique; why he was singled out from all mankind and stood alone in his damnation. But that loneliness had a strange effect—since he was no longer capable of help or direction he was free. The Rev. John Newton could no longer guide his pen or inspire his muse. Since doom had been pronounced and damnation was inevitable, he might sport with hares, cultivate cucumbers, listen to village gossip, weave nets, make tables; all that could be hoped was to while away the dreadful years without the ability to enlighten others or to be helped himself. Never had Cowper written more enchantingly, more gaily, to his friends than now that he knew himself condemned. It was only at moments, when he wrote to Newton or to Unwin, that the terror raised its horrid head above the surface and that he cried aloud: "My days are spent in vanity. . . . Nature revives again; but a soul once slain lives no more." For the most part, as he idled his time away in pleasant pastimes, as he looked with amusement at what passed in the street below, one might think him the happiest of men. There was Geary Ball going to the "Royal Oak" to drink his dram—that happened as regularly as Cowper brushed his teeth; but behold—two ladies were going into the draper's shop opposite. That was an event.

One of the ladies he knew already—she was Mrs. Jones, the wife of a neighbouring clergyman. But the other was a stranger. She was arch and sprightly, with dark hair and round dark eyes. Though a widow—she had been the wife of a Sir Robert Austen—she was far from old and not at all solemn. When she talked, for she and Cowper were soon drinking tea together, "she laughs and makes laugh, and keeps up a conversation without seeming to labour at it". She was a lively, well-bred woman who had lived much in France, and, having seen much of the world, "accounts it a great simpleton as it is". Such were Cowper's first impressions of Ann Austen. Ann's first impressions of the queer couple who lived in the large house in the village street were even more enthusiastic. But that was natural—Ann was an enthusiast by nature. Moreover, though she had seen a great deal of the world and had a town house in Queen Anne Street, she had no friends or relations in that world much to her liking. Clifton Reynes, where her sister lived, was a rude, rough English village where the inhabitants broke into the house if a lady were left unprotected. Lady Austen was dissatisfied; she wanted society, but she also wanted to be settled and to be serious. Neither Clifton Reynes nor Queen Anne Street gave her altogether what she wanted. And then in the most opportune way—quite by chance—she met a refined, well-bred couple who were ready to appreciate what she had to give and ready to invite her to share the quiet pleasures of the countryside which were so dear to them. She could heighten those pleasures deliciously. She made the days seem full of movement and laughter. She organised picnics—they went to the Spinnie and ate their dinner in the root-house and drank their tea on the top of a wheelbarrow. And when autumn came and the evenings drew in, Ann Austen enlivened them too; she it was who stirred William to write a poem about a sofa, and told him, just as he was sinking into one of his fits of melancholy, the story of John Gilpin, so that he leapt out of bed, shaking with laughter. But beneath her sprightliness they were glad to find that she was seriously inclined. She longed for peace and quietude, "for with all that gaiety", Cowper wrote, "she is a great thinker".

And with all that melancholy, to paraphrase his words, Cowper was a man of the world. As he said himself, he was not by nature a recluse. He was no lean and solitary hermit. His limbs were sturdy; his cheeks were ruddy; he was growing plump. In his younger days he, too, had known the world, and provided, of course, that you have seen through it, there is something to be said for having known it. Cowper, at any rate, was a little proud of his gentle birth. Even at Olney he kept certain standards of gentility. He must have an elegant box for his snuff and silver buckles for his shoes; if he wanted a hat it must be "not a round slouch, which I abhor, but a smart, well-cocked, fashionable affair". His letters preserve this serenity, this good sense, this sidelong, arch humour embalmed in page after page of beautiful clear prose. As the post went only three times a week he had plenty of time to smooth out every little crease in daily life to perfection. He had time to tell how a farmer was thrown from his cart and one of the pet hares had escaped; Mr. Grenville had called; they had been caught in a shower and Mrs. Throckmorton had asked them to come into the house—some little thing of the kind happened every week very aptly for his purpose. Or if nothing happened and it was true that the days went by at Olney "shod with felt", then he was able to let his mind play with rumours that reached him from the outer world. There was talk of flying. He would write a few pages on the subject of flying and its impiety; he would express his opinion of the wickedness, for Englishwomen at any rate, of painting the cheeks. He would discourse upon Homer and Virgil and perhaps attempt a few translations himself. And when the days were dark and even he could no longer trudge through the mud, he would open one of his favourite travellers and dream that he was voyaging with Cook or with Anson, for he travelled widely in imagination, though in body he moved no further than from Buckingham to Sussex and from Sussex back to Buckingham again.

His letters preserve what must have made the charm of his company. It is easy to see that his wit, his stories, his sedate, considerate ways, must have made his morning visits—and he had got into the habit of visiting Lady Austen at eleven every morning—delightful. But there was more in his society than that—there was some charm some peculiar fascination, that made it indispensable. His cousin Theodora had loved him—she still loved him anonymously; Mrs. Unwin loved him; and now Ann Austen was beginning to feel something stronger than friendship rise within her. That strain of intense and perhaps inhuman passion which rested with tremulous ecstasy like that of a hawk-moth over a flower, upon some tree, some hill-side— did that not tensify the quiet of the country morning, and give to intercourse with him some keener interest than belonged to the society of other men? "The very stones in the garden walls are my intimate acquaintance", he wrote. "Everything I see in the fields is to me an object, and I can look at the same rivulet, or at a handsome tree, every day of my life with new pleasure." It is this intensity of vision that gives his poetry, with all its moralising and didacticism, its unforgettable qualities. It is this that makes passages in *The Task* like clear windows let into the prosaic fabric of the rest. It was this that gave the edge and zest to his talk. Some finer vision suddenly seized and possessed him. It must have given to the long winter evenings, to the early morning visits, an indescribable combination of pathos and charm. Only, as Theodora could have warned Ann Austen, his passion was not for men and women; it was an abstract ardour; he was a man singularly without thought of sex.

Already early in their friendship Ann Austen had been warned. She adored her friends, and she expressed her adoration with the enthusiasm that was natural to her. At once Cowper wrote to her kindly but firmly admonishing her of the folly of her ways. "When we embellish a creature with colours taken from our fancy," he wrote, "we make it an idol . . . and shall derive nothing from it but a painful conviction of our error." Ann read the letter, flew into a rage, and left the country in a huff. But the breach was soon healed; she worked him ruffles; he acknowledged them with a present of his book. Soon she had embraced Mary Unwin and was back again on more intimate terms than ever. In another month indeed, with such rapidity did her plans take effect, she had sold the lease of her town house, taken part of the vicarage next door to Cowper, and declared that she had now no home but Olney and no friends but Cowper and Mary Unwin. The door between the gardens was opened; the two families dined together on alternate nights; William called Ann sister; and Ann called William brother. What arrangement could have been more idyllic? "Lady Austen and we pass our days alternately at each other's chateau. In the morning I walk with one or other of the ladies, and in the afternoon wind thread", wrote Cowper, playfully comparing himself to Hercules and Samson. And then the evening came, the winter evening which he loved best, and he dreamt in the firelight and watched the shadows dance uncouthly and the sooty films play upon the bars until the lamp was brought, and in that level light he had out his netting, or wound silk, and then, perhaps, Ann sang to the harpsichord and Mary and William played battledore and shuttlecock together. Secure, innocent, peaceful, where then was that "thistly sorrow" that grows inevitably, so Cowper said, beside human happiness? Where would discord come, if come it must? The danger lay perhaps with the women. It might be that Mary would notice one evening that Ann wore a lock of William's hair set in diamonds. She might find a poem to Ann in which he expressed more than a brotherly affection. She would grow jealous. For Mary Unwin was no country simpleton, she was a well-read woman with "the manners of a Duchess"; she had nursed and consoled William for years before Ann came to flutter the "still life" which they both loved best. Thus the two ladies would compete; discord would enter at that point. Cowper would be forced to choose between them.

But we are forgetting another presence at that innocent evening's entertainment. Ann might sing; Mary might play; the fire might burn brightly and the frost and the wind outside make the fireside calm all the sweeter. But there was a shadow among them. In that tranquil room a gulf opened. Cowper trod on the verge of an abyss. Whispers mingled with the singing, voices hissed in his ear words of doom and damnation. He was haled by a terrible voice to perdition. And then Ann Austen expected him to make love to her! Then Ann Austen wanted him to marry her! The thought was odious; it was indecent; it was intolerable. He wrote her another letter, a letter to which there could be no reply. In her bitterness Ann burnt it. She left Olney and no word ever passed between them again. The friendship was over.

And Cowper did not mind very much. Everybody was extremely kind to him. The Throckmortons gave him the key of their garden. An anonymous friend—he never guessed her name—gave him fifty pounds a year. A cedar desk with silver handles was sent him by another friend who wished also to remain unknown. The kind people at Olney supplied him with almost too many tame hares. But if you are damned, if you are solitary, if you are cut off from God and man, what does human kindness avail? "It is all vanity. . . . Nature revives again; but a soul once slain lives no more." He sank from gloom to gloom, and died in misery. As for Lady Austen, she married a Frenchman. She was happy—so people said.

II
BEAU BRUMMELL

When Cowper, in the seclusion of Olney, was roused to anger by the thought of the Duchess of Devonshire and predicted a time when "instead of a girdle there will be a rent, and instead of beauty, baldness", he was acknowledging the power of the lady whom he thought so despicable. Why, otherwise, should she haunt the damp solitudes of Olney? Why should the rustle of her silken skirts disturb those gloomy meditations? Undoubtedly the Duchess was a good haunter. Long after those words were written, when she was dead and buried beneath a tinsel coronet, her ghost mounted the stairs of a very different dwelling-place. An old man was sitting in his arm-chair at Caen. The door opened, and the servant announced, "The Duchess of Devonshire". Beau Brummell at once rose, went to the door and made a bow that would have graced the Court of St. James's.

Only, unfortunately, there was nobody there. The cold air blew up the staircase of an Inn. The Duchess was long dead, and Beau Brummell, in his old age and imbecility, was dreaming that he was back in London again giving a party. Cowper's curse had come true for both of them. The Duchess lay in her shroud, and Brummell, whose clothes had been the envy of kings, had now only one pair of much-mended trousers, which he hid as best he could under a tattered cloak. As for his hair, that had been shaved by order of the doctor.

But though Cowper's sour predictions had thus come to pass, both the Duchess and the dandy might claim that they had had their day. They had been great figures in their time. Of the two, perhaps Brummell might boast the more miraculous career. He had no advantage of birth, and but little of fortune. His grandfather had let rooms in St. James's Street. He had only a moderate capital of thirty thousand pounds to begin with, and his beauty, of figure rather than of face, was marred by a broken nose. Yet without a single noble, important, or valuable action to his credit he cuts a figure; he stands for a symbol; his ghost walks among us still. The reason for this eminence is now a little difficult to determine. Skill of hand and nicety of judgment were his, of course, otherwise he would not have brought the art of tying neck-cloths to perfection. The story is, perhaps, too well known—how he drew his head far back and sunk his chin slowly down so that the cloth wrinkled in perfect symmetry, or if one wrinkle were too deep or too shallow, the cloth was thrown into a basket and the attempt renewed, while the Prince of Wales sat, hour after hour, watching. Yet skill of hand and nicety of judgment were not enough. Brummell owed his ascendency to some curious combination of wit, of taste, of insolence, of independence—for he was never a toady— which it were too heavy-handed to call a philosophy of life, but served the purpose. At any rate, ever since he was the most popular boy at Eton, coolly jesting when they were for throwing a bargee into the river, "My good fellows, don't send him into the river; the man is evidently in a high state of perspiration, and it almost amounts to a certainty that he will catch cold", he floated buoyantly and gaily and without apparent effort to the top of whatever society he found himself among. Even when he was a captain in the Tenth Hussars and so scandalously inattentive to duty that he only knew his troop by "the very large blue nose" of one of the men, he was liked and tolerated. When he resigned his commission, for the regiment was to be sent to Manchester—and "I really could not go—think, your Royal Highness, Manchester!"—he had only to set up house in Chesterfield Street to become the head of the most jealous and exclusive society of his time. For example, he was at Almack's one night talking to Lord ——. The Duchess of —— was there, escorting her young daughter, Lady Louisa. The Duchess caught sight of Mr. Brummell, and at once warned her daughter that if that gentleman near the door came and spoke to them she was to be careful to impress him favourably, "for", and she sank her voice to a whisper, "he is the celebrated Mr. Brummell". Lady Louisa might well have wondered why a Mr. Brummell was celebrated, and why a Duke's daughter need take care to impress a Mr. Brummell. And then, directly he began to move towards them, the reason of her mother's warning became apparent. The grace of his carriage was so astonishing; his bows were so exquisite. Everybody looked overdressed or badly dressed—some, indeed, looked positively dirty—beside him. His clothes seemed to melt into each other with the perfection of their cut and the quiet harmony of their colour. Without a single point of emphasis everything was distinguished—from his bow to the way he opened his snuff-box, with his left hand invariably. He was the personification of freshness and cleanliness and order. One could well believe that he had his chair brought into his dressing-room and was deposited at Almack's without letting a puff of wind disturb his curls or a spot of mud stain his shoes. When he actually spoke to her, Lady Louisa would be at first enchanted—no one was more agreeable, more amusing, had a manner that was more flattering and enticing—and then she would be puzzled. It was quite possible that before the evening was out he would ask her to marry him, and yet his manner of doing it was such that the most ingenuous debutante could not believe that he meant it seriously. His odd grey eyes seemed to contradict his lips; they had a look in them which made the sincerity of his compliments very doubtful. And then he said very cutting things about other people. They were not exactly witty; they were certainly not profound; but they were so skilful, so adroit—they had a twist in them which made them slip into the mind and stay there when more important phrases were forgotten. He had downed the Regent himself with his dexterous "Who's your fat friend?" and his method was the same with humbler people who snubbed him or bored him. "Why, what could I do, my good fellow, but cut the connection? I discovered that Lady Mary actually ate cabbage!"—so he explained to a friend his failure to marry a lady. And, again, when some dull citizen pestered him about his tour to the North, "Which of the lakes do I admire?" he asked his valet. "Windermere, sir." "Ah, yes—Windermere, so it is—Windermere." That was his style, flickering, sneering, hovering on the verge of insolence, . skimming the edge of nonsense, but always keeping within some curious mean, so that one knew the false Brummell story from the true by its exaggeration. Brummell could never have said, "Wales, ring the bell", any more than he could have worn a brightly coloured waistcoat or a glaring necktie. That "certain exquisite propriety" which Lord Byron remarked in his dress stamped his whole being, and made him appear cool, refined, and debonair among the gentlemen who talked only of sport, which Brummell detested, and smelt of the stable, which Brummell never visited. Lady Louisa might well be on tenter-hooks to impress Mr. Brummell favourably. Mr. Brummell's good opinion was of the utmost importance in the world of Lady Louisa.

And unless that world fell into ruins his rule seemed

assured. Handsome, heartless, and cynical, the Beau seemed invulnerable. His taste was impeccable, his health admirable, and his figure as fine as ever. His rule had lasted many years and survived many vicissitudes. The French Revolution had passed over his head without disordering a single hair. Empires had risen and fallen while he experimented with the crease of a neck-cloth and criticised the cut of a coat. Now the battle of Waterloo had been fought and peace had come. The battle left him untouched; it was the peace that undid him. For some time past he had been winning and losing at the gaming-tables. Harriette Wilson had heard that he was ruined, and then, not without disappointment, that he was safe again. Now, with the armies disbanded, there was let loose upon London a horde of rough, ill-mannered men who had been fighting all those years and were determined to enjoy themselves. They flooded the gaming-houses. They played very high. Brummell was forced into competition. He lost and won and vowed never to play again, and then he did play again. At last his remaining ten thousand pounds was gone. He borrowed until he could borrow no more. And finally, to crown the loss of so many thousands, he lost the sixpenny-bit with a hole in it which had always brought him good luck. He gave it by mistake to a hackney coachman: that rascal Rothschild got hold of it, he said, and that was the end of his luck. Such was his own account of the affair—other people put a less innocent interpretation on the matter. At any rate there came a day, 16th May 1816, to be precise—it was a day upon which everything was precise—when he dined alone off a cold fowl and a bottle of claret at Watier's, attended the opera, and then took coach for Dover. He drove rapidly all through the night and reached Calais the day after. He never set foot in England again.

And now a curious process of disintegration set in. The peculiar and highly artificial society of London had acted as a preservative; it had kept him in being; it had concentrated him into one single gem. Now that the pressure was removed, the odds and ends, so trifling separately, so brilliant in combination, which had made up the being of the Beau, fell asunder and revealed what lay beneath. At first his lustre seemed undiminished. His old friends crossed the water to see him and made a point of standing him a dinner and leaving a little present behind them at his bankers. He held his usual levee at his lodgings; he spent the usual hours washing and dressing; he rubbed his teeth with a red root, tweezed out hairs with a silver tweezer, tied his cravat to admiration, and issued at four precisely as perfectly equipped as if the Rue Royale had been St. James's Street and the Prince himself had hung upon his arm. But the Rue Royale was not St. James's Street; the old French Countess who spat on the floor was not the Duchess of Devonshire; the good bourgeois who pressed him to dine off goose at four was not Lord Alvanley; and though he soon won for himself the title of Roi de Calais, and was known to workmen as "George, ring the bell", the praise was gross, the society coarse, and the amusements of Calais very slender. The Beau had to fall back upon the resources of his own mind. These might have been considerable. According to Lady Hester Stanhope, he might have been, had he chosen, a very clever man; and when she told him so, the Beau admitted that he had wasted his talents because a dandy's way of life was the only one "which could place him in a prominent light, and enable him to separate himself from the ordinary herd of men, whom he held in considerable contempt". That way of life allowed of verse-making—his verses, called "The Butterfly's Funeral", were much admired; and of singing, and of some dexterity with the pencil. But now, when the summer days were so long and so empty, he found that such accomplishments hardly served to while away the time. He tried to occupy himself with writing his memoirs; he bought a screen and spent hours pasting it with pictures of great men and beautiful ladies whose virtues and frailties were symbolised by hyenas, by wasps, by profusions of cupids, fitted together with extraordinary skill; he collected Buhl furniture;

he wrote letters in a curiously elegant and elaborate style to ladies. But these occupations palled. The resources of his mind had been whittled away in the course of years; now they failed him. And then the crumbling process went a little farther, and another organ was laid bare—the heart. He who had played at love all these years and kept so adroitly beyond the range of passion, now made violent advances to girls who were young enough to be his daughters. He wrote such passionate letters to Mademoiselle Ellen of Caen that she did not know whether to laugh or to be angry. She was angry, and the Beau, who had tryannised over the daughters of Dukes, prostrated himself before her in despair. But it was too late—the heart after all these years was not a very engaging object even to a simple country girl, and he seems at last to have lavished his affections upon animals. He mourned his terrier Vick for three weeks; he had a friendship with a mouse; he became the champion of all the neglected cats and starving dogs in Caen. Indeed, he said to a lady that if a man and a dog were drowning in the same pond he would prefer to save the dog—if, that is, there were nobody looking. But he was still persuaded that everybody was looking; and his immense regard for appearances gave him a certain stoical endurance. Thus, when paralysis struck him at dinner he left the table without a sign; sunk deep in debt as he was, he still picked his way over the cobbles on the points of his toes to preserve his shoes, and when the terrible day came and he was thrown into prison he won the admiration of murderers and thieves by appearing among them as cool and courteous as if about to pay a morning call. But if he were to continue to act his part, it was essential that he should be supported— he must have a sufficiency of boot polish, gallons of eau-de-Cologne, and three changes of linen every day. His expenditure upon these items was enormous. Generous as his old friends were, and persistently as he supplicated them, there came a time when they could be squeezed no longer. It was decreed that he was to content himself with one change of linen daily, and his allowance was to admit of necessaries only. But how could a Brummell exist upon necessaries only? The demand was absurd. Soon afterwards he showed his sense of the gravity of the situation by mounting a black silk neck-cloth. Black silk neck-cloths had always been his aversion. It was a signal of despair, a sign that the end was in sight. After that everything that had supported him and kept him in being dissolved. His self-respect vanished. He would dine with anyone who would pay the bill. His memory weakened and he told the same story over and over again till even the burghers of Caen were bored. Then his manners degenerated. His extreme cleanliness lapsed into carelessness, and then into positive filth. People objected to his presence in the dining-room of the hotel. Then his mind went—he thought that the Duchess of Devonshire was coming up the stairs when it was only the wind. At last but one passion remained intact among the crumbled debris of so many— an immense greed. To buy Rheims biscuits he sacrificed the greatest treasure that remained to him—he sold his snuff-box. And then nothing was left but a heap of disagreeables, a mass of corruption, a senile and disgusting old man fit only for the charity of nuns and the protection of an asylum. There the clergyman begged him to pray. "'I do try', he said, but he added something which made me doubt whether he understood me." Certainly, he would try; for the clergyman wished it and he had always been polite. He had been polite to thieves and to duchesses and to God Himself. But it was no use trying any longer. He could believe in nothing now except a hot fire, sweet biscuits, and another cup of coffee if he asked for it. And so there was nothing for it but that the Beau who had been compact of grace and sweetness should be shuffled into the grave like any other ill-dressed, ill-bred, unneeded old man. Still, one must remember that Byron, in his moments of dandyism, "always pronounced the name of Brummell with a mingled emotion of respect and jealousy".

NOTE:

Mr. Berry of St. James's Street has courteously drawn my attention to the fact that Beau Brummell certainly visited England in 1822. He came to the famous wine-shop on 26th July 1822 and was weighed as usual. His weight was then 10 stones 13 pounds. On the previous occasion, 6th July 1815, his weight was 12 stones 10 pounds. Mr. Berry adds that there is no record of his coming after 1822.

III
MARY WOLLSTONECRAFT

Great wars are strangely intermittent in their effects. The French Revolution took some people and tore them asunder; others it passed over without disturbing a hair of their heads. Jane Austen, it is said, never mentioned it; Charles Lamb ignored it; Beau Brummell never gave the matter a thought. But to Wordsworth and to Godwin it was the dawn; unmistakably they saw

France standing on the top of golden hours,
And human nature seeming born again.

Thus it would be easy for a picturesque historian to lay side by side the most glaring contrasts—here in Chesterfield Street was Beau Brummell letting his chin fall carefully upon his cravat and discussing in a tone studiously free from vulgar emphasis the proper cut of the lapel of a coat; and here in Somers Town was a party of ill-dressed, excited young men, one with a head too big for his body and a nose too long for his face, holding forth day by day over the tea-cups upon human perfectibility, ideal unity, and the rights of man. There was also a woman present with very bright eyes and a very eager tongue, and the young men, who had middle-class names, like Barlow and Holcroft and Godwin, called her simply "Wollstonecraft", as if it did not matter whether she were married or unmarried, as if she were a young man like themselves.

Such glaring discords among intelligent people—for Charles Lamb and Godwin, Jane Austen and Mary Wollstonecraft were all highly intelligent—suggest how much influence circumstances have upon opinions. If Godwin had been brought up in the precincts of the Temple and had drunk deep of antiquity and old letters at Christ's Hospital, he might never have cared a straw for the future of man and his rights in general. If Jane Austen had lain as a child on the landing to prevent her father from thrashing her mother, her soul might have burnt with such a passion against tyranny that all her novels might have been consumed in one cry for justice.

Such had been Mary Wollstonecraft's first experience of the joys of married life. And then her sister Everina had been married miserably and had bitten her wedding ring to pieces in the coach. Her brother had been a burden on her; her father's farm had failed, and in order to start that disreputable man with the red face and the violent temper and the dirty hair in life again she had gone into bondage among the aristocracy as a governess—in short, she had never known what happiness was, and, in its default, had fabricated a creed fitted to meet the sordid misery of real human life. The staple of her doctrine was that nothing mattered save independence. "Every obligation we receive from our fellow-creatures is a new shackle, takes from our native freedom, and debases the mind." Independence was the first necessity for a woman; not grace or charm, but energy and courage and the power to put her will into effect, were her necessary qualities. It was her highest boast to be able to say, "I never yet resolved to do anything of consequence that I did not adhere readily to it". Certainly Mary could say this with truth. When she was a little more than thirty she could look back upon a series of actions which she had carried out in the teeth of opposition. She had taken a house by prodigious efforts for her friend Fanny, only to find that Fanny's mind was changed and she did not want a house after all. She had started a school. She had persuaded Fanny into marrying Mr. Skeys. She had thrown up her school and gone to Lisbon alone to nurse Fanny when she died. On the voyage back she had forced the captain of the ship to rescue a wrecked French vessel by threatening to expose him if he refused. And when, overcome by a passion for Fuseli, she declared her wish to live with him and been refused flatly by his wife, she had put her principle of decisive action instantly into effect, and had gone to Paris determined to make her living by her pen.

The Revolution thus was not merely an event that had happened outside her; it was an active agent in her own blood. She had been in revolt all her life—against tyranny, against law, against convention. The reformer's love of humanity, which has so much of hatred in it as well as love, fermented within her. The outbreak of revolution in France expressed some of her deepest theories and convictions, and she dashed off in the heat of that extraordinary moment those two eloquent and daring books— the *Reply to Burke* and the *Vindication of the Rights of Woman*, which are so true that they seem now to contain nothing new in them—their originality has become our commonplace. But when she was in Paris lodging by herself in a great house, and saw with her own eyes the King whom she despised driving past surrounded by National Guards and holding himself with greater dignity than she expected, then, "I can scarcely tell you why", the tears came to her eyes. "I am going to bed," the letter ended, "and, for the first time in my life, I cannot put out the candle." Things were not so simple after all. She could not understand even her own feelings. She saw the most cherished of her convictions put into practice—and her eyes filled with tears. She had won fame and independence and the right to live her own life—and she wanted something different. "I do not want to be loved like a goddess," she wrote, "but I wish to be necessary to you." For Imlay, the fascinating American to whom her letter was addressed, had been very good to her. Indeed, she had fallen passionately in love with him. But it was one of her theories that love should be free—"that mutual affection was marriage and that the marriage tie should not bind after the death of love, if love should die". And yet at the same time that she wanted freedom she wanted certainty. "I like the word affection," she wrote, "because it signifies something habitual."

The conflict of all these contradictions shows itself in her face, at once so resolute and so dreamy, so sensual and so intelligent, and beautiful into the bargain with its great coils of hair and the large bright eyes that Southey thought the most expressive he had ever seen. The life of such a woman was bound to be tempestuous. Every day she made theories by which life should be lived; and every day she came smack against the rock of other people's prejudices. Every day too—for she was no pedant, no cold-blooded theorist—something was born in her that thrust aside her theories and forced her to model them afresh. She acted upon her theory that she had no legal claim upon Imlay; she refused to marry him; but when he left her alone week after week with the child she had borne him her agony was unendurable.

Thus distracted, thus puzzling even to herself, the plausible and treacherous Imlay cannot be altogether blamed for failing to follow the rapidity of her changes and the alternate reason and unreason of her moods. Even friends whose liking was impartial were disturbed by her discrepancies. Mary had a passionate, an exuberant, love of Nature, and yet one night when the colours in the sky were so exquisite that Madeleine Schweizer could not help saying to her, "Come, Mary—come, nature-lover—and enjoy this wonderful spectacle—this constant transition from colour to colour", Mary never took her eyes off the Baron de Wolzogen. "I must confess," wrote Madame Schweizer, "that this erotic absorption made such a disagreeable impression on me, that all my pleasure vanished." But if the sentimental Swiss was disconcerted by Mary's sensuality, Imlay, the shrewd man of business, was exasperated by her intelligence. Whenever he saw her he yielded to her charm, but then her quickness, her penetration, her uncompromising idealism harassed him. She saw through his excuses; she met all his reasons; she was even capable of managing his business. There was no peace with her—he must be off again. And then her letters followed him, torturing him with their sincerity and their insight. They were so outspoken; they pleaded so passionately to be told the truth; they showed such a contempt for soap and alum and wealth and comfort; they repeated, as he suspected, so truthfully that he had only to say the word, "and you shall never hear of me more", that he could not endure it. Tickling minnows he had hooked a dolphin, and the creature rushed him through the waters till he was dizzy and only wanted to escape. After all, though he had played at theory-making too, he was a business man, he depended upon soap and alum; "the secondary pleasures of life", he had to admit, "are very necessary to my comfort". And among them was one that for ever evaded Mary's jealous scrutiny. Was it business, was it politics, was it a woman, that perpetually took him away from her? He shillied and shallied; he was very charming when they met; then he disappeared again. Exasperated at last, and half insane with suspicion, she forced the truth from the cook. A little actress in a strolling company was his mistress, she learnt. True to her own creed of decisive action, Mary at once soaked her skirts so that she might sink unfailingly, and threw herself from Putney Bridge. But she was rescued; after unspeakable agony she recovered, and then her "unconquerable greatness of mind", her girlish creed of independence, asserted itself again, and she determined to make another bid for happiness and to earn her living without taking a penny from Imlay for herself or their child.

It was in this crisis that she again saw Godwin, the little man with the big head, whom she had met when the French Revolution was making the young men in Somers Town think that a new world was being born. She met him—but that is a euphemism, for in fact Mary Wollstonecraft actually visited him in his own house. Was it the effect of the French Revolution? Was it the blood she had seen spilt on the pavement and the cries of the furious crowd that had rung in her ears that made it seem a matter of no importance whether she put on her cloak and went to visit Godwin in Somers Town, or waited in Judd Street West for Godwin to come to her? And what strange upheaval of human life was it that inspired that curious man, who was so queer a mixture of meanness and magnanimity, of coldness and deep feeling—for the memoir of his wife could not have been written without unusual depth of heart—to hold the view that she did right—that he respected Mary for trampling upon the idiotic convention by which women's lives were tied down? He held the most extraordinary views on many subjects, and upon the relations of the sexes in particular. He thought that reason should influence even the love between men and women. He thought that there was something spiritual in their relationship. He had written that "marriage is a law, and the worst of all laws . . . marriage is an affair of property, and the worst of all properties". He held the belief that if two people of the opposite sex like each other, they should live together without any ceremony, or, for living together is apt to blunt love, twenty doors off, say, in the same street. And he went further; he said that if another man liked your wife "this will create no difficulty. We may all enjoy her conversation, and we shall all be wise enough to consider the sensual intercourse a very trivial object." True, when he wrote those words he had never been in love; now for the first time he was to experience that sensation. It came very quietly and naturally, growing "with equal advances in the mind of each" from those talks in Somers Town, from those discussions upon everything under the sun which they held so improperly alone in his rooms. "It was friendship melting into love . . .", he wrote. "When, in the course of things, the disclosure came, there was nothing in a manner for either party to disclose to the other."

Certainly they were in agreement upon the most essential points; they were both of opinion, for instance, that marriage was unnecessary. They would continue to live apart. Only when Nature again intervened, and Mary found herself with child, was it worth while to lose valued friends, she asked, for the sake of a theory? She thought not, and they were married. And then that other theory—that it is best for husband and wife to live apart—was not that also incompatible with other feelings that were coming to birth in her? "A husband is a convenient part of the furniture of the house", she wrote. Indeed, she discovered that she was passionately domestic. Why not, then, revise that theory too, and share the same roof. Godwin should have a room some doors off to work in; and they should dine out separately if they liked—their work, their friends, should be separate. Thus they settled it, and the plan worked admirably. The arrangement combined "the novelty and lively sensation of a visit with the more delicious and heart-felt pleasures of domestic life". Mary admitted that she was happy; Godwin confessed that, after all one's philosophy, it was "extremely gratifying" to find that "there is someone who takes an interest in one's happiness". All sorts of powers and emotions were liberated in Mary by her new satisfaction. Trifles gave her an exquisite pleasure—the sight of Godwin and Imlay's child playing together; the thought of their own child who was to be born; a day's jaunt into the country. One day, meeting Imlay in the New Road, she greeted him without bitterness. But, as Godwin wrote, "Ours is not an idle happiness, a paradise of selfish and transitory pleasures". No, it too was an experiment, as Mary's life had been an experiment from the start, an attempt to make human conventions conform more closely to human needs. And their marriage was only a beginning; all sorts of things were to follow after. Mary was going to have a child. She was going to write a book to be called *The Wrongs of Women*. She was going to reform education. She was going to come down to dinner the day after her child was born. She was going to employ a midwife and not a doctor at her confinement—but that experiment was her last. She died in child-birth. She whose sense of her own existence was so intense, who had cried out even in her misery, "I cannot bear to think of being no more—of losing myself—nay, it appears to me impossible that I should cease to exist", died at the age of thirty-six. But she has her revenge. Many millions have died and been forgotten in the hundred and thirty years that have passed since she was buried; and yet as we read her letters and listen to her arguments and consider her experiments, above all, that most fruitful experiment, her relation with Godwin, and realise the high-handed and hot-blooded manner in which she cut her way to the quick of life, one form of immortality is hers undoubtedly: she is alive and active, she argues and experiments, we hear her voice and trace her influence even now among the living.

IV
DOROTHY WORDSWORTH

Two highly incongruous travellers, Mary Wollstonecraft and Dorothy Wordsworth, followed close upon each other's footsteps. Mary was in Altona on the Elbe in 1795 with her baby; three years later Dorothy came there with her brother and Coleridge. Both kept a record of their travels; both saw the same places, but the eyes with which they saw them were very different. Whatever Mary saw served to start her mind upon some theory, upon the effect of government, upon the state of the people, upon the mystery of her own soul. The beat of the oars on the waves made her ask, "Life, what are you? Where goes this breath? This *I* so much alive? In what element will it mix, giving and receiving fresh energy?" And sometimes she forgot to look at the sunset and looked instead at the Baron Wolzogen. Dorothy, on the other hand, noted what was before her accurately, literally, and with prosaic precision. "The walk very pleasing between Hamburgh and Altona. A large piece of ground planted with trees, and intersected by gravel walks. . . . The ground on the opposite side of the Elbe appears marshy." Dorothy never railed against "the cloven hoof of despotism". Dorothy never asked "men's questions" about exports and imports; Dorothy never confused her own soul with the sky. This "*I* so much alive" was ruthlessly subordinated to the trees and the grass. For if she let "I" and its rights and its wrongs and its passions and its suffering get between her and the object, she would be calling the moon "the Queen of the Night"; she would be talking of dawn's "orient beams"; she would be soaring into reveries and rhapsodies and forgetting to find the exact phrase for the ripple of moonlight upon the lake. It was like "herrings in the water"—she could not have said that if she had been thinking about herself. So while Mary dashed her head against wall after wall, and cried out, "Surely something resides in this heart that is not perishable—and life is more than a dream", Dorothy went on methodically at Alfoxden noting the approach of spring. "The sloe in blossom, the hawthorn green, the larches in the park changed from black to green, in two or three days." And next day, 14th April 1798, "the evening very stormy, so we staid indoors. Mary Wollstonecraft's life, &c., came." And the day after they walked in the squire's grounds and noticed that "Nature was very successfully striving to make beautiful what art had deformed—ruins, hermitages, &c., &c.". There is no reference to Mary Wollstonecraft; it seems as if her life and all its storms had been swept away in one of those compendious et ceteras, and yet the next sentence reads like an unconscious comment. "Happily we cannot shape the huge hills, or carve out the valleys according to our fancy." No, we cannot re-form, we must not rebel; we can only accept and try to understand the message of Nature. And so the notes go on.

Spring passed; summer came; summer turned to autumn; it was winter, and then again the sloes were in blossom and the hawthorns green and spring had come. But it was spring in the North now, and Dorothy was living alone with her brother in a small cottage at Grasmere in the midst of the hills. Now after the hardships and separations of youth they were together under their own roof; now they could address themselves undisturbed to the absorbing occupation of living in the heart of Nature and trying, day by day, to read her meaning. They had money enough at last to let them live together without the need of earning a penny. No family duties or professional tasks distracted them. Dorothy could ramble all day on the hills and sit up talking to Coleridge all night without being scolded by her aunt for unwomanly behaviour. The hours were theirs from sunrise to sunset, and could be altered to suit the season. If it was fine, there was no need to come in; if it was wet, there was no need to get up. One could go to bed at any hour. One could let the dinner cool if the cuckoo were shouting on the hill and William had not found the exact epithet he wanted. Sunday was a day like any other. Custom, convention, everything was subordinated to the absorbing, exacting, exhausting task of living in the heart of Nature and writing poetry. For exhausting it was. William would make his head ache in the effort to find the right word. He would go on hammering at a poem until Dorothy was afraid to suggest an alteration. A chance phrase of hers would run in his head and make it impossible for him to get back into the proper mood. He would come down to breakfast and sit "with his shirt neck unbuttoned, and his waistcoat open", writing a poem on a Butterfly which some story of hers had suggested, and he would eat nothing, and then he would begin altering the poem and again would be exhausted.

It is strange how vividly all this is brought before us, considering that the diary is made up of brief notes such as any quiet woman might make of her garden's changes and her brother's moods and the progress of the seasons. It was warm and mild, she notes, after a day of rain. She met a cow in a field. "The cow looked at me, and I looked at the cow, and whenever I stirred the cow gave over eating." She met an old man who walked with two sticks—for days on end she met nothing more out of the way than a cow eating and an old man walking. And her motives for writing are common enough—"because I will not quarrel with myself, and because I shall give William pleasure by it when he comes home again". It is only gradually that the difference between this rough notebook and others discloses itself; only by degrees that the brief notes unfurl in the mind and open a whole landscape before us, that the plain statement proves to be aimed so directly at the object that if we look exactly along the line that it points we shall see precisely what she saw. "The moonlight lay upon the hills like snow." "The air was become still, the lake of a bright slate colour, the hills darkening. The bays shot into the low fading shores. Sheep resting. All things quiet." "There was no one waterfall above another—it was the sound of waters in the air—the voice of the air." Even in such brief notes one feels the suggestive power which is the gift of the poet rather than of the naturalist, the power which, taking only the simplest facts, so orders them that the whole scene comes before us, heightened and composed, the lake in its quiet, the hills in their splendour. Yet she was no descriptive writer in the usual sense. Her first concern was to be truthful—grace and symmetry must be made subordinate to truth. But then truth is sought because to falsify the look of the stir of the breeze on the lake is to tamper with the spirit which inspires appearances. It is that spirit which goads her and urges her and keeps her faculties for ever on the stretch. A sight or a sound would not let her be till she had traced her perception along its course and fixed it in words, though they might be bald, or in an image, though it might be angular. Nature was a stern taskmistress. The exact prosaic detail must be rendered as well as the vast and visionary outline. Even when the distant hills trembled before her in the glory of a dream she must note with literal accuracy "the glittering silver line on the ridge of the backs of the sheep", or remark how "the crows at a little distance from us became white as silver as they flew in the sunshine, and when they went still further, they looked like shapes of water passing over the green fields". Always trained and in use, her powers of observation became in time so expert and so acute that a day's walk stored her mind's eye with a vast assembly of curious objects to be sorted at leisure. How strange the sheep looked mixed with the soldiers at Dumbarton Castle! For some reason the sheep looked their real size, but the soldiers looked like puppets. And then the movements of the sheep were so natural and fearless, and the motion of the dwarf soldiers was so restless and apparently without meaning. It was extremely queer. Or lying in bed she would look up at the ceiling and think how the varnished beams were "as glossy as black rocks on a sunny day cased in ice". Yes, they

> crossed each other in almost as intricate and fantastic a manner as I have seen the underboughs of a large beech-tree withered by the depth of the shade above. . . . It was like what I should suppose an underground cave or temple to be, with a dripping or moist roof, and the moonlight entering in upon it by some means or other, and yet the colours were more like melted gems. I lay looking up till the light of the fire faded away. . . . I did not sleep much.

Indeed, she scarcely seemed to shut her eyes. They looked and they looked, urged on not only by an indefatigable curiosity but also by reverence, as if some secret of the utmost importance lay hidden beneath the surface. Her pen sometimes stammers with the intensity of the emotion that she controlled, as De Quincey said that her tongue stammered with the conflict between her ardour and her shyness when she spoke. But controlled she was. Emotional and impulsive by nature, her eyes "wild and starting", tormented by feelings which almost mastered her, still she must control, still she must repress, or she would fail in her task—she would cease to see. But if one subdued oneself, and resigned one's private agitations, then, as if in reward, Nature would bestow an exquisite satisfaction. "Rydale was very beautiful, with spear-shaped streaks of polished steel. . . . It calls home the heart to quietness. I had been very melancholy", she wrote. For did not Coleridge come walking over the hills and tap at the cottage door late at night—did she not carry a letter from Coleridge hidden safe in her bosom?

Thus giving to Nature, thus receiving from Nature, it seemed, as the arduous and ascetic days went by, that Nature and Dorothy had grown together in perfect sympathy—a sympathy not cold or vegetable or inhuman because at the core of it burnt that other love for "my beloved", her brother, who was indeed its heart and inspiration. William and Nature and Dorothy herself, were they not one being? Did they not compose a trinity, self-contained and self-sufficient and independent whether indoors or out? They sit indoors. It was

> about ten o'clock and a quiet night. The fire flickers and the watch ticks. I hear nothing but the breathing of my Beloved as he now and then pushes his book forward, and turns over a leaf.

And now it is an April day, and they take the old cloak and lie in John's grove out of doors together.

> William heard me breathing, and rustling now and then, but we both lay still and unseen by one another. He thought that it would be sweet thus to lie in the grave, to hear the peaceful sounds of the earth, and just to know that our dear friends were near. The lake was still; there was a boat out.

It was a strange love, profound, almost dumb, as if brother and sister had grown together and shared not the speech but the mood, so that they hardly knew which felt, which spoke, which saw the daffodils or the sleeping city; only Dorothy stored the mood in prose, and later William came and bathed in it and made it into poetry. But one could not act without the other.

They must feel, they must think, they must be together. So now, when they had lain out on the hill-side they would rise and go home and make tea, and Dorothy would write to Coleridge, and they would sow the scarlet beans together, and William would work at his "Leech Gatherer", and Dorothy would copy the lines for him. Rapt but controlled, free yet strictly ordered, the homely narrative moves naturally from ecstasy on the hills to baking bread and ironing linen and fetching William his supper in the cottage.

The cottage, though its garden ran up into the fells, was on the highroad. Through her parlour window Dorothy looked out and saw whoever might be passing—a tall beggar woman perhaps with her baby on her back; an old soldier; a coroneted landau with touring ladies peering inquisitively inside. The rich and the great she would let pass—they interested her no more than cathedrals or picture galleries or great cities; but she could never see a beggar at the door without asking him in and questioning him closely. Where had he been? What had he seen? How many children had he? She searched into the lives of the poor as if they held in them the same secret as the hills. A tramp eating cold bacon over the kitchen fire might have been a starry night, so closely she watched him; so clearly she noted how his old coat was patched "with three bell-shaped patches of darker blue behind, where the buttons had been", how his beard of a fortnight's growth was like "grey *plush*". And then as they rambled on with their tales of seafaring and the press-gang and the Marquis of Granby, she never failed to capture the one phrase that sounds on in the mind after the story is forgotten, "What, you are stepping westward?" "To be sure there is great promise for virgins in Heaven." "She could trip lightly by the graves of those who died when they were young." The poor had their poetry as the hills had theirs. But it was out of doors, on the road or on the moor, not in the cottage parlour, that her imagination had freest play. Her happiest moments were passed tramping beside a jibbing horse on a wet Scottish road without certainty of bed or supper. All she knew was that there was some sight ahead, some grove of trees to be noted, some waterfall to be inquired into. On they tramped hour after hour in silence for the most part, though Coleridge, who was of the party, would suddenly begin to debate aloud the true meaning of the words majestic, sublime, and grand. They had to trudge on foot because the horse had thrown the cart over a bank and the harness was only mended with string and pocket-handkerchiefs. They were hungry, too, because Wordsworth had dropped the chicken and the bread into the lake, and they had nothing else for dinner. They were uncertain of the way, and did not know where they would find lodging: all they knew was that there was a waterfall ahead. At last Coleridge could stand it no longer. He had rheumatism in the joints; the Irish jaunting car provided no shelter from the weather; his companions were silent and absorbed. He left them. But William and Dorothy tramped on. They looked like tramps themselves. Dorothy's cheeks were brown as a gipsy's, her clothes were shabby, her gait was rapid and ungainly. But still she was indefatigable; her eye never failed her; she noticed everything. At last they reached the waterfall. And then all Dorothy's powers fell upon it. She searched out its character, she noted its resemblances, she defined its differences, with all the ardour of a discoverer, with all the exactness of a naturalist, with all the rapture of a lover. She possessed it at last—she had laid it up in her mind for ever. It had become one of those "inner visions" which she could call to mind at any time in their distinctness and in their particularity. It would come back to her long years afterwards when she was old and her mind had failed her; it would come back stilled and heightened and mixed with all the happiest memories of her past—with the thought of Racedown and Alfoxden and Coleridge reading "Christabel", and her beloved, her brother William. It would bring with it what no human being could give, what no human relation could offer—consolation and quiet. If, then, the passionate cry of Mary Wollstonecraft had reached her ears—"Surely something resides in this heart that is not perishable—and life is more than a dream"—she would have had no doubt whatever as to her answer. She would have said quite simply, "We looked about us, and felt that we were happy".

WILLIAM HAZLITT

First published in 1935

Had one met Hazlitt no doubt one would have liked him on his own principle that "We can scarcely hate anyone we know". But Hazlitt has been dead now a hundred years, and it is perhaps a question how far we can know him well enough to overcome those feelings of dislike, both personal and intellectual, which his writings still so sharply arouse. For Hazlitt—it is one of his prime merits—was not one of those noncommittal writers who shuffle off in a mist and die of their own insignificance. His essays are emphatically himself. He has no reticence and he has no shame. He tells us exactly what he thinks, and he tells us— the confidence is less seductive—exactly what he feels. As of all men he had the most intense consciousness of his own existence, since never a day passed without inflicting on him some pang of hate or of jealousy, some thrill of anger or of pleasure, we cannot read him for long without coming in contact with a very singular character—ill-conditioned yet high-minded; mean yet noble; intensely egotistical yet inspired by the most genuine passion for the rights and liberties of mankind.

Soon, so thin is the veil of the essay as Hazlitt wore it, his very look comes before us. We see him as Coleridge saw him, "brow-hanging, shoe-contemplative, strange". He comes shuffling into the room, he looks nobody straight in the face, he shakes hands with the fin of a fish; occasionally he darts a malignant glance from his corner. "His manners are 99 in 100 singularly repulsive", Coleridge said. Yet now and again his face lit up with intellectual beauty, and his manner became radiant with sympathy and

227

understanding. Soon, too, as we read on, we become familiar with the whole gamut of his grudges and his grievances. He lived, one gathers, mostly at inns. No woman's form graced his board. He had quarrelled with all his old friends, save perhaps with Lamb. Yet his only fault had been that he had stuck to his principles and "not become a government tool". He was the object of malignant persecution—Blackwood's reviewers called him "pimply Hazlitt", though his cheek was pale as alabaster. These lies, however, got into print, and then he was afraid to visit his friends because the footman had read the newspaper and the housemaid tittered behind his back. He had—no one could deny it—one of the finest minds, and he wrote indisputably the best prose style of his time. But what did that avail with women? Fine ladies have no respect for scholars, nor chambermaids either—so the growl and plaint of his grievances keeps breaking through, disturbing us, irritating us; and yet there is something so independent, subtle, fine, and enthusiastic about him—when he can forget himself he is so rapt in ardent speculation about other things—that dislike crumbles and turns to something much warmer and more complex. Hazlitt was right:

It is the mask only that we dread and hate; the man
may have something human about him! The notions in
short which we entertain of people at a distance, or from
partial representation, or from guess-work, are simple,
uncompounded ideas, which answer to nothing in reality;
those which we derive from experience are mixed modes,
the only true and, in general, the most favourable ones.

Certainly no one could read Hazlitt and maintain a simple and uncompounded idea of him. From the first he was a twy-minded man—one of those divided natures which are inclined almost equally to two quite opposite careers. It is significant that his first impulse was not to essay-writing but to painting and philosophy. There was something in the remote and silent art of the painter that offered a refuge to his tormented spirit. He noted enviously how happy the old age of painters was—"their minds keep alive to the last"; he turned longingly to the calling that takes one out of doors, among fields and woods, that deals with bright pigments, and has solid brush and canvas for its tools and not merely black ink and white paper. Yet at the same time he was bitten by an abstract curiosity that would not let him rest in the contemplation of concrete beauty. When he was a boy of fourteen he heard his father, the good Unitarian minister, dispute with an old lady of the congregation as they were coming out of Meeting as to the limits of religious toleration, and, he said, "it was this circumstance that decided the fate of my future life". It set him off "forming in my head . . . the following system of political rights and general jurisprudence". He wished "to be satisfied of the reason of things". The two ideals were ever after to clash. To be a thinker and to express in the plainest and most accurate of terms "the reason of things", and to be a painter gloating over blues and crimsons, breathing fresh air and living sensually in the emotions—these were two different, perhaps incompatible ideals, yet like all Hazlitt's emotions both were tough and each strove for mastery. He yielded now to one, now to the other. He spent months in Paris copying pictures at the Louvre. He came home and toiled laboriously at the portrait of an old woman in a bonnet day after day, seeking by industry and pains to discover the secret of Rembrandt's genius; but he lacked some quality—perhaps it was invention—and in the end cut the canvas to ribbons in a rage or turned it against the wall in despair. At the same time he was writing the "Essay on the Principles of Human Action" which he preferred to all his other works. For there he wrote plainly and truthfully, without glitter or garishness, without any wish to please or to make money, but solely to gratify the urgency of his own desire for truth. Naturally, "the book dropped still-born from the press". Then, too, his political hopes, his belief that the age of freedom had come and that the tyranny of kingship was over, proved vain. His friends deserted to the Government, and he was left to uphold the doctrines of liberty, fraternity, and revolution in that perpetual minority which requires so much self-approval to support it.

Thus he was a man of divided tastes and of thwarted ambition; a man whose happiness, even in early life, lay behind. His mind had set early and bore for ever the stamp of first impressions. In his happiest moods he looked not forwards but backwards—to the garden where he had played as a child, to the blue hills of Shropshire and to all those landscapes which he had seen when hope was still his, and peace brooded upon him and he looked up from his painting or his book and saw the fields and woods as if they were the outward expression of his own inner quietude. It is to the books that he read then that he returns—to Rousseau and to Burke and to the *Letters of Junius*. The impression that they made upon his youthful imagination was never effaced and scarcely overlaid; for after youth was over he ceased to read for pleasure, and youth and the pure and intense pleasures of youth were soon left behind.

Naturally, given his susceptibility to the charms of the other sex, he married; and naturally, given his consciousness of his own "misshapen form made to be mocked", he married unhappily. Miss Sarah Stoddart pleased him when he met her at the Lambs by the common sense with which she found the kettle and boiled it when Mary absentmindedly delayed. But of domestic talents she had none. Her little income was insufficient to meet the burden of married life, and Hazlitt soon found that instead of spending eight years in writing eight pages he must turn journalist and write articles upon politics and plays and pictures and books of the right length, at the right moment. Soon the mantelpiece of the old house at York Street where Milton had lived was scribbled over with ideas for essays. As the habit proves, the house was not a tidy house, nor did geniality and comfort excuse the lack of order. The Hazlitts were to be found eating breakfast at two in the afternoon, without a fire in the grate or a curtain to the window. A valiant walker and a clear-sighted woman, Mrs. Hazlitt had no delusions about her husband. He was not faithful to her, and she faced the fact with admirable common sense. But "he said that I had always despised him and his abilities", she noted in her diary, and that was carrying common sense too far. The prosaic marriage came lamely to an end. Free at last from the encumbrance of home and husband, Sarah Hazlitt pulled on her boots and set off on a walking tour through Scotland, while Hazlitt, incapable of attachment or comfort, wandered from inn to inn, suffered tortures of humiliation and disillusionment, but, as he drank cup after cup of very strong tea and made love to the innkeeper's daughter, he wrote those essays that are of course among the very best that we have.

That they are not quite the best—that they do not haunt the mind and remain entire in the memory as the essays of Montaigne or Lamb haunt the mind—is also true. He seldom reaches the perfection of these great writers or their unity. Perhaps it is the nature of these short pieces that they need unity and a mind at harmony with itself. A little jar there makes the whole composition tremble. The essays of Montaigne, Lamb, even Addison, have the reticence which springs from composure, for with all their familiarity they never tell us what they wish to keep hidden. But with Hazlitt it is different. There is always something divided and discordant even in his finest essays, as if two minds were at work who never succeed save for a few moments in making a match of it. In the first place there is the mind of the inquiring boy who wishes to be satisfied of the reason of things—the mind of the thinker. It is the thinker for the most part who is allowed the choice of the subject. He chooses some abstract idea, like Envy, or Egotism, or Reason and Imagination. He treats it with energy and independence. He explores its ramifications and scales its narrow paths as if it were a mountain road and the ascent both difficult and inspiring. Compared with this athletic progress, Lamb's seems the flight of

231

a butterfly cruising capriciously among the flowers and perching for a second incongruously here upon a barn, there upon a wheelbarrow. But every sentence in Hazlitt carries us forward. He has his end in view and, unless some accident intervenes, he strides towards it in that "pure conversational prose style" which, as he points out, is so much more difficult to practise than fine writing.

There can be no question that Hazlitt the thinker is an admirable companion. He is strong and fearless; he knows his mind and he speaks his mind forcibly yet brilliantly too, for the readers of newspapers are a dull-eyed race who must be dazzled in order to make them see. But besides Hazlitt the thinker there is Hazlitt the artist. There is the sensuous and emotional man, with his feeling for colour and touch, with his passion for prizefighting and Sarah Walker, with his sensibility to all those emotions which disturb the reason and make it often seem futile enough to spend one's time slicing things up finer and finer with the intellect when the body of the world is so firm and so warm and demands so imperatively to be pressed to the heart. To know the reason of things is a poor substitute for being able to feel them. And Hazlitt felt with the intensity of a poet. The most abstract of his essays will suddenly glow red-hot or white-hot if something reminds him of his past. He will drop his fine analytic pen and paint a phrase or two with a full brush brilliantly and beautifully if some landscape stirs his imagination or some book brings back the hour when he first read it. The famous passages about reading *Love for Love* and drinking coffee from a silver pot, and reading *La Nouvelle Héloïse* and eating a cold chicken, are known to all, and yet how oddly they often break into the context, how violently we are switched from reason to rhapsody—how embarrassingly our austere thinker falls upon our shoulders and demands our sympathy! It is this disparity and the sense of two forces in conflict that trouble the serenity and cause the inconclusiveness of some of Hazlitt's finest essays. They set out to give us a proof and they end by giving us a picture. We are about to plant our feet upon the solid rock of Q.E.D., and behold the rock turns to quagmire and we are knee-deep in mud and water and flowers. "Faces pale as the primrose with hyacinthine locks" are in our eyes; the woods of Tuderly breathe their mystic voices in our ears. Then suddenly we are recalled, and the thinker, austere, muscular, and sardonic, leads us on to analyse, to dissect, and to condemn.

Thus if we compare Hazlitt with the other great masters in his line it is easy to see where his limitations lie. His range is narrow and his sympathies few if intense. He does not open the doors wide upon all experience like Montaigne, rejecting nothing, tolerating everything, and watching the play of the soul with irony and detachment. On the contrary, his mind shut hard with egotistic tenacity upon his first impressions and froze them to unalterable convictions. Nor was it for him to make play, like Lamb, with the figures of his friends, creating them afresh in fantastic flights of imagination and reverie. His characters are seen with the same quick sidelong glance full of shrewdness and suspicion which he darted upon people in the flesh. He does not use the essayist's licence to circle and meander. He is tethered by his egotism and by his convictions to one time and one place and one being. We never forget that this is England in the early days of the nineteenth century; indeed, we feel ourselves in the Southampton Buildings or in the inn parlour that looks over the downs and on to the high road at Winterslow. He has an extraordinary power of making us contemporary with himself. But as we read on through the many volumes which he filled with so much energy and yet with so little love of his task, the comparison with the other essayists drops from us. These are not essays, it seems, independent and self-sufficient, but fragments broken off from some larger book—some searching enquiry into the reason for human actions or into the nature of human institutions. It is only accident that has cut them short, and only deference to the public taste that has decked them out with gaudy images and bright colours. The phrase which occurs in one form or another so frequently and indicates the structure which if he were free he would follow—"I will here try to go more at large into the subject and then give such instances and illustrations of it as occur to me"—could by no possibility occur in the *Essays of Elia* or *Sir Roger de Coverley*. He loves to grope among the curious depths of human psychology and to track down the reason of things. He excels in hunting out the obscure causes that lie behind some common saying or sensation, and the drawers of his mind are well stocked with illustrations and arguments. We can believe him when he says that for twenty years he had thought hard and suffered acutely. He is speaking of what he knows from experience when he exclaims, "How many ideas and trains of sentiment, long and deep and intense, often pass through the mind in only one day's thinking or reading!" Convictions are his life-blood; ideas have formed in him like stalactites, drop by drop, year by year. He has sharpened them in a thousand solitary walks; he has tested them in argument after argument, sitting in his corner, sardonically observant, over a late supper at the Southampton Inn. But he has not changed them. His mind is his own and it is made up.

Thus however threadbare the abstraction—*Hot and Cold*, or *Envy*, or *The Conduct of Life*, or *The Picturesque and the Ideal*—he has something solid to write about. He never lets his brain slacken or trusts to his great gift of picturesque phrasing to float him over a stretch of shallow thought. Even when it is plain from the savagery and contempt with which he attacks his task that he is out of the mood and only keeps his mind to the grindstone by strong tea and sheer force of will, we still find him mordant and searching and acute. There is a stir and trouble, a vivacity and conflict in his essays as if the very contrariety of his gifts kept him on the stretch. He is always hating, loving, thinking, and suffering. He could never come to terms with authority or doff his own idiosyncrasy in deference to opinion. Thus chafed and goaded the level of his essays is extraordinarily high. Often dry, garish in their bright imagery, monotonous in the undeviating energy of their rhythm—for Hazlitt believed too implicitly in his own saying, "mediocrity, insipidity, want of character, is the great fault", to be an easy writer to read for long at a stretch— there is scarcely an essay without its stress of thought, its thrust of insight, its moment of penetration. His pages are full of fine sayings and unexpected turns and independence and originality. "All that is worth remembering of life is the poetry of it." "If the truth were known, the most disagreeable people are the most amiable." "You will hear more good things on the outside of a stage-coach from London to Oxford, than if you were to pass a twelve-month with the undergraduates or heads of colleges of that famous University." We are constantly plucked at by sayings that we would like to put by to examine later.

But besides the volumes of Hazlitt's essays there are the volumes of Hazlitt's criticism. In one way or another, either as lecturer or reviewer, Hazlitt strode through the greater part of English literature and delivered his opinion of the majority of famous books. His criticism has the rapidity and the daring, if it has also the looseness and the roughness, which arise from the circumstances in which it was written. He must cover a great deal of ground, make his points clear to an audience not of readers but of listeners, and has time only to point to the tallest towers and the brightest pinnacles in the landscape. But even in his most perfunctory criticism of books we feel that faculty for seizing on the important and indicating the main outline which learned critics often lose and timid critics never acquire. He is one of those rare critics who have thought so much that they can dispense with reading. It matters very little that Hazlitt had read only one poem by Donne; that he found Shakespeare's sonnets unintelligible; that he never read a book through after he was thirty; that he came indeed to dislike reading altogether. What he had read he had read with fervour. And since in his view it was the duty of a critic to "reflect the colours, the light and shade, the soul and body of a work", appetite, gusto, enjoyment were far more important than analytic subtlety or prolonged and extensive study. To communicate his own fervour was his aim. Thus he first cuts out with vigorous and direct strokes the figure of one author and contrasts it with another, and next builds up with the freest use of imagery and colour the brilliant ghost that the book has left glimmering in his mind. The poem is re-created in glowing phrases—"A rich distilled perfume emanates from it like the breath of genius; a golden cloud envelops it; a honeyed paste of poetic diction encrusts it, like the candied coat of the auricula". But since the analyst in Hazlitt is never far from the surface, this painter's imagery is kept in check by a nervous sense of the hard and lasting in literature, of what a book means and where it should be placed, which models his enthusiasm and gives it angle and outline. He singles out the peculiar quality of his author and stamps it vigorously. There is the "deep, internal, sustained sentiment" of Chaucer; "Crabbe is the only poet who has attempted and succeeded in the *still life* of tragedy". There is nothing flabby, weak, or merely ornamental in his criticism of Scott—sense and enthusiasm run hand in hand. And if such criticism is the reverse of final, if it is initiatory and inspiring rather than conclusive and complete, there is something to be said for the critic who starts the reader on a journey and fires him with a phrase to shoot off on adventures of his own. If one needs an incentive to read Burke, what is better than "Burke's style was forked and playful like the lightning, crested like the serpent"? Or again, should one be trembling on the brink of a dusty folio, the following passage is enough to plunge one in midstream:

It is delightful to repose on the wisdom of the ancients; to have some great name at hand, besides one's own initials always staring one in the face; to travel out of one's self into the Chaldee, Hebrew, and Egyptian characters; to have the palm-trees waving mystically in the margin of the page, and the camels moving slowly on in the distance of three thousand years. In that dry desert of learning, we gather strength and patience, and a strange and insatiable thirst of knowledge. The ruined monuments of antiquity are also there, and the fragments of buried cities (under which the adder lurks) and cool springs, and green sunny spots, and the whirlwind and the lion's roar, and the shadow of angelic wings.

Needless to say that is not criticism. It is sitting in an armchair and gazing into the fire, and building up image after image of what one has seen in a book. It is loving and taking the liberties of a lover. It is being Hazlitt.

But it is likely that Hazlitt will survive not in his lectures, nor in his travels, nor in his *Life of Napoleon,* nor in his *Conversations of Northcote,* full as they are of energy and integrity, of broken and fitful splendour and shadowed with the shape of some vast unwritten book that looms on the horizon. He will live in a volume of essays in which is distilled all those powers that are dissipated and distracted elsewhere, where the parts of his complex and tortured spirit come together in a truce of amity and concord. Perhaps a fine day was needed, or a game of fives or a long walk in the country, to bring about this consummation. The body has a large share in everything that Hazlitt writes. Then a mood of intense and spontaneous reverie came over him; he soared into what Patmore called "a calm so pure and serene that one did not like to interrupt it". His brain worked smoothly and swiftly and without consciousness of its own operations; the pages dropped without an erasure from his pen. Then his mind ranged in a rhapsody of well-being over books and love, over the past and its beauty, the present and its comfort, and the future that would bring a partridge hot from the oven or a dish of sausages sizzling in the pan.

I look out of my window and see that a shower has just fallen: the fields look green after it, and a rosy cloud hangs over the brow of the hill; a lily expands its petals in the moisture, dressed in its lovely green and white; a shepherd-boy has just brought some pieces of turf with daisies and grass for his young mistress to make a bed for her skylark, not doomed to dip his wings in the dappled dawn—my cloudy thoughts draw off, the storm of angry politics has blown over—Mr. Blackwood, I am yours—Mr. Croker, my service to you—Mr. T. Moore, I am alive and well.

There is then no division, no discord, no bitterness. The different faculties work in harmony and unity. Sentence follows sentence with the healthy ring and chime of a blacksmith's hammer on the anvil; the words glow and the sparks fly; gently they fade and the essay is over. And as his writing had such passages of inspired description, so, too, his life had its seasons of intense enjoyment. When he lay dying a hundred years ago in a lodging in Soho his voice rang out with the old pugnacity and conviction: "Well, I have had a happy life." One has only to read him to believe it.

REFLECTIONS
AT SHEFFIELD PLACE

Written in May, 1937

The great ponds at Sheffield Place at the right season of the year are bordered with red, white and purple reflections, for rhododendrons are massed upon the banks and when the wind passes over the real flowers the water flowers shake and break into each other. But there, in an opening among the trees stands a great fantastic house, and since it was there that John Holroyd, Lord Sheffield, lived, since it was there that Gibbon stayed, another reflection imposes itself upon the water trance. Did the historian himself ever pause here to cast a phrase, and if so what words would he have found for those same floating flowers? Great lord of language as he was, no doubt he filled his mind from the fountain of natural beauty. The exactions of the *Decline and Fall* meant, of course, the death and dismissal of many words deserving of immortal life. Order and seemliness were drastically imposed. It was a question, he reflected, "whether some flowers of fancy, some grateful errors, have not been eradicated with the weeds of prejudice." Still his mind was a whispering gallery of words; the famous "barefooted friars" singing vespers may have been a recollection of Marlowe's "And ducke as low as any bare-foot Fryar," murmuring in the background. Be this as it may, to consider what Gibbon would have said had he seen the rhododendrons reflected in the water is an idle exercise, for in his day, late in the eighteenth century, a girl who looked out of the window of Sheffield Place saw not rhododendrons "but four young swans . . . now entirely grey" floating upon the water. Moreover, it is unlikely that he ever bestirred himself to walk in the grounds. "Gib," that same girl, Maria Josepha Holroyd, remarked, "is a mortal enemy to any person taking a walk, and he is so frigid that he makes us sit by a good roasting Christmas fire every evening." There he sat in the summer evening talking endlessly, delightfully, in the best of spirits, for no place was more like home to him than Sheffield Place, and he looked upon the Holroyds as his own flesh and blood.

Seen through Maria's eyes Gibbon—she called him sometimes "Gib," sometimes "le grand Gibbon," sometimes "The Historian"—looked different from Gibbon seen by himself. In 1792 she was a girl of twenty-one; he was a man of fifty-five. To him she was "the tall and blooming Maria"; "the soft and stately Maria," a niece by adoption, whose manners he could correct; whose future he could forecast—"That establishment must be splendid; that life must be happy"; whose style, especially one metaphor about the Rhine escaping its banks, he could approve. But to her he was often an object of ridicule; he was so fat; such a figure of fun "waddling across the room whenever she [Madame da Silva] appeared, and sitting by her and looking at her, till his round eyes run down with water"; rather testy too, an old bachelor, who lived like clockwork and hated to have his plans upset; but at the same time, she had to admit, the most delightful of talkers. That summer night he drew out the two young men who were staying in the house, Fred North and Mr. Douglas, and made them far more entertaining than they would have been without him. "It was impossible to have selected three Beaux who could have been more agreeable, whether their conversation was trifling or serious," whether they talked about Greek and Latin or turtle soup. For that summer Mr. Gibbon was "raving" about turtles and wanted Lord Sheffield to have one brought from London. Maria's gaze rested upon him with a mixture of amusement and respect; but it did not rest upon him alone. For not only were Fred North and Mr. Douglas in the room, and the swans on the pond outside and the woods; but soldiers were tramping past the Park gates; the Prince himself was holding a review; they were going over to inspect the camp; Mr. Gibbon and Aunt Serena in the post chaise; she, if only her father would let her, on horseback. But the sight of her father suggested other cares; he was wildly hospitable; he had asked the Prince and the Duke to stay; and as her mother was dead, all the catering, all the entertaining fell upon her. There was too something in her father's face that made her look at Mr. Gibbon as if for support; he was the only man who could influence her father; who could bring him to reason; who could check his extravagance, restrain . . . But here she paused, for there was some weakness in her father's character that could not be put into plain language by a daughter. At any rate she was very glad when he married a second time "for I feel delighted to think when sooner or later troubles come, as we who know the gentleman must fear . . . " Whatever frailty of her father's she hinted at, Mr. Gibbon was the only one of his friends whose good sense could restrain him.

The relation between the Peer and the Historian was very singular. They were devoted. But what tie was it that attached the downright, self-confident, perhaps loose-living man of the world to the suave, erudite sedentary historian? —the attraction of opposites perhaps. Sheffield, with his finger in every pie, his outright, downright man of-the-world's good sense, supplied the historian with what he must sometimes have needed—someone to call him "you damned beast," someone to give him a solid footing on English earth. In Parliament Gibbon was dumb; in love he was ineffective. But his friend Holroyd was a member of a dozen committees; before one wife was two years in the grave he had married another. If it is true that friends are chosen partly in order to live lives that we cannot live in our own persons, then we can understand why the Peer and the Historian were devoted; why the great writer divested himself of his purple language and wrote racy colloquial English to Sheffield; why Sheffield curbed his extravagance and restrained his passions in deference to Gibbon; why Gibbon crossed Europe, in a post chaise to console Sheffield for his wife's death; and why Sheffield, though always busied with a thousand affairs of his own, yet found time to manage Gibbon's tangled money matters; and was now indeed engaged in arranging the business of Aunt Hester's legacy.

Considering Hester Gibbon's low opinion of her nephew and her own convictions it was surprising that she had left him any thing at all. To her Gibbon stood for all those lusts of the flesh, all those vanities of the intellect which many years previously she had renounced. Many years ago, many years before the summer night when they sat round the fire in the Library and discussed Latin and Greek and turtle soup, Hester Gibbon had put all such vanities behind her. She had left Putney and the paternal house to follow her brother's tutor William Law to his home in Northamptonshire. There in the village of King's Cliffe she lived with him trying to understand his mystic philosophy, more successfully putting it into practice; teaching the ignorant; living frugally; feeding beggars, spending her substance on charity. There at last, for she made no haste to join the Saints as her nephew observed, at the age of eighty-six she lay by Law's side in his grave; while Mrs. Hutcheson, who had shared his house but not his love, lay in an inferior position at their feet. Every difference that could divide two human beings seems to have divided the aunt from the nephew; and yet they had something in common. The suburban world of Putney had called her mad because she believed too much; the learned world of divinity had called him wicked because he believed too little. Both aunt and nephew found it impossible to hit off the exact degree of scepticism and belief which the world holds reasonable. And this very difference perhaps had not been without its effect upon the nephew. When he was a young man practising the graces which were to conciliate the world he adored, his eccentric aunt had roused his ridicule. "Her dress and figure exceed anything we had at the masquerade; her language and ideas belong to

242

the last century," he wrote. In fact, though his urbanity never deserted him in writing to her—he was her heir-at-law we are reminded—his comments to others upon the Saint, the Holy Matron of Northamptonshire, as he called her, were of an acutely ironical kind; nor did he fail to note maliciously those little frailties—her anger when Mrs. Hutcheson forgot her in her will; her reprehensible desire to borrow from a nephew whom she refused to meet—which were to him so marked a feature of the saintly temper, so frequent an accompaniment of a mind clouded by enthusiasm. As Maria Holroyd observed, and others have observed after her, the great historian had a round mouth but an extremely pointed tongue; and—who knows?—it may have been Aunt Hester herself who first sharpened that weapon. Edward's father, for instance, may have talked about William Law, his tutor—an admirable man of course; far too great a man, to have been the tutor of a scatter-brained spendthrift like himself; still William Law had made himself very comfortable at the Gibbon's house in Putney, had filled it with his own friends; had allowed Hester to fall passionately in love with him, but had never married her, since marriage was against his creed—had only accepted her devotion and her income, conduct which in another might have been condemned—so he may have gossiped. From very early days at any rate Edward must have had a private view of the eccentricities of the unworldly, of the inconsistencies of the devout. At last, however, Aunt Hester, as her nephew irreverently remarked, had "gone to sing Hallelujahs." She lay with William Law in the grave, after a life of what ecstasies, of what tortures, of what jealousies, of what safisfactions who can say? The only fact that was certain was that she had left one hundred pounds and an estate at Newhaven to her "poor though unbelieving nephew." "She might have done better, she might have done worse," he observed. And by an odd coincidence her land lay not far from the Holroyd property; Lord Sheffield was eager to buy it. He could easily pay for it, he was sure, by cutting down some of the timber.

If then we accept Aunt Hester's view, Gibbon was a worldling, wallowing in the vanities of the flesh, scoffing at the holiness of the faith. But his other aunt, his mother's sister, took a very different view of him. To his Aunt Kitty he had been ever since he was a babe a source of acute anxiety—he was so weakly; and of intense pride—he was such a prodigy. His mother was one of those flyaway women who make great use of their unmarried sisters, since they are frequently in childbed themselves and have an appetite for pleasure when they can escape the cares of the nursery. She died, moreover, in her prime; and Kitty of course took charge of the only survivor of all those cradles, nursed him, petted him, and was the first to inspire him with that love of pagan literature which was to bring the glitter of minarets and the flash of eastern pageantry so splendidly into his sometimes too pale and pompous prose. It was Aunt Kitty who, with a prodigality that would have scandalized Aunt Hester, flung open the door of that enchanted world—the world of *The Cavern of the Winds*, of the *Palace of Felicity*, of Pope's *Homer*, and of the *Arabian Nights* in which Edward was to roam for ever. "Where a title attracted my eye, without fear or awe I snatched the volume from the shelf; and Mrs. Porten, who indulged herself in moral and religious speculations, was more prone to encourage. than to check a curiosity above the strength of a boy." And it was she who first loosened his lips. "Her indulgent tenderness, the frankness of her temper, and my innate rising curiosity, soon removed all distance between us; like friends of an equal age, we freely conversed on every topic, familiar or abstruse." It was she who began the conversation which was still continuing in front of the fire in the library that summer night.

What would have happened if the child had fallen into the hands of his other aunt and her companion? Should we have had the *Decline and Fall* if they had controlled his reading and checked his curiosity, as William Law checked all reading and condemned all curiosity? It is an interesting question. But the effect on the man of his two incompatible aunts developed a conflict in his nature. Aunt Hester, from whom he expected a fortune, encouraged, it would seem from his letters, a streak of hypocrisy, a vein of smooth and calculating conventionality. He sneered to Sheffield at her religion; when she died he hailed her departure with a flippant joke. Aunt Kitty on the other hand brought out a strain of piety, of filial devotion. When she died he wrote, as if it were she and not the Saint who made him think kindly for a moment of Christianity, "The immortality of the soul is on some occasions a very comfortable doctrine." And it was she certainly who made him bethink him when she was asked to stay at Sheffield Place, that "Aunt Kitty has a secret wish to lye in my room; if it is not occupied, it might be indulged." So while Aunt Hester lay with William Law in the grave, Aunt Kitty hoisted herself into the great four-poster with the help of the stool which the little man always used, and lay there, seeing the very cupboards and chairs that her nephew saw when he slept there, and the pond perhaps and the trees out of the window. The great historian, whose gaze swept far horizons and surveyed the processions of the Roman Emperors, could also fix them minutely upon a rather tedious old lady and guess her fancy to sleep in a certain bed. He was a strange mixture.

Very strange, Maria may have thought as she sat there listening to his talk while she stitched: selfish yet tender; ridiculous but sublime. Perhaps human nature was like that—by no means all of a piece; different at different moments; changing, as the furniture changed in the firelight, as the waters of the lake changed when the night wind swept over them. But it was time for bed; the party broke up. Mr. Gibbon, she noted with concern, for she was genuinely fond of him, had some difficulty in climbing the stairs. He was unwell; a slight operation for an old complaint was necessary, and he left them with regret to go to town. The operation was over; the news was good; they hoped that he would soon be with them again. Then suddenly between five and six of a January evening an express arrived at Sheffield Place to say that he was dangerously ill. Lord Sheffield and his

245

sister Serena started immediately for London. It was fine, luckily, and the moon was up. "The night was light as day," Serena wrote to Maria. "The beauty of it was solemn and almost melancholy with our train of ideas, but it seemed to calm our minds." They reached Gibbon's lodging at midnight and "poor Dussot came to the door the picture of despair to tell me *he* was no more . . . " He had died that morning; he was already laid in the shell of his coffin. A few days later they brought him back to Sheffield Place; carried him through the Park, past the ponds, and laid him under a crimson cloth among the Holroyds in the Mausoleum.

As for the "soft and stately Maria" she survived to the year 1863; and her granddaughter Kate, the mother of Bertrand Russell, marvelled that an old woman of that age should mind dying—an old woman who had lived through the French Revolution, who had entertained Gibbon at Sheffield Place.

THE HISTORIAN
AND "THE GIBBON"

Written in March, 1937

"Yet, upon the whole, the *History of the Decline and Fall* seems to have struck root, both at home and abroad, and may, perhaps, a hundred years hence still continue to be abused." So Gibbon wrote in the calm confidence of immortality; and let us confirm him in his own opinion of his book by showing, in the first place, that it has one quality of permanence—it still excites abuse. Few people can read the whole of the *Decline and Fall* without admitting that some chapters have glided away without leaving a trace; that many pages are no more than a concussion of sonorous sounds; and that innumerable figures have passed across the stage without printing even their names upon our memories. We seem, for hours on end, mounted on a celestial rocking-horse which, as it gently sways up and down, remains rooted to a single spot. In the soporific idleness thus induced we recall with regret the vivid partisanship of Macaulay, the fitful and violent poetry of Carlyle. We suspect that the vast fame with which the great historian is surrounded is one of those vague diffusions of acquiescence which gather when people are too busy, too lazy or too timid to see things for themselves. And to justify this suspicion it is easy to gather pomposities of diction— the Church has become "the sacred edifice"; and sentences so stereotyped that they chime like bells—"destroyed the confidence" must be followed by "and excited the resentment"; while characters are daubed in with single epithets like "the vicious" or "the virtuous," and are so crudely jointed that they seem capable only of the extreme antics of puppets dangling from a string. It is easy, in short, to suppose that Gibbon owed some part of his fame to the gratitude of journalists on whom he bestowed the gift of a style singularly open to imitation and well adapted to invest little ideas with large bodies. And then we turn to the book again, and to our amazement we find that the rocking-horse has left the ground; we are mounted on a winged steed; we are sweeping in wide circles through the air and below us Europe unfolds; the ages change and pass; a miracle has taken place.

But miracle is not a word to use in writing of Gibbon. If miracle there was it lay in the inexplicable fact which Gibbon, who seldom stresses a word, himself thought worthy of italics: " . . . I *know* by experience, that from my early youth I aspired to the character of an historian." Once that seed was planted so mysteriously in the sickly boy whose erudition amazed his tutor there was more of the rational than of the miraculous in the process by which that gift was developed and brought to fruition. Nothing, in the first place, could have been more cautious, more deliberate and more far-sighted than Gibbon's choice of a subject. A historian he had to be; but historian of what? The history of the Swiss was rejected; the history of Florence was rejected; for a long time he played with the idea of a life of Sir Walter Raleigh. Then that, too, was rejected and for reasons that are extremely illuminating:

. . . I should shrink with terror from the modern history of England, where every character is a problem, and every reader a friend or an enemy; where a writer is supposed to hoist a flag of party, and is devoted to damnation by the adverse faction . . . I must embrace a safer and more extensive theme.

But once found, how was he to treat the distant, the safe, the extensive theme? An attitude, a style had to be adopted; one presumably that generalized, since problems of character were to be avoided; that abolished the writer's personality, since he was not dealing with his own times and contemporary questions;

that was rhythmical and fluent, rather than abrupt and intense, since vast stretches of time had to be covered, and the reader carried smoothly through many folios of print.

At last the problem was solved; the fusion was complete; matter and manner became one; we forget the style, and are only aware that we are safe in the keeping of a great artist. He is able to make us see what he wants us to see and in the right proportions. Here he compresses; there he expands. He transposes, emphasizes, omits in the interests of order and drama. The features of the individual faces are singularly conventionalized. Here are none of those violent gestures and unmistakable voices that fill the pages of Carlyle and Macaulay with living human beings who are related to ourselves. There are no Whigs and Tories here; no eternal verities and implacable destinies. Time has cut off those quick reactions that make us love and hate. The innumerable figures are suffused in the equal blue of the far distance. They rise and fall and pass away without exciting our pity or our anger. But if the figures are small, they are innumerable; if the scene is dim it is vast. Armies wheel; hordes of barbarians are destroyed; forests are huge and dark; processions are splendid; altars rise and fall; one dynasty succeeds another. The richness, the variety of the scene absorb us. He is the most resourceful of entertainers. Without haste or effort he swings his lantern where he chooses. If sometimes the size of the whole is oppressive, and the unemphatic story monotonous, suddenly in the flash of a phrase a detail is lit up: we see the monks "in the lazy gloom of their convents"; statues become unforgettably "that inanimate people"; the "gilt and variegated armour" shines out: the splendid names of kings and countries are sonorously intoned; or the narrative parts and a scene opens:

By the order of Probus, a great quantity of large trees, torn up by the roots, were transplanted into the midst of the circus. The spacious and shady forest was immediately filled with a thousand ostriches, a thousand stags, a thousand fallow deer, and a thousand wild boars; and all this variety of game was abandoned to the riotous impetuosity of the multitude . . . The air was continually refreshed by the playing of fountains, and profusely impregnated by the grateful scent of aromatics. In the centre of the edifice, the arena, or stage, was strewed with the finest sand, and successively assumed the most different forms. At one moment it seemed to rise out of the earth, like the garden of Hesperides, and was afterwards broken into the rocks and caverns of Thrace . . .

But it is only when we come to compress and dismember one of Gibbon's pictures that we realize how carefully the parts have been chosen, how firmly the sentences, composed after a certain number of turns round the room and then tested by the ear and only then written down, adhere together.

But these are qualities, it might be said, that belong to the historical novelist—to Scott or to Flaubert. And Gibbon was an historian, so religiously devoted to the truth that he felt an aspersion upon his accuracy as an aspersion upon his character. Flights of notes at the bottom of the page check his pageants and verify his characters. Thus they have a different quality from scenes and characters composed from a thousand hints and suggestions in the freedom of the imagination. They are inferior, perhaps, in subtlety and in intensity. On the other hand, as Gibbon pointed out, "The Cyropaedia is vague and languid; the Anabasis circumstantial and animated. Such is the eternal difference between fiction and truth."

The imagination of the novelist must often fail; but the historian can repose himself upon fact. And even if those facts are sometimes dubious and capable of more than one interpretation, they bring the reason into play and widen our range of interest. The vanished generations, invisible separately, have collectively spun round them intricate laws, erected marvellous structures of ceremony and belief. These can be described, analysed, recorded. The interest with which we follow him in his patient and impartial examination has an excitement peculiar to itself. History may be, as he tells us, "little more than the register of the crimes, follies, and misfortunes of mankind"; but we seem, at least, as we read him raised above the tumult and the chaos into a clear and rational air.

The victories and the civilization of Constantine no longer influence the state of Europe; but a considerable portion of the globe still retains the impression which it received from the conversion of that monarch; and the ecclesiastical institutions of his reign are still connected, by an indissoluble chain, with the opinions, the passions, and the interests of the present generation.

He is not merely a master of the pageant and the story; he is also the critic and the historian of the mind.

It is here of course that we become conscious of the idiosyncrasy and of the limitations of the writer. Just as we know that Macaulay was a nineteenth-century Whig, and Carlyle a Scottish peasant with the gift of prophecy, so we know that Gibbon was rooted in the eighteenth century and indelibly stamped with its character and his own. Gradually, stealthily, with a phrase here, a gibe there, the whole solid mass is leavened with the peculiar quality of his temperament. Shades of meaning reveal themselves; the pompous language becomes delicate and exact. Sometimes a phrase is turned edgewise, so that as it slips with the usual suavity into its place it leaves a scratch. "He was even destitute of a sense of honour, which so frequently supplies the sense of public virtue." Or the solemn rise and fall of the text above is neatly diminished by the demure particularity of a note. "The ostrich's neck is three feet long, and composed of seventeen vertebrae. See Buffon. Hist. Naturelle." The infallibility of historians is gravely mocked. " . . . their knowledge will appear gradually to increase, as their means of information must have diminished, a circumstance which frequently occurs in historical disquisitions." Or we are urbanely asked to reflect how,

in our present state of existence, the body is so inseparably connected with the soul, that it seems to be to our interest to taste, with innocence and moderation, the enjoyments of which that faithful companion is susceptible.

The infirmities of that faithful companion provide him with a fund of perpetual amusement. Sex, for some reason connected, perhaps, with his private life, always excites a demure smile:

Twenty-two acknowledged concubines, and a library of sixty-two thousand volumes, attested the variety of his inclinations; and from the productions which he left behind him, it appears that the former as well as the latter were designed for use rather than for ostentation.

The change upon such phrases is rung again and again. Few virgins or matrons, nuns or monks leave his pages with their honour entirely unscathed. But his most insidious raillery, his most relentless reason, are directed, of course, against the Christian religion.

Fanaticism, asceticism, superstition were naturally antipathetic to him. Wherever he found them, in life or in religion, they roused his contempt and derision. The two famous chapters in which he examined "the *human* causes of the progress and establishment of Christianity," though inspired by the same love of truth which in other connections excited the admiration of scholars, roused great scandal at the time. Even the eighteenth century, that "age of light and liberty," was not entirely open to the voice of reason. "How many souls have his writings polluted!" Hannah More exclaimed when she heard of his death. "Lord preserve others from their contagion!" In such circumstances irony was the obvious weapon; the pressure of public opinion forced him to be covert, not open. And irony is a dangerous weapon; it easily becomes sidelong and furtive; the ironist seems to be darting a poisoned tongue from a place of concealment. However grave and temperate Gibbon's irony at its best, however searching his logic and robust his contempt for the cruelty and intolerance of superstition, we sometimes feel, as he pursues his victim with incessant scorn, that he is a little limited, a little superficial, a little earthy, a little too positively and imperturbably a man of the eighteenth century and not of our own.

But then he is Gibbon; and even historians, as Professor Bury reminds us, have to be themselves. History "is in the last resort somebody's image of the past, and the image is conditioned by the mind and experience of the person who forms it." Without his satire, his irreverence, his mixture of sedateness and slyness, of majesty and mobility, and above all that belief in reason which pervades the whole book and gives it unity, an implicit if unspoken message, the *Decline and Fall* would be the work of another man. It would be the work indeed of two other men. For as we read we are perpetually creating another book, perceiving another figure. The sublime person of "the historian" as the Sheffields called him is attended by a companion whom they called, as if he were the solitary specimen of some extinct race, "the Gibbon." The Historian and the Gibbon go hand in hand. But it is not easy to draw even a thumbnail sketch of this strange being because the autobiography, or rather the six autobiographies, compose a portrait of such masterly completeness and authority that it defies our attempts to add to it. And yet no autobiography is ever final; there is always something for the reader to add from another angle.

There is the body, in the first place—the body with all those little physical peculiarities that the outsider sees and uses to interpret what lies within. The body in Gibbon's case was ridiculous—prodigiously fat, enormously top-heavy, precariously balanced upon little feet upon which he spun round with astonishing alacrity. Like Goldsmith he over-dressed, and for the same reason perhaps—to supply the dignity which nature denied him. But unlike Goldsmith, his ugliness caused him no embarrassment or, if so, he had mastered it completely. He talked incessantly, and in sentences composed as carefully as his writing. To the sharp and irreverent eyes of contemporaries his vanity was perceptible and ridiculous; but it was only on the surface. There was something hard and muscular in the obese little body which turned aside the sneers of the fine gentlemen. He had roughed it, not only in the Hampshire Militia, but among his equals. He had supped "at little tables covered with a napkin, in the middle of a coffee room, upon a bit of cold meat or a Sandwich," with twenty or thirty of the first men in the kingdom, before he retired to rule supreme over the first families of Lausanne. It was in London, among the distractions of society and politics, that he achieved that perfect poise, that perfect balance between work, society and the pleasures of the senses which composed his wholly satisfactory existence. And the balance had not been arrived at without a struggle. He was sickly; he had a spendthrift for a father; he was expelled from Oxford; his love affair was thwarted; he was short of money and had none of the advantages of birth. But he turned everything to profit. From his lack of health he learnt the love of books; from the barrack and the guardroom he learnt to understand the common people; from his exile he learnt the smallness of the English cloister; and from poverty and obscurity how to cultivate the amenities of human intercourse.

At last it seemed as if life itself were powerless to unseat this perfect master of her uncertain paces. The final buffet—the loss of his sinecure—was turned to supreme advantage; a perfect house, a perfect friend, a perfect society at once placed themselves at his service, and without loss of time or temper Gibbon entered a post-chaise with Caplin his valet and Muff his dog and bowled over Westminster Bridge to finish his history and enjoy his maturity in circumstances that were ideal.

But as we run over the familiar picture there is something that eludes us. It may be that we have not been able to find out anything for ourselves. Gibbon has always been before us. His self-knowledge was consummate; he had no illusions either about himself or about his work. He had chosen his part and he played it to perfection. Even that characteristic attitude, with his snuff-box in his hand and his body stretched out, he had noted himself, and perhaps he had adopted it as consciously as he observed it. But it is his silence that is most baffling. Even in the letters, where he drops the Historian and shortens himself now and then to "the Gib," there are long pauses when nothing is heard even at Sheffield Place of what is going on in the study at Lausanne.

The artist after all is a solitary being. Twenty years spent in the society of the *Decline and Fall* are twenty years spent in solitary communion with distant events, with intricate problems of arrangement, with the minds and bodies of the dead. Much that is important to other people loses its importance; the perspective is changed when the eyes are fixed not upon the foreground but upon the mountains, not upon a living woman but upon "my other wife, the *Decline and Fall of the Roman Empire.*" And it is difficult, after casting firm sentences that will withstand the tread of time. to say "in three words, I am alone." It is only now and then that we catch a phrase that has not been stylized, or see a little picture that he has not been able to include in the majestic design. For example, when Lord Sheffield bursts out in his downright way, "You are a right good friend . . . ," we see the obese little man impetuously and impulsively hoisting himself into a post-chaise and crossing a Europe ravaged by revolution to comfort a widower. And again when the old stepmother at Bath takes up her pen and quavers out a few uncomposed and unliterary sentences we see him:

I truly rejoice, & congratulate you on your being once more safely arrived in your native Country. I wish'd to tell you so yesterday, but the joy your letter gave would not suffer my hand to be steady enough to write . . . Many has been the disappointments I have borne with fortitude, but the fear of having my last and only friend torn from me was very near overseting my reason . . . Madame Ely and Mrs. Bonfoy are here. Mrs. Holroyd has probably told you that Miss Gould is now Mrs. Horneck. I wish she had been Mrs. Gibbon . . .

so the old lady rambles on, and for a moment we see him as in a cracked mirror held in a trembling hand. For a moment, a cloud crosses that august countenance. It was true. He had sometimes on returning home in the evening, sighed for a companion. He had sometimes felt that "domestic solitude . . . is a comfortless state." He had conceived the romantic idea of adopting and educating a young female relative called Charlotte. But there were difficulties; the idea was abandoned. Then the cloud drifts away; common sense, indomitable cheerfulness return; once more the serene figure of the historian emerges triumphant. He had every reason to be content. The great building was complete; the mountain was off his breast; the slave was freed from the toil of the oar.

And he was by no means exhausted. Other tasks less laborious, perhaps more delightful, lay before him. His love of literature was unsated; his love of life—of the young, of the innocent, of the gay—was unblunted. It was the faithful companion, the body, unfortunately, that failed him. But his composure was unshaken. He faced death with an equanimity that speaks well for "the profane virtues of sincerity and moderation." And as he sank into a sleep that was probably eternal, he could remember with satisfaction the view across the plain to the stupendous mountains beyond; the white acacia that grew beside the study window, and the great work which, he was not wrong in thinking, will immortalize his name.

SARA COLERIDGE

Written in September, 1940

Coleridge also left children of his body. One, his daughter, Sara, was a continuation of him, not of his flesh inded, for she was minute, aetherial, but of his mind, his temperament. The whole of her forty-eight years were lived in the light of his sunset, so that, like other children of great men, she is a chequered dappled figure flitting between a vanished radiance and the light of every day. And, like so many of her father's works, Sara Coleridge remains unfinished. Mr. Griggs[7] has written her life, exhaustively, sympathetically; but still . . . dots intervene. That extremely interesting fragment, her autobiography, ends with three rows of dots after twenty-six pages. She intended, she says, to end every section with a moral, or a reflection. And then "on reviewing my earlier childhood I find the predominant reflection . . . " There she stops. But she said many things in those twenty-six pages, and Mr. Griggs has added others that tempt us to fill in the dots, though not with the facts that she might have given us.

"Send me the very feel of her sweet Flesh, the very look and motion of that mouth—O, I could drive myself mad about her," Coleridge wrote when she was a baby. She was a lovely child, delicate, large-eyed, musing but active, very still but always in motion, like one of her father's poems. She remembered how he took her as a child to stay with the Wordsworths at Allan Bank.

---

7   *Coleridge Fille: A Biography of Sara Coleridge.* By Earl
Leslie Griggs.

The rough farmhouse life was distasteful to her, and to her shame they bathed her in a room where men came in and out. Delicately dressed in lace and muslin, for her father liked white for girls, she was a contrast to Dora, with her wild eyes and floating yellow hair and frock of deep Prussian blue or purple— for Wordsworth liked clothes to be coloured. The visit was full of such contrasts and conflicts. Her father cherished her and petted her. "I slept with him and he would tell me fairy stories when he came to bed at twelve or one o'clock . . . " Then her mother, Mrs. Coleridge, arrived, and Sara flew to that honest, homely, motherly woman and "wished never to be separated from her." At that—the memory was still bitter—"my father showed displeasure and accused me of want of affection. I could not understand why . . . I think my father's motive," she reflected later, "must have been a wish to fasten my affections on him . . . I slunk away and hid myself in the wood behind the house."

But it was her father who, when she lay awake terrified by a horse with eyes of flame, gave her a candle. He, too, had been afraid of the dark. With his candle beside her, she lost her fear, and lay awake, listening to the sound of the river, to the thud of the forge hammer, and to the cries of stray animals in the fields. The sounds haunted her all her life. No country, no garden, no house ever compared with the Fells and the horse-shoe lawn and the room with three windows looking over the lake to the mountains. She sat there while her father, Wordsworth and De Quincey paced up and down talking. What they said she could not understand, but she "used to note the handkerchief hanging out of the pocket and long to clutch it." When she was a child the handkerchief vanished and her father with it. After that, "I never lived with him for more than a few weeks at a time," she wrote. A room at Greta Hall was always kept ready for him but he never came. Then the brothers, Hartley and Derwent, vanished, too; and Mrs. Coleridge and Sara stayed on with Uncle Southey, feeling their dependence and resenting it. "A house of bondage Greta Hall was to her," Hartley wrote. Yet there was

Uncle Southey's library; and thanks to that admirable, erudite and indefatigable man, Sara became mistress of six languages, translated Dobritzhoffer from the Latin, to help pay for Hartley's education, and qualified herself, should the worst come, to earn her living. "Should it be necessary," Wordsworth wrote, "she will be well fitted to become a governess in a nobleman's or gentleman's family . . . She is remarkably clever."

But it was her beauty that took her father by surprise when at last at the age of twenty she visited him at Highgate. She was learned he knew, and he was proud of it; but he was unprepared, Mr. Griggs says, "for the dazzling vision of loveliness which stepped across the threshold one cold December day." People rose in a public hall when she came in. "I have seen Miss Coleridge," Lamb wrote, "and I wish I had just such a—daughter." Did Coleridge wish to keep such a daughter? Was a father's jealousy roused in that will-less man of inordinate susceptibility when Sara met her cousin Henry up at Highgate and almost instantly, but secretly, gave him her coral necklace in exchange for a ring with his hair? What right had a father who could not offer his daughter even a room to be told of the engagement or to object to it? He could only quiver with innumerable conflicting sensations at the thought that his nephew, whose book on the West Indies had impressed him unfavourably, was taking from him the daughter who, like Christabel, was his masterpiece, but, like Christabel, was unfinished. All he could do was to cast his magic spell. He talked. For the first time since she was a woman, Sara heard him talk. She could not remember a word of it afterwards. And she was penitent. It was partly that

my father generally discoursed on such a very extensive scale . . . Henry could sometimes bring him down to narrower topics, but when alone with me he was almost always on the star-paved road, taking in the whole heavens in his circuit.

She was a heaven-haunter, too; but at the moment "I was anxious about my brothers and their prospects—about Henry's health, and upon the subject of my engagement generally." Her father ignored such things. Sara's mind wandered.

The young couple, however, made ample amends for that momentary inattention. They listened to his voice for the rest of their lives. At the christening of their first child Coleridge talked for six hours without stopping. Hard-worked as Henry was, and delicate, sociable and pleasure-loving, the spell of Uncle Sam was on him, and so long as he lived he helped his wife. He annotated, he edited, he set down what he could remember of the wonderful voice. But the main labour fell on Sara. She made herself, she said, the housekeeper in that littered palace. She followed his reading; verified his quotations; defended his character; traced notes on innumerable margins; ransacked bundles; pieced beginnings together and supplied them not with ends but with continuations. A whole day's work would result in one erasure. Cab fares to newspaper offices mounted; eyes, for she could not afford a secretary, felt the strain; but so long as a page remained obscure, a date doubtful, a reference unverified, an aspersion not disproved, "poor, dear, indefatigable Sara," as Mrs. Wordsworth called her, worked on. And much of her work was done lastingly; editors still stand on the foundations she truly laid.

Much of it was not self-sacrifice, but self-realization. She found her father, in those blurred pages, as she had not found him in the flesh; and she found that he was herself. She did not copy him, she insisted; she was him. Often she continued his thoughts as if they had been her own. Did she not even shuffle a little in her walk, as he did, from side to side? Yet though she spent half her time in reflecting that vanished radiance, the other half was spent in the light of common day—at Chester Place, Regents Park. Children were born and children died. Her health broke down; she had her father's legacy of harassed nerves; and, like her farther, had need of opium. Pathetically she wished that she could be given "three years' respite from child bearing." But she wished in vain. Then Henry, whose gaiety had so often dragged her from the dark abyss, died young; leaving his notes unfinished, and two children also, and very little money, and many apartments in Uncle Sam's great house still unswept. She worked on. In her desolation it was her solace, her opium perhaps. "Things of the mind and intellect give me intense pleasure; they delight and amuse me as they are in themselves . . . and sometimes I think, the result has been too large, the harvest too abundant, in inward satisfaction. This is dangerous . . . " Thoughts proliferated. Like her father she had a Surinam toad in her head, breeding other toads. But his were jewelled; hers were plain. She was diffuse, unable to conclude, and without the magic that does instead of a conclusion. She would have liked, had she been able to make an end, to have written—on metaphysics, on theology, some book of criticism. Or again, politics interested her intensely, and Turner's pictures. But "whatever subject I commence, I feel discomfort unless I could pursue it in every direction to the farthest bounds of thought . . . This was the reason why my father wrote by snatches. He could not bear to complete incompletely." So, book in hand, pen suspended, large eyes filled with a dreamy haze, she mused—"picking flowers, and finding nests, and exploring some particular nook, as I used to be when a child walking with my Uncle Southey . . . "

Then her children interrupted. With her son, the brilliant Herbert, she read, straight through the classics. Were there not, Mr. Justice Coleridge objected, passages in Aristophanes that they had better skip? Perhaps . . . Still, Herbert took all the prizes, won all the scholarships, almost drove her to distraction with his horn-playing and, like his father, loved parties. Sara went to balls, and watched him dance waltz after waltz. She had the old lovely clothes that Henry had given her altered for her daughter, Edith. She found herself eating supper twice, she was so bored. She preferred dinner parties where she held her own with Macaulay, who was so like her father in the face, and with Carlyle —"A precious Arch-charlatan," she called him. The young poets, like Aubrey de Vere, sought her out. She was one of those, he said, "whose thoughts are growing while they speak." After he had gone, her thoughts followed him, in long, long letters, rambling over baptism, regenerations, metaphysics, theology, and poetry, past, present and to come. As a critic she never, like her father, grazed paths of light; she was a fertilizer, not a creator, a burrowing, tunnelling reader, throwing up molehills as she read her way through Dante, Virgil, Aristophanes, Crashaw, Jane Austen, Crabbe, to emerge suddenly, unafraid, in the very face of Keats and Shelley. "Fain would mine eyes," she wrote, "discern the Future in the past."

Past, present, future dappled her with a strange light. She was mixed in herself, still divided, as in the wood behind the house, between two loyalties, to the father who told her fairy stories in bed; and to the mother—Frettikins she called her—to whom she clung in the flesh. "Dear mother," she exclaimed, "what an honest, simple, lively minded affectionate woman she was, how free from disguise or artifice . . . " Why, even her wig—she had cut her hair off as a girl—" was as dry and rough and dull as a piece of stubble, and as short and stumpy." The wig and the brow—she understood them both. Could she have skipped the moral she could have told us much about that strange marriage. She meant to write her life. But she was interrupted. There was a lump on her breast. Mr. Gilman, consulted, detected cancer. She did not want to die. She had not finished editing her father's works, she had not written her own, for she did not like to complete incompletely. But she died at forty-eight, leaving, like her father, a blank page covered with dots, and two lines:

> Father, no amaranths e'er shall wreathe my brow—
> Enough that round thy grave they flourish now.

THE MAN
AT THE GATE

Written in September, 1940

The man was Coleridge as De Quincey saw him, standing in a gateway. For it is vain to put the single word Coleridge at the head of a page—Coleridge the innumerable, the mutable, the atmospheric; Coleridge who is part of Wordsworth, Keats and Shelley; of his age and of our own; Coleridge whose written words fill hundreds of pages and overflow innumerable margins; whose spoken words still reverberate, so that as we enter his radius he seems not a man, but a swarm, a cloud, a buzz of words, darting this way and that, clustering, quivering and hanging suspended. So little of this can be caught in any reader's net that it is well before we become dazed in the labyrinth of what we call Coleridge to have a clear picture before us—the picture of a man standing at a gate:

... his person was broad and full, and tended even to corpulence, his complexion was fair ... his eyes were large and soft in their expression; and it was from the peculiar appearance of haze or dreaminess which mixed with their light, that I recognized my object.

That was in 1807. Coleridge was already incapable of movement. The Kendal black drop had robbed him of his will. "You bid me rouse myself—go, bid a man paralytic in both arms rub them briskly together." The arms already hung flabby at his side; he was powerless to raise them. But the disease which

263

paralysed his will left his mind unfettered. In proportion as he became incapable of action, he became capable of feeling. As he stood at the gate his vast expanse of being was a passive target for innumerable arrows, all of them sharp, many of them poisoned. To confess, to analyse, to describe was the only alleviation of his appalling torture—the prisoner's only means of escape.

Thus there shapes itself in the volumes of Coleridge's letters an immense mass of quivering matter, as if the swarm had attached itself to a bough and hung there pendent. Sentences roll like drops down a pane, drop collecting drop, but when they reach the bottom, the pane is smeared. A great novelist, Dickens for preference, could have formed out of this swarm and diffusion a prodigious, an immortal character. Dickens, could he have been induced to listen, would have noted —perhaps this:

> Deeply wounded by very disrespectful words used
> concerning me, and which struggling as I have been
> thro' life, and still maintaining a character and holding
> connections no way unworthy of my Family

Or again:

> The worst part of the charges were that I had been
> imprudent enough and in the second place gross and
> indelicate enough to send out a gentleman's servant in his
> own house to a public house for a bottle of brandy . . .

Or again:

> What joy would it not be to you or to me, Miss Betham! to
> meet a Milton in a future state

And again, on accepting a loan:

I can barely collect myself sufficiently to convey to you—
first, that I receive this proof of your filial kindness with
feelings not unworthy of the same ... but that, whenever
(if ever) my circumstances shall improve, you must permit
me to remind you that what was, and *forever* under *all*
conditions of fortune will be, *felt* as a *gift*, has become
a Loan—and lastly, that you must let me have you as a
frequent friend on whose visits I may rely as often as
convenience will permit you ...

The very voice (drastically cut short) of Micawber himself!

But there is a difference. For this Micawber knows that he is
Micawber. He holds a looking-glass in his hand. He is a man
of exaggerated self-consciousness, endowed with an astonishing
power of self-analysis. Dickens would need to be doubled with
Henry James, to be trebled with Proust, in order to convey the
complexity and the conflict of a Pecksniff who despises his
own hypocrisy, of a Micawber who is humiliated by his own
humiliation. He is so made that he can hear the crepitation of
a leaf, and yet remains obtuse to the claims of wife and child.
An unopened letter brings great drops of sweat to his forehead;
yet to lift a pen and answer it is beyond his power. The Dickens
Coleridge and the Henry James Coleridge perpetually tear him
asunder. The one sends out surreptitiously to Mr. Dunn the
chemist for another bottle of opium; and the other analyses
the motives that have led to this hypocrisy into an infinity of
fine shreds.

Thus often in reading the "gallop scrawl" of the letters from
Highgate in 1820 we seem to be reading notes for a late work by
Henry James. He is the forerunner of all who have tried to reveal
the intricacies, to take the faintest creases of the human soul.
The great sentences pocketed with parentheses, expanded with
dash after dash, break their walls under the strain of including
and qualifying and suggesting all that Coleridge feels, fears and
glimpses. Often he is prolix to the verge of incoherence, and his

meaning dwindles and fades to a wisp on the mind's horizon. Yet in our tongue-tied age there is a joy in this reckless abandonment to the glory of words. Cajoled, caressed, tossed up in handfuls, words yield those flashing phrases that hang like ripe fruit in the many-leaved tree of his immense volubility. "Brow-hanging, shoe-contemplative, *strange*"; there is Hazlitt. Of Dr. Darwin: "He was like a pigeon picking up peas, and afterwards voiding them with excremental additions." Anything may tumble out of that great maw; the subtlest criticism, the wildest jest, the exact condition of his intestines. But he uses words most often to express the crepitations of his apprehensive susceptibility. They serve as a smoke-screen between him and the menace of the real world. The word screen trembles and shivers. What enemy is approaching? Nothing visible to the naked eye. And yet how he trembles and quivers! Hartley, "poor Hartley . . . in shrinking from the momentary pain of telling the plain truth, a truth not discreditable to him or to me, has several times inflicted an agitating pain and confusion"—by what breach of morality or dereliction of duty?—"by bringing up Mr. Bourton unexpectedly on Sundays with the intention of dining here." Is that all? Ah, but a diseased body feels the stab of anguish if only a corn is trod upon. Anguish shoots through every fibre of his being. Has he not himself often shrunk from the momentary pain of telling the plain truth? Why has he no home to offer his son, no table to which Hartley could bring his friends uninvited? Why does he live a stranger in the house of friends, and be (at present) unable to discharge his share of the housekeeping expenses? The old train of bitter thoughts is set in motion once more. He is one hum and vibration of painful emotion. And then, giving it all the slip, he takes refuge in thought and provides Hartley with "in short, the sum of all my reading and reflections on the vast Wheel of the Mythology of the earliest and purest Heathenism." Hartley must feed upon that and take a snack of cold meat and pickles at some inn.

Letter-writing was in its way a substitute for opium. In his letters he could persuade others to believe what he did not altogether believe himself—that he had actually written the folios, the quartos, the octavos that he had planned. Letters also relieved him of those perpetually pullulating ideas which, like Surinam toads, as he said, were always giving birth to little toads that "grow quickly and draw off attention from the mother toad." In letters thoughts need not be brought to a conclusion. Somebody was always interrupting, and then he could throw down his pen and indulge in what was, after all, better than writing—the "insemination" of ideas without the intermediary of any gross impediment by word of mouth into the receptive, the acquiescent, the entirely passive ear, say, of Mr. Green who arrived punctually at three. Later, if it were Thursday, in came politicians, economists, musicians, business men, fine ladies, children— it mattered not who they were so long as he could talk and they would listen.

Two pious American editors have collected the comments of this various company,[8] and they are, of course, various. Yet it is the only way of getting at the truth—to have it broken into many splinters by many mirrors and so select. The truth about Coleridge the talker seems to have been that he rapt some listeners to the seventh heaven; bored others to extinction; and made one foolish girl giggle irrepressibly. In the same way his eyes were brown to some, grey to others, and again a very bright blue. But there is one point upon which all who listened are agreed; not one of them could remember a single word he said. All, however, with astonishing unanimity are agreed that it was "like"—the waves of the ocean, the flowing of a mighty river, the splendour of the Aurora Borealis, the radiance of the Milky Way. Almost all are equally agreed that waves, river, Borealis, and Milky Way lacked, as Lady Jerningham tersely put it, "behind." From their accounts it is clear that he avoided contradiction;

---

8   *Coleridge the Talker.* Edited by Richard W. Armour and Raymond F. Howes.

detested personality; cared nothing who you were; only needed some sound of breathing or rustle of skirts to stir his flocks of dreaming thoughts into motion and light the glitter and magic that lay sunk in the torpid flesh. Was it the mixture of body and mind in his talk that gave off some hypnotic fume that lulled the audience into drowsiness? He acted as he talked; now, if he felt the interest flag, pointing to a picture, or caressing a child, and then, as the time to make an exit approached, majestically possessed himself of a bedroom candlestick and, still discoursing, disappeared. Thus played upon by gesture and voice, brow and glittering eye, no one, as Crabb Robinson remarks, could take a note. It is then in his letters, where the body of the actor was suppressed, that we have the best record of the siren's song. There we hear the voice that began talking at the age of two—"Nasty Doctor Young" are his first recorded words; and went on in barracks, on board ship, in pulpits, in stage coaches—it mattered not where he found himself or with whom, Keats it might be or the baker's boy—on he went, on and on, talking about nightingales, dreams, the will, the volition, the reason, the understanding, monsters, and mermaids, until a little girl, overcome by the magic of the incantation, burst into tears when the voice ceased and left her alone in a silent world.

We too, when the voice stops only half an hour before he passed that July day in 1834 into silence, feel bereft. Is it for hours or for years that this heavily built man standing in a gate has been pouring forth this passionate soliloquy, while his "large soft eyes with a peculiar expression of haze or dreaminess mixed in their light" have been fixed upon a far-away vision that filled a very few pages with poems in which every word is exact and every image as clear as crystal?

THE ART
OF BIOGRAPHY

First published in 1942

I

The art of biography, we say—but at once go on to ask, is biography an art? The question is foolish perhaps, and ungenerous certainly, considering the keen pleasure that biographers have given us. But the question asks itself so often that there must be something behind it. There it is, whenever a new biography is opened, casting its shadow on the page; and there would seem to be something deadly in that shadow, for after all, of the multitude of lives that are written, how few survive!

But the reason for this high death rate, the biographer might argue, is that biography, compared with the arts of poetry and fiction, is a young art. Interest in our selves and in other people's selves is a late development of the human mind. Not until the eighteenth century in England did that curiosity express itself in writing the lives of private people. Only in the nineteenth century was biography fully grown and hugely prolific. If it is true that there have been only three great biographers— Johnson, Boswell, and Lockhart—the reason, he argues, is that the time was short; and his plea, that the art of biography has had but little time to establish itself and develop itself, is certainly borne out by the textbooks. Tempting as it is to explore the reason—why, that is, the self that writes a book of prose came into being so many centuries after the self that writes a

269

poem, why Chaucer preceded Henry James—it is better to leave that insoluble question unasked, and so pass to his next reason for the lack of masterpieces. It is that the art of biography is the most restricted of all the arts. He has his proof ready to hand. Here it is in the preface in which Smith, who has written the life of Jones, takes this opportunity of thanking old friends who have lent letters, and "last but not least" Mrs. Jones, the widow, for that help "without which," as he puts it, "this biography could not have been written." Now the novelist, he points out, simply says in his foreword, "Every character in this book is fictitious." The novelist is free; the biographer is tied.

There, perhaps, we come within hailing distance of that very difficult, again perhaps insoluble, question: What do we mean by calling a book a work of art? At any rate, here is a distinction between biography and fiction—a proof that they differ in the very stuff of which they are made. One is made with the help of friends, of facts; the other is created without any restrictions save those that the artist, for reasons that seem good to him, chooses to obey. That is a distinction; and there is good reason to think that in the past biographers have found it not. only a distinction but a very cruel distinction.

The widow and the friends were hard taskmasters. Suppose, for example, that the man of genius was immoral, ill-tempered, and threw the boots at the maid's head. The widow would say, "Still I loved him—he was the father of my children; and the public, who love his books, must on no account be disillusioned. Cover up; omit." The biographer obeyed. And thus the majority of Victorian biographies are like the wax figures now preserved in Westminster Abbey, that were carried in funeral processions through the street—effigies that have only a smooth superficial likeness to the body in the coffin.

Then, towards the end of the nineteenth century, there was a change. Again for reasons not easy to discover, widows became broader-minded, the public keener-sighted; the effigy no longer carried conviction or satisfied curiosity. The biographer certainly won a measure of freedom. At least he could hint that there were scars and furrows on the dead man's face. Froude's Carlyle is by no means a wax mask painted rosy red. And following Froude there was Sir Edmund Gosse, who dared to say that his own father was a fallible human being. And following Edmund Gosse in the early years of the present century came Lytton Strachey.

II

The figure of Lytton Strachey is so important a figure in the history of biography, that it compels a pause. For his three famous books, *Eminent Victorians, Queen Victoria*, and *Elizabeth and Essex*, are of a stature to show both what biography can do and what biography cannot do. Thus they suggest many possible answers to the question whether biography is an art, and if not why it fails. Lytton Strachey came to birth as an author at a lucky moment. In 1918, when he made his first attempt, biography, with its new liberties, was a form that offered great attractions. To a writer like himself, who had wished to write poetry or plays but was doubtful of his creative power, biography seemed to offer a promising alternative. For at last it was possible to tell the truth about the dead; and the Victorian age was rich in remarkable figures many of whom had been grossly deformed by the effigies that had been plastered over them. To recreate them, to show them as they really were, was a task that called for gifts analogous to the poet's or the novelist's, yet did not ask that inventive power in which he found himself lacking.

It was well worth trying. And the anger and the interest that his short studies of Eminent Victorians aroused showed that he was able to make Manning, Florence Nightingale, Gordon, and the rest live as they had not lived since they were actually in the flesh. Once more they were the centre of a buzz of discussion. Did Gordon really drink, or was that an invention? Had Florence

271

Nightingale received the Order of Merit in her bedroom or in her sitting room? He stirred the public, even though a European war was raging, to an astonishing interest in such minute matters. Anger and laughter mixed; and editions multiplied.

But these were short studies with something of the over-emphasis and the foreshortening of caricatures. In the lives of the two great Queens, Elizabeth and Victoria, he attempted a far more ambitious task. Biography had never had a fairer chance of showing what it could do. For it was now being put to the test by a writer who was capable of making use of all the liberties that biography had won: he was fearless; he had proved his brilliance; and he had learned his job. The result throws great light upon the nature of biography. For who can doubt after reading the two books again, one after the other, that the Victoria is a triumphant success, and that the *Elizabeth* by comparison is a failure? But it seems too, as we compare them, that it was not Lytton Strachey who failed; it was the art of biography. In the *Victoria* he treated biography as a craft; he submitted to its limitations. In the *Elizabeth* he treated biography as an art; he flouted its limitations.

But we must go on to ask how we have come to this conclusion and what reasons support it. In the first place it is clear that the two Queens present very different problems to their biographer. About Queen Victoria everything was known. Everything she did, almost everything she thought, was a matter of common knowledge. No one has ever been more closely verified and exactly authenticated than Queen Victoria. The biographer could not invent her, because at every moment some document was at hand to check his invention. And, in writing of Victoria, Lytton Strachey submitted to the conditions. He used to the full the biographer's power of selection and relation, but he kept strictly within the world of fact. Every statement was verified; every fact was authenticated. And the result is a life which, very possibly, will do for the old Queen what Boswell did for the old dictionary maker. In time to come Lytton Strachey's Queen

Victoria will be Queen Victoria, just as Boswell's Johnson is now Dr. Johnson. The other versions will fade and disappear. It was a prodigious feat, and no doubt, having accomplished it, the author was anxious to press further. There was Queen Victoria, solid, real, palpable. But undoubtedly she was limited. Could not biography produce something of the intensity of poetry, something of the excitement of drama, and yet keep also the peculiar virtue that belongs to fact—its suggestive reality, its own proper creativeness?

Queen Elizabeth seemed to lend herself perfectly to the experiment. Very little was known about her. The society in which she lived was so remote that the habits, the motives, and even the actions of the people—of that age were full of strangeness and obscurity. "By what art are we to worm our way into those strange spirits? those even stranger bodies? The more clearly we perceive it, the more remote that singular universe becomes," Lytton Strachey remarked on one of the first pages. Yet there was evidently a "tragic history" lying dormant, half revealed, half concealed, in the story of the Queen and Essex. Everything seemed to lend itself to the making of a book that combined the advantages of both worlds, that gave the artist freedom to invent, but helped his invention with the support of facts—a book that was not only a biography but also a work of art.

Nevertheless, the combination proved unworkable; fact and fiction refused to mix. Elizabeth never became real in the sense that Queen Victoria had been real, yet she never became fictitious in the sense that Cleopatra or Falstaff is fictitious. The reason would seem to be that very little was known—he was urged to invent; yet something was known— his invention was checked. The Queen thus moves in an ambiguous world, between fact and fiction, neither embodied nor disembodied. There is a sense of vacancy and effort, of a tragedy that has no crisis, of characters that meet but do not clash.

If this diagnosis is true we are forced to say that the trouble lies with biography itself. It imposes conditions, and those conditions are that it must be based upon fact. And by fact in biography we mean facts that can be verified by other people besides the artist. If he invents facts as an artist invents them— facts that no one else can verify—and tries to combine them with facts of the other sort, they destroy each other.

Lytton Strachey himself seems in the *Queen Victoria* to have realized the necessity of this condition, and to have yielded to it instinctively. "The first forty-two years of the Queen's life," he wrote, "are illuminated by a great and varied quantity of authentic information. With Albert's death a veil descends." And when with Albert's death the veil descended and authentic information failed, he knew that the biographer must follow suit. "We must be content with a brief and summary relation," he wrote; and the last years are briefly disposed of. But the whole of Elizabeth's life was lived behind a far thicker veil than the last years of Victoria. And yet, ignoring his own admission, he went on to write, not a brief and summary relation, but a whole book about those strange spirits and even stranger bodies of whom authentic information was lacking. On his own showing, the attempt was doomed to failure.

III

It seems, then, that when the biographer complained that he was tied by friends, letters, and documents he was laying his finger upon a necessary element in biography; and that it is also a necessary limitation. For the invented character lives in a free world where the facts are verified by one person only— the artist himself. Their authenticity lies in the truth of his own vision. The world created by that vision is rarer, intenser, and more wholly of a piece than the world that is largely made of authentic information supplied by other people. And because of this difference the two kinds of fact will not mix; if they touch they destroy each other. No one, the conclusion seems to be, can make the best of both worlds; you must choose, and you must abide by your choice.

But though the failure of *Elizabeth and Essex* leads to this conclusion, that failure, because it was the result of a daring experiment carried out with magnificent skill, leads the way to further discoveries. Had he lived, Lytton Strachey would no doubt himself have explored the vein that he had opened. As it is, he has shown us the way in which others may advance. The biographer is bound by facts—that is so; but, if it is so, he has the right to all the facts that are available. If Jones threw boots at the maid's head, had a mistress at Islington, or was found drunk in a ditch after a night's debauch, he must be free to say so—so far at least as the law of libel and human sentiment allow.

But these facts are not like the facts of science—once they are discovered, always the same. They are subject to changes of opinion; opinions change as the times change. What was thought a sin is now known, by the light of facts won for us by the psychologists, to be perhaps a misfortune; perhaps a curiosity; perhaps neither one nor the other, but a trifling foible of no great importance one way or the other. The accent on sex has changed within living memory. This leads to the destruction of a great deal of dead matter still obscuring the true features of the human face. Many of the old chapter headings—life at college, marriage, career—are shown to be very arbitrary and artificial distinctions. The real current of the hero's existence took, very likely, a different course.

Thus the biographer must go ahead of the rest of us, like the miner's canary, testing the atmosphere, detecting falsity, unreality, and the presence of obsolete conventions. His sense of truth must be alive and on tiptoe. Then again, since we live in an age when a thousand cameras are pointed, by newspapers, letters, and diaries, at every character from every angle, he must be prepared to admit contradictory versions of the same face. Biography will enlarge its scope by hanging up looking glasses

275

at odd corners. And yet from all this diversity it will bring out, not a riot of confusion, but a richer unity. And again, since so much is known that used to be unknown, the question now inevitably asks itself, whether the lives of great men only should be recorded. Is not anyone who has lived a life, and left a record of that life, worthy of biography—the failures as well as the successes, the humble as well as the illustrious? And what is greatness? And what smallness? We must revise our standards of merit and set up new heroes for our admiration.

IV

Biography thus is only at the beginning of its career; it has a long and active life before it, we may be sure—a life full of difficulty, danger, and hard work. Nevertheless, we can also be sure that it is a different life from the life of poetry and fiction—a life lived at a lower degree of tension. And for that reason its creations are not destined for the immortality which the artist now and then achieves for his creations.

There would seem to be certain proof of that already. Even Dr. Johnson as created by Boswell will not live as long as Falstaff as created by Shakespeare. Micawber and Miss Bates we may be certain will survive Lockhart's Sir Walter Scott and Lytton Strachey's Queen Victoria. For they are made of more enduring matter. The artist's imagination at its most intense fires out what is perishable in fact; he builds with what is durable; but the biographer must accept the perishable, build with it, imbed it in the very fabric of his work. Much will perish; little will live. And thus we come to the conclusion, that he is a craftsman, not an artist; and his work is not a work of art, but something betwixt and between.

Yet on that lower level the work of the biographer is invaluable; we cannot thank him sufficiently for what he for us. For we are incapable of living wholly in the intense world of the imagination. The imagination is a faculty that soon tires and needs rest and refreshment. But for a tired imagination the proper food is not inferior poetry or minor fiction —indeed they blunt and debauch it—but sober fact, that "authentic information" from which, as Lytton Strachey has shown us, good biography is made. When and where did the real man live; how did he look; did he wear laced boots or elastic-sided; who were his aunts, and his friends; how did he blow his nose whom did he love, and how; and when he came to die did he die in his bed like a Christian, or . . .

By telling us the true facts, by sifting the little from the big, and shaping the whole so that we perceive the outline, the biographer does more to stimulate the imagination than any poet or novelist save the very greatest. For few poets and novelists are capable of that high degree of tension which gives us reality. But almost any biographer, if he respects facts, can give us much more than another fact to add to our collection. He can give us the creative fact; the fertile fact; the fact that suggests and engenders. Of this, too, there is certain proof. For how often, when a biography is read and tossed aside, some scene remains bright, some figure lives on in the depths of the mind, and causes us, when we read a poem or a novel, to feel a start of recognition, as if we remembered something that we had known before.

THE NOVELS
OF E. M. FORSTER

First published in 1942

I

There are many reasons which should prevent one from criticizing the work of contemporaries. Besides the obvious uneasiness—the fear of hurting feelings—there is too the difficulty of being just. Coming out one by one, their books seem like parts of a design which is slowly uncovered. Our appreciation may be intense, but our curiosity is even greater. Does the new fragment add anything to what went before? Does it carry out our theory of the author's talent, or must we alter our forecast? Such questions ruffle what should be the smooth surface of our criticism and make it full of argument and interrogation. With a novelist like Mr. Forster this is specially true, for he is in any case an author about whom there is considerable disagreement. There is something baffling and evasive in the very nature of his gifts. So, remembering that we are at best only building up a theory which may be knocked down in a year or two by Mr. Forster himself, let us take Mr. Forster's novels in the order in which they were written, and tentatively and cautiously try to make them yield us an answer.

The order in which they were written is indeed of some importance, for at the outset we see that Mr. Forster is extremely susceptible to the influence of time. He sees his people much at the mercy of those conditions which change with the years. He is acutely conscious of the bicycle and of the motor car; of the public school and of the university; of the suburb and of the city. The social historian will find his books full of illuminating information. In 1905 Lilia learned to bicycle, coasted down the High Street on Sunday evening, and fell off at the turn by the church. For this she was given a talking to by her brother-in-law which she remembered to her dying day. It is on Tuesday that the housemaid cleans out the drawing-room at Sawston. Old maids blow into their gloves when they take them off. Mr. Forster is a novelist, that is to say, who sees his people in close contact with their surroundings. And therefore the colour and constitution of the year 1905 affect him far more than any year in the calendar could affect the romantic Meredith or the poetic Hardy. But we discover as we turn the page that observation is not an end in itself; it is rather the goad, the gadfly driving Mr. Forster to provide a refuge from this misery, an escape from this meanness. Hence we arrive at that balance of forces which plays so large a part in the structure of Mr. Forster's novels. Sawston implies Italy; timidity, wildness; convention, freedom; unreality, reality. These are the villains and heroes of much of his writing. In *Where Angels Fear to Tread* the disease, convention, and the remedy, nature, are provided if anything with too eager a simplicity, too simple an assurance, but with what a freshness, what a charm! Indeed it would not be excessive if we discovered in this slight first novel evidence of powers which only needed, one might hazard, a more generous diet to ripen into wealth and beauty. Twenty-two years might well have taken the sting from the satire and shifted the proportions of the whole. But, if that is to some extent true, the years have had no power to obliterate the fact that, though Mr. Forster may be sensitive to the bicycle and the duster, he is also the most persistent devotee of the soul. Beneath bicycles and dusters, Sawston and Italy, Philip, Harriet, and Miss Abbott, there always lies for him—it is this which makes him so tolerant a satirist—a burning core. It is the soul; it is reality; it is truth; it is poetry; it is love; it decks itself in many shapes, dresses itself in many disguises. But get at it he must; keep from it he cannot. Over brakes and byres, over drawing-room carpets and mahogany sideboards, he flies in pursuit. Naturally the spectacle is sometimes comic, often fatiguing; but there are moments—and his first novel provides several instances—when he lays his hands on the prize.

Yet, if we ask ourselves upon which occasions this happens and how, it will seem that those passages which are least didactic, least conscious of the pursuit of beauty, succeed best in achieving it. When he allows himself a holiday—some phrase like that comes to our lips; when he forgets the vision and frolics and sports with the fact; when, having planted the apostles of culture in their hotel, he creates airily, joyfully, spontaneously, Gino the dentist's son sitting in the cafe with his friends, or describes—it is a masterpiece of comedy—the performance of *Lucia Di Lammermoor*, it is then that we feel that his aim is achieved. Judging, therefore, on the evidence of this first book, with its fantasy, its penetration, its remarkable sense of design, we should have said that once Mr. Forster had acquired freedom, had passed beyond the boundaries of Sawston, he would stand firmly on his feet among the descendants of Jane Austen and Peacock. But the second novel, *The Longest Journey*, leaves us baffled and puzzled. The opposition is still the same: truth and untruth; Cambridge and Sawston; sincerity and sophistication. But everything is accentuated. He builds his Sawston of thicker bricks and destroys it with stronger blasts. The contrast between poetry and realism is much more precipitous. And now we see much more clearly to what a task his gifts commit him. We see that what might have been a passing mood is in truth a conviction. He believes that a novel must take sides in the human conflict. He sees beauty—none more keenly; but beauty imprisoned in a fortress of brick and mortar whence he must extricate her. Hence he is always constrained to build the cage— society in all its intricacy and triviality—before he can free the prisoner. The omnibus, the villa, the suburban residence, are an essential part of his design. They are required to imprison and impede the flying flame which is so remorselessly caged behind them. At the same time, as we read *The Longest Journey* we are aware of a mocking spirit of fantasy which flouts his seriousness. No one seizes more deftly the shades and shadows of the social comedy; no one more amusingly hits off the comedy of luncheon and tea party and a game of tennis at the rectory. His old maids, his clergy, are the most lifelike we have had since Jane Austen laid down the pen. But he has into the bargain what Jane Austen had not—the impulses of a poet. The neat surface is always being thrown into disarray by an outburst of lyric poetry. Again and again in *The Longest Journey* we are delighted by some exquisite description of the country; or some lovely sight—like that when Rickie and Stephen send the paper boats burning through the arch—is made visible to us forever. Here, then, is a difficult family of gifts to persuade to live in harmony together: satire and sympathy; fantasy and fact; poetry and a prim moral sense. No wonder that we are often aware of contrary currents that run counter to each other and prevent the book from bearing down upon us and overwhelming us with the authority of a masterpiece. Yet if there is one gift more essential to a novelist than another it is the power of combination—the single vision. The success of the masterpieces seems to lie not so much in their freedom from faults—indeed we tolerate the grossest errors in them all—but in the immense persuasiveness of a mind which has completely mastered its perspective.

II

We look then, as time goes on, for signs that Mr. Forster is committing himself; that he is allying himself to one of the two great camps to which most novelists belong. Speaking roughly, we may divide them into the preachers and the teachers, headed by Tolstoy and Dickens, on the one hand, and the pure artists, headed by Jane Austen and Turgenev, on the other. Mr. Forster, it seems, has a strong impulse to belong to both camps at once. He has many of the instincts and aptitudes of the pure artist (to adopt the old classification)—an exquisite prose style, an acute sense of comedy, a power of creating characters in a few strokes which live in an atmosphere of their own; but he is at the same time highly conscious of a message. Behind the rainbow of wit and sensibility there is a vision which he is determined that we shall see. But his vision is of a peculiar kind and his message of an elusive nature. He has not great interest in institutions. He has none of that wide social curiosity which marks the work of Mr. Wells. The divorce law and the poor law come in for little of his attention. His concern is with the private life; his message is addressed to the soul. "It is the private life that holds out the mirror to infinity; personal intercourse, and that alone, that ever hints at a personality beyond our daily vision." Our business is not to build in brick and mortar, but to draw together the seen and the unseen. We must learn to build the "rainbow bridge that should connect the prose in us with the passion. Without it we are meaningless fragments, half monks, half beasts." This belief that it is the private life that matters, that it is the soul that is eternal, runs through all his writing. It is the conflict between Sawston and Italy in *Where Angels Fear to Tread*; between Rickie and Agnes in *The Longest Journey*; between Lucy and Cecil in *A Room with a View*. It deepens, it becomes more insistent as time passes. It forces him on from the lighter and more whimsical short novels past that curious interlude, *The Celestial Omnibus*, to the two large books, *Howards End* and A Passage to India, which mark his prime.

But before we consider those two books let us look for a moment at the nature of the problem he sets himself. It is the soul that matters; and the soul, as we have seen, is caged in a solid villa of red brick somewhere in the suburbs of London. It seems, then, that if his books are to succeed in their mission his reality must at certain points become irradiated; his brick must be lit up; we must see the whole building saturated with light.

We have at once to believe in the complete reality of the suburb and in the complete reality of the soul. In this combination of realism and mysticism his closest affinity is, perhaps, with Ibsen. Ibsen has the same realistic power. A room is to him a room, a writing table a writing table, and a waste-paper basket a waste-paper basket. At the same time, the paraphernalia of reality have at certain moments to become the veil through which we see infinity. When Ibsen achieves this, as he certainly does, it is not by performing some miraculous conjuring trick at the critical moment. He achieves it by putting us into the right mood from the very start and by giving us the right materials for his purpose. He gives us the effect of ordinary life, as Mr. Forster does, but he gives it us by choosing a very few facts and those of a highly relevant kind. Thus when the moment of illumination comes we accept it implicitly. We are neither roused nor puzzled; we do not have to ask ourselves, What does this mean? We feel simply that the thing we are looking at is lit up, and its depths revealed. It has not ceased to be itself by becoming something else.

Something of the same problem lies before Mr. Forster—how to connect the actual thing with the meaning of the thing and to carry the reader's mind across the chasm which divides the two without spilling a single drop of its belief. At certain moments on the Arno, in Hertfordshire, in Surrey, beauty leaps from the scabbard, the fire of truth flames through the crusted earth; we must see the red brick villa in the suburbs of London lit up. But it is in these great scenes which are the justification of the huge elaboration of the realistic novel that we are most aware of failure. For it is here that Mr. Forster makes the change from realism to symbolism; here that the object which has been so uncompromisingly solid becomes, or should become, luminously transparent. He fails, one is tempted to think, chiefly because that admirable gift of his for observation has served him too well. He has recorded too much and too literally. He has given us an almost photographic picture on one side of the page; on the other he asks us to see the same view transformed and radiant with eternal fires. The bookcase which falls upon Leonard Bast in *Howards End* should perhaps come down upon him with all the dead weight of smoke-dried culture; the Marabar caves should appear to us not real caves but, it may be, the soul of India. Miss Quested should be transformed from an English girl on a picnic to arrogant Europe straying into the heart of the East and getting lost there. We qualify these statements, for indeed we are not quite sure whether we have guessed aright. Instead of getting that sense of instant certainty which we get in *The Wild Duck* or in *The Master Builder*, we are puzzled, worried. What does this mean? we ask ourselves. What ought we to understand by this? And the hesitation is fatal. For we doubt both things—the real and the symbolical: Mrs. Moore, the nice old lady, and Mrs. Moore, the sibyl. The conjunction of these two different realities seems to cast doubt upon them both. Hence it is that there is so often an ambiguity at the heart of Mr. Forster's novels. We feel that something has failed us at the critical moment; and instead of seeing, as we do in *The Master Builder*, one single whole we see two separate parts.

The stories collected under the title of *The Celestial Omnibus* represent, it may be, an attempt on Mr. Forster's part to simplify the problem which so often troubles him of connecting the prose and poetry of life. Here he admits definitely if discreetly the possibility of magic. Omnibuses drive to Heaven; Pan is heard in the brushwood; girls turn into trees. The stories are extremely charming. They release the fantasticality which is laid under such heavy burdens in the novels. But the vein of fantasy is not deep enough or strong enough to fight single-handed against those other impulses which are part of his endowment. We feel that he is an uneasy truant in fairyland. Behind the hedge he always hears the motor horn and the shuffling feet of tired wayfarers, and soon he must return. One slim volume indeed contains all that he has allowed himself of pure fantasy. We pass from the freakish land where boys leap into the arms of Pan and girls become trees to the two Miss Schlegels, who have an income of six hundred pounds apiece and live in Wickham Place.

III

Much though we may regret the change, we cannot doubt that it was right. For none of the books before *Howards End* and *A Passage To India* altogether drew upon the full range of Mr. Forster's powers. With his queer and in some ways contradictory assortment of gifts, he needed, it seemed, some subject which would stimulate his highly sensitive and active intelligence, but would not demand the extremes of romance or passion; a subject which gave him material for criticism, and invited investigation; a subject which asked to be built up of an enormous number of slight yet precise observations, capable of being tested by an extremely honest yet sympathetic mind; yet, with all this, a subject which when finally constructed would show up against the torrents of the sunset and the eternities of night with a symbolical significance. In *Howards End* the lower middle, the middle, the upper middle classes of English society are so built up into a complete fabric. It is an attempt on a larger scale than hitherto, and, if it fails, the size of the attempt is largely responsible. Indeed, as we think back over the many pages of this elaborate and highly skilful book, with its immense technical accomplishment, and also its penetration, its wisdom and its beauty, we may wonder in what mood of the moment we can have been prompted to call it a failure. By all the rules, still more by the keen interest with which we have read it from start to finish, we should have said success. The reason is suggested perhaps by the manner of one's praise. Elaboration, skill, wisdom, penetration, beauty—they are all there, but they lack fusion; they lack cohesion; the book as a whole lacks force. Schlegels, Wilcoxes, and Basts, with all that they stand for of class and environment, emerge with extraordinary verisimilitude, but the whole effect is less satisfying than that of the much slighter but beautifully harmonious *Where Angels Fear to Tread*. Again we have the sense that there is some perversity in Mr. Forster's endowment so that his gifts in their variety and number tend to trip each other up. If he were less scrupulous, less just, less sensitively aware of the different aspects of every case, he could, we feel, come down with greater force on one precise point. As it is, the strength of his blow is dissipated. He is like a light sleeper who is always being woken by something in the room. The poet is twitched away by the satirist; the comedian is tapped on the shoulder by the moralist; he never loses himself or forgets himself for long in sheer delight in the beauty or the interest of things as they are. For this reason the lyrical passages in his books, often of great beauty in themselves, fail of their due effect in the context. Instead of flowering naturally—as in Proust, for instance—from an overflow of interest and beauty in the object itself, we feel that they have been called into existence by some irritation, are the effort of a mind outraged by ugliness to supplement it with a beauty which, because it originates in protest, has something a little febrile about it.

Yet in *Howards End* there are, one feels, in solution all the qualities that are needed to make a masterpiece. The characters are extremely real to us. The ordering of the story is masterly. That indefinable but highly important thing, the atmosphere of the book, is alight with intelligence; not a speck of humbug, not an atom of falsity is allowed to settle. And again, but on a larger battlefield, the struggle goes forward which takes place in all Mr. Forster's novels— the struggle between the things that matter and the things that do not matter, between reality and sham, between the truth and the lie. Again the comedy is exquisite and the observation faultless. But again, just as we are yielding ourselves to the pleasures of the imagination, a little jerk rouses us. We are tapped on the shoulder. We are to notice this, to take heed of that. Margaret or Helen, we are made to understand, is not speaking simply as herself; her words have another and a larger intention. So, exerting ourselves to find out the meaning, we step from the enchanted world of imagination, where our faculties work freely, to the twilight world of theory, where only our intellect functions dutifully. Such moments of disillusionment have the habit of coming when Mr. Forster is most in earnest, at the crisis of the book, where the sword falls or the bookcase drops. They bring, as we have noted already, a curious insubstantiality into the "great scenes" and the important figures. But they absent themselves entirely from the comedy. They make us wish, foolishly enough, to dispose Mr. Forster's gifts differently and to restrict him to write comedy only. For directly he ceases to feel responsible for his characters' behaviour, and forgets that he should solve the problem of the universe, he is the most diverting of novelists. The admirable Tibby and the exquisite Mrs. Munt in *Howards End*, though thrown in largely to amuse us, bring a breath of fresh air in with them. They inspire us with the intoxicating belief that they are free to wander as far from their creator as they choose. Margaret, Helen, Leonard Bast, are closely tethered and vigilantly overlooked lest they may take matters into their own hands and upset the theory. But Tibby and Mrs. Munt go where they like, say what they like, do what they like. The lesser characters and the unimportant scenes in Mr. Forster's novels thus often remain more vivid than those with which, apparently, most pain has been taken. But it would be unjust to part from this big, serious, and highly interesting book without recognizing that it is an important if unsatisfactory piece of work which may well be the prelude to something as large but less anxious.

IV

Many years passed before *A Passage to India* appeared. Those who hoped that in the interval Mr. Forster might have developed his technique so that it yielded rather more easily to the impress of his whimsical mind and gave freer outlet to the poetry and fantasy which play about in him were disappointed. The attitude is precisely the same four-square attitude which walks up to life as if it were a house with a front door, puts its hat on the table in the hall and proceeds to visit all the rooms in an orderly manner. The house is still the house of the British middle classes. But there is a change from *Howards End*. Hitherto Mr. Forster has been apt to pervade his books like a careful hostess who is anxious to introduce, to explain, to warn her guests of a step here, of a draught there. But here, perhaps in some disillusionment both with his guests and with his house, he seems to have relaxed these cares. We are allowed to ramble over this extraordinary continent almost alone. We notice things, about the country especially, spontaneously, accidentally almost, as if we were actually there; and now it was the sparrows flying about the pictures that caught our eyes, now the elephant with the painted forehead, now the enormous but badly designed ranges of hills. The people too, particularly the Indians, have something of the same casual, inevitable quality. They are not perhaps quite so important as the land, but they are alive; they are sensitive. No longer do we feel, as we used to feel in England, that they will be allowed to go only so far and no further lest they may upset some theory of the author's. Aziz is a free agent. He is the most imaginative character that Mr. Forster has yet created, and recalls Gino the dentist in his first book, *Where Angels Fear to Tread*. We may guess indeed that it has helped Mr. Forster to have put the ocean between him and Sawston. It is a relief, for a time, to be beyond the influence of Cambridge. Though it is still a necessity for him to build a model world which he can submit to delicate and precise criticism,

289

the model is on a larger scale. The English society, with all its pettiness and its vulgarity and its streak of heroism, is set against a bigger and a more sinister background. And though it is still true that there are ambiguities in important places, moments of imperfect symbolism, a greater accumulation of facts than the imagination is able to deal with, it seems as if the double vision which troubled us in the earlier books was in process of becoming single. The saturation is much more thorough. Mr. Forster has almost achieved the great feat of animating this dense, compact body of observation with a spiritual light. The book shows signs of fatigue and disillusionment; but it has chapters of clear and triumphant beauty, and above all it makes us wonder, What will he write next?

GEORGE MOORE

First published in 1942

The only criticism worth having at present is that which is spoken, not written—spoken over wine-glasses and coffee-cups late at night, flashed out on the spur of the moment by people passing who have not time to finish their sentences, let alone consider the dues of editors or the feelings of friends. About living writers these talker's (it is one of their most engaging peculiarities) are always in violent disagreement. Take George Moore, for example. George Moore is the best living novelist— and the worst; writes the most beautiful prose of his time—and the feeblest; has a passion for literature which none of those dismal pundits, his contemporaries, shares; but how whimsical his judgments are, how ill-balanced, childish and egotistical, into the bargain! So they hammer the horseshoe out; so the sparks fly; and the worth of the criticism lies not so much in the accuracy of each blow as in the heat it engenders, the sense it kindles that the matter of George Moore and his works is of the highest importance, which, without waiting another instant, we must settle for ourselves.

Perhaps it is not accident only, but a vague recollection of dipping and dallying in *Esther Waters, Evelyn Innes, The Lake,* which makes us take down in its new and stately form *Hail and Farewell* (Heinemann)—the two large volumes which George Moore has written openly and directly about himself. For all his novels are written, covertly and obliquely, about himself, so at least memory would persuade us, and it may help us to understand them if we steep ourselves in the pure waters which are elsewhere tinged with fictitious flavours. But are not all novels about the writer's self, we might ask? It is only as he sees people that we can see them; his fortunes colour and his oddities shape his vision until what we see is not the thing itself, but the thing seen and the seer inextricably mixed. There are degrees, however. The great novelist feels, sees, believes with such intensity of conviction that he hurls his belief outside himself and it flies off and lives an independent life of its own, becomes Natasha, Pierre, Levin, and is no longer Tolstoy. When, however, Mr. Moore creates a Natasha she may be charming, foolish, lovely, but her beauty, her folly, her charm are not hers, but Mr. Moore's. All her qualities refer to him. In other words, Mr. Moore is completely lacking in dramatic power. On the face of it, *Esther Waters* has all the appearance of a great novel; it has sincerity, shapeliness, style; it has surpassing seriousness and integrity; but because Mr. Moore has not the strength to project Esther from himself its virtues collapse and fall about it like a tent with a broken pole. There it lies, this novel without a heroine, and what remains of it is George Moore himself, a ruin of lovely language and some exquisite descriptions of the Sussex downs. For the novelist who has no dramatic power, no fire of conviction within, leans upon nature for support; she lifts him up and enhances his mood without destroying it.

But the defects of a novelist may well be the glories of his brother the autobiographer, and we find, to our delight, that the very qualities which weaken Mr. Moore's novels are the making of his memoirs. This complex character, at once diffident and self-assertive, this sportsman who goes out shooting in ladies' high-heeled boots, this amateur jockey who loves literature beyond the apple of his eye, this amorist who is so innocent, this sensualist who is so ascetic, this complex and uneasy character, in short, with its lack of starch and pomp and humbug, its pliability and malice and shrewdness and incompetence, is made of too many incompatible elements to concentrate into the diamond of a great artist, and is better occupied in exploring its own vagaries than in explaining those of other people. For one thing, Mr. Moore is without that robust belief in himself which leads men to prophesy and create. Nobody was ever more diffident. As a little boy they told him that only an ugly old woman would marry him, and he has never got over it. "For it is difficult for me to believe any good of myself. Within the oftentimes bombastic and truculent appearance that I present to the world trembles a heart shy as a wren in the hedgerow or a mouse along the wainscoting." The least noise startles him, and the ordinary proceedings of mankind fill him with wonder and alarm. Their streets have so many names; their coats have so many buttons; the ordinary business of life is altogether beyond him. But with the timidity of the mouse he has also its gigantic boldness. This meek grey innocent creature runs right over the lion's paws. There is nothing that Mr. Moore will not say; by his own confession he ought to be excluded from every drawing-room in South Kensington. If his friends forgive him it is only because to Mr. Moore all things are forgiven. Once when he was a child, "inspired by an uncontrollable desire to break the monotony of infancy," he threw all his clothes into a hawthorn tree and "ran naked in front of my nurse or governess screaming with delight at the embarrassment I was causing her." The habit has remained with him. He loves to take off his clothes and run screaming with delight at the fuss and blush and embarrassment which he is causing that dear old governess, the British Public. But the antics of Mr. Moore, though impish and impudent, are, after all, so amusing and so graceful that the governess, it is said, sometimes hides behind a tree to watch. That scream of his, that garrulous chuckle as of small birds chattering in a nest, is a merry sound; and then how melodiously he draws out his long notes when dusk descends and the stars rise! Always you will find him haunting the evening, when the downs are fading into waves of silver and the grey Irish fields are melting into the grey Irish hills. The storm never breaks over his head, the thunder never roars in his cars, the rain never drenches him. No; the worst that befalls him is that Teresa has not filled the Moderator lamp sufficiently full, so that the company which is dining in the garden under the apple tree must adjourn to the dining-room, where Mr. Osborne, Mr. Hughes, Mr. Longworth, Mr. Seumas O'Sullivan, Mr. Atkinson and Mr. Yeats are awaiting them.

And then in the dining-room, Mr. Moore sitting down and offering a cigar to his friends, takes up again the thread of that interminable discourse, which, if it lapses into the gulfs of reverie for a moment, begins anew wherever he finds a bench or chair to sit on or can link his arm in a friend's, or can find even some discreet sympathetic animal who will only occasionally lift a paw in silence. He talks incessantly about books and politics; of the vision that came to him in the Chelsea road; how Mr. Colville bred Belgian hares on the Sussex downs; about the death of his cat; the Roman Catholic religion; how dogma is the death of literature; how the names of poets determine their poetry; how Mr. Yeats is like a crow, and he himself has been forced to sit on the window sill in his pyjamas. One thing follows another; out of the, present flowers the past; it is as easy, inconsequent, melodious as the smoke of those fragrant cigars. But as one listens more attentively one perceives that while each topic floats up as easily as cigar smoke into the air, the blue wreaths have a strange fixity; they do not disperse, they unite; they build up the airy chambers of a lifetime, and as we listen in the Temple Gardens, in Ebury Street, in Paris, in Dublin to Mr. Moore talking, we explore from start to finish, from those earliest days in Ireland to these latest in London, the habitation of his soul.

But let us apply Mr. Moore's own test to Mr. Moore's own work. What interests him, he says, is not the three or four beautiful poems that a man may have written, but the mind that he brings into the world; and "by a mind I mean a new way of feeling and seeing." When the fierce tide of talk once more washes the battlements of Mr. Moore's achievement let us throw into mid-stream these remarks; not one of his novels is a masterpiece; they are silken tents which have no poles; but he has brought a new mind into the world; he has given us a new way of feeling and seeing; he has devised—very painfully, for he is above all things painstaking, eking out a delicate gift laboriously—a means of liquidating the capricious and volatile essence of himself and decanting it in these memoirs; and that, whatever the degree, is triumph, achievement, immortality. If, further, we try to establish the degree we shall go on to say that no one so inveterately literary is among the great writers; literature has wound itself about him like a veil, forbidding him the free use of his limbs; the phrase comes to him before the emotion; but we must add that he is nevertheless a born writer, a man who detests meals, servants, ease, respectability or anything that gets between him and his art; who has kept his freedom when most of his contemporaries have long ago lost theirs; who is ashamed of nothing but of being ashamed; who says whatever he has it in his mind to say, and has taught himself an accent, a cadence, indeed a language, for saying it in which, though they are not English, but Irish, will give him his place among the lesser immortals of our tongue.

JONES AND WILKINSON[9]

First published in 1942

Whether Jones should come before Wilkinson or Wilkinson before Jones is not a matter likely to agitate many breasts at the present moment, seeing that more than a hundred and fifty years have rolled over the gentlemen in question and diminished a lustre which, even in their own time, round about the year 1750, was not very bright. The Rev. Dr. Wilkinson might indeed claim precedence by virtue of his office. He was His Majesty's Chaplain of the Savoy and Chaplain also to his late Royal Highness, Frederick Prince of Wales. But then Dr. Wilkinson was transported. Captain James Jones might assert that, as Captain of His Majesty's third regiment of Guards with a residence by virtue of his office in Savoy Square, his social position was equal to the Doctor's. But Captain Jones had to seclude himself beyond the reach of the law at Mortlake. What, however, renders these comparisons peculiarly odious is the fact that the Captain and the Doctor were boon companions whose tastes were congenial, whose incomes were insufficient, whose wives drank tea together, and whose houses in the Savoy were not two hundred yards apart. Dr. Wilkinson, for all his sacred offices (he was Rector of Coyty in Glamorgan, stipendiary curate of Wise in Kent, and, through Lord Galway, had the right to "open plaister-pits in the honour of Pontefract"), was a convivial spirit who cut a splendid figure in the pulpit, preached and read prayers in a voice that was clear, strong and sonorous so that many a lady of

---

9   Drawn from the *Memoirs of Tate Wilkinson*, 4 vols., 1790.

fashion never "missed her pew near the pulpit," and persons of title remembered him many years after misfortune had removed the handsome preacher from their sight.

Captain Jones shared many of his friend's qualities. He was vivacious, witty, and generous, well made and elegant in person and, if he was not quite as handsome as the doctor, he was perhaps rather his superior in intellect. Compare them as we may, however, there can be little doubt that the gifts and tastes of both gentlemen were better adapted for pleasure than for labour, for society than for solitude, for the hazards and pleasures of the table rather than for the rigours of religion and war. It was the gaming-table that seduced Captain Jones, and here, alas, his gifts and graces stood him in little stead. His affairs became more and more hopelessly embarrassed, so that shortly, instead of being able to take his walks at large, he was forced to limit them to the precincts of St. James's, where, by ancient prerogative, such unfortunates as he were free from the attentions of the bailiffs.

To so gregarious a spirit the confinement was irksome. His only resource, indeed, was to get into talk with any such "parksaunterers" as misfortunes like his own had driven to perambulate the Park, or, when the weather allowed, to bask and loiter and gossip on its benches. As chance would have it (and the Captain was a devotee of that goddess) he found himself one day resting on the same bench with an elderly gentleman of military aspect and stern demeanour, whose ill-temper the wit and humour which all allowed to Captain Jones presumably beguiled, so that whenever the Captain appeared in the Park, the old man sought his company, and they passed the time until dinner very pleasantly in talk. On no occasion, however, did the General—for it appeared that the name of this morose old man was General Skelton—ask Captain Jones to his house; the acquaintance went no further than the bench in St. James's Park; and when, as soon fell out, the Captain's difficulties forced him to the greater privacy of a little cabin at Mortlake, he forgot entirely the military gentleman who, presumably, still sought an appetite for dinner or some alleviation of his own sour mood in loitering and gossiping with the park-saunterers of St. James's.

But among the amiable characteristics of Captain Jones was a love of wife and child, scarcely to be wondered at, indeed, considering his wife's lively and entertaining disposition and the extraordinary promise of that little girl who was later to become the wife of Lord Cornwallis. At whatever risk to himself, Captain Jones would steal back to revisit his wife and to hear his little girl recite the part of Juliet which, under his teaching, she had perfectly by heart. On one such secret journey he was hurrying to get within the royal sanctuary of St. James's when a voice called on him to stop. His fears obsessing him, he hurried the faster, his pursuer close at his heels. Realizing that escape was impossible, Jones wheeled about and facing his pursuer, whom he recognized as the Attorney Brown, demanded what his enemy wanted of him. Far from being his enemy, said Brown, he was the best friend he had ever had, which he would prove if Jones would accompany him to the first tavern that came to hand. There, in a private room over a fire, Mr. Brown disclosed the following astonishing story. An unknown friend, he said, who had scrutinized Jones's conduct carefully and concluded that his deserts outweighed his misdemeanours, was prepared to settle all his debts and indeed to put him beyond the reach of such tormentors in future. At these words a load was lifted from Jones's heart, and he cried out "Good God! Who can this paragon of friendship be?" It was none other, said Brown, than General Skelton. General Skelton, the man whom he had only met to chat with on a bench in St. James's Park? Jones asked in wonderment. Yes, it was the General, Brown assured him. Then let him hasten to throw himself in gratitude at his benefactor's knee! Not so fast, Brown replied; General Skelton will never speak to you again. General Skelton died last night.

The extent of Captain Jones's good fortune was indeed magnificent. The General had left Captain Jones sole heir to all his possessions on no other condition than that he should assume the name of Skelton instead of Jones. Hastening through streets no longer dreadful, since every debt of honour could now be paid, Captain Jones brought his wife the astonishing news of their good fortune, and they promptly set out to view that part which lay nearest to hand—the General's great house in Henrietta Street. Gazing about her, half in dream, half in earnest, Mrs. Jones Was so overcome with the tumult of her emotions that she could not stay to gather in the extent of her possessions, but ran to Little Bedford Street, where Mrs. Wilkinson was then living, to impart her joy. Meanwhile, the news that General Skelton lay dead in Henrietta Street without a son to succeed him spread abroad, and those who thought themselves his heirs arrived in the house of death to take stock of their inheritance, among them one great and beautiful lady whose avarice was her undoing, whose misfortunes were equal to her sins, Kitty Chudleigh, Countess of Bristol, Duchess of Kingston. Miss Chudleigh, as she then called herself, believed, and who can doubt that with her passionate nature, her lust for wealth and property, her pistols and her parsimony, she believed with vehemence and asserted her belief with arrogance, that all General Skelton's property had legally descended to her. Later, when the will was read and the truth made public that not only the house in Henrietta Street, but Pap Castle in Cumberland and the lands and lead mines pertaining to it, were left without exception to an unknown Captain Jones, she burst out in "terms exceeding all bounds of delicacy." She cried that her relative the General was an old fool in his dotage, that Jones and his wife were impudent low upstarts beneath her notice, and so flounced into her coach "with a scornful quality toss" to carry on that life of deceit and intrigue and ambition which drove her later to wander in ignominy, an outcast from her country.

What remains to be told of the fortunes of Captain Jones can be briefly despatched. Having new furnished the house in Henrietta Street, the Jones family set out when summer came to visit their estates in Cumberland. The country was so fair, the Castle so stately, the thought that now all belonged to them so gratifying that their progress for three weeks was one of unmixed pleasure and the spot where they were now to live seemed a paradise. But there was an eagerness, an impetuosity about James Jones which made him impatient to suffer even the smiles of fortune passively. He must be active —he must be up and doing. He must be "let down," for all his friends could do to dissuade him, to view a lead mine. The consequences as they foretold were disastrous. He was drawn up, indeed, but already infected with a deadly sickness of which in a few days he died, in the arms of his wife, in the midst of that paradise which he had toiled so long to reach and now was to die without enjoying.

Meanwhile the Wilkinsons—but that name, alas, was no longer applicable to them, nor did the Dr. and his wife any more inhabit the house in the Savoy—the Wilkinsons had suffered more extremities at the hands of Fate than the Joneses themselves. Dr. Wilkinson, it has been said, resembled his friend Jones in the conviviality of his habits and his inability to keep within the limits of his income. Indeed, his wife's dowry of two thousand pounds had gone to pay off the debts of his youth. But by what means could he pay off the debts of his middle age? He was now past fifty, and what with good company and good living, was seldom free from duns, and always pressed for money. Suddenly, from an unexpected quarter, help appeared. This was none other than the Marriage Act, passed in 1755, which laid it down that if any person solemnized a marriage without publishing the banns, unless a marriage licence had already been obtained, he should be subject to transportation for fourteen years. Dr. Wilkinson, looking at the matter, it is to be feared, from his own angle, and with a view to his own necessities, argued that as Chaplain of the Savoy, which was extra-Parochial and Royal-exempt, he could grant licences as usual—a privilege which at once brought him such a glut of business, such a crowd of couples wishing to be married in a hurry, that the rat-tat-tat never ceased on his street door, and cash flooded the family exchequer so that even his little boy's pockets were lined with gold. The duns were paid; the table sumptuously spread. But Dr. Wilkinson shared another failing with his friend Jones; he would not take advice. His friends warned him; the Government plainly hinted that if he persisted they would be forced to act. Secure in what he imagined to be his right, enjoying the prosperity it brought him to the full, the Doctor paid no heed. On Easter Day he was engaged in marrying from eight in the morning till twelve at night. At last, one Sunday, the King's Messengers appeared. The Doctor escaped by a secret walk over the leads of the Savoy, made his way to the river bank, where he slipped upon some logs and fell, heavy and elderly as he was, in the mud; but nevertheless got to Somerset stairs, took a boat, and reached the Kentish shore in safety. Even now he brazened it out that the law was on his side, and came back four weeks later prepared to stand his trial. Once more, for the last time, company overflowed the house in the Savoy; lawyers abounded, and, as they ate and drank, assured Dr. Wilkinson that his case was already won. In July 1756 the trial began. But what conclusion could there be? The crime had been committed and persisted in openly in spite of warning. The Doctor was found guilty and sentenced to fourteen years' transportation.

It remained for his friends to fit him out, like the gentleman he was, for his voyage to America. There, they argued, his gifts of speech and person would make him welcome, and later his wife and son could join him. To them he bade farewell in the dismal precincts of Newgate in March 1757. But contrary winds beat the ship back to shore; the gout seized on a body enfeebled by pleasure and adversity; at Plymouth Dr. Wilkinson was transported finally and for ever. The lead mine undid Jones; the Marriage Act was the downfall of Wilkinson. Both now sleep in peace, Jones in Cumberland, Wilkinson, far from his friend (and if their failings were great, great too were their gifts and graces) on the shores of the melancholy Atlantic.

MADAME DE SÉVIGNÉ

First published in 1942

This great lady, this robust and fertile letter writer, who in our age would probably have been one of the great novelists, takes up presumably as much space in the consciousness of living readers as any figure of her vanished age. But it is more difficult to fix that figure within an outline than so to sum up many of her contemporaries. That is partly because she created her being, not in plays or poems, but in letters—touch by touch, with repetitions, amassing daily trifles, writing down what came into her head as if she were talking. Thus the fourteen volumes of her letters enclose a vast open space, like one of her own great woods; the rides are crisscrossed with the intricate shadows of branches, figures roam down the glades, pass from sun to shadow, are lost to sight, appear again, but never sit down in fixed attitudes to compose a group.

Thus we live in her presence, and often fall, as with living people, into unconsciousness. She goes on talking, we half listen. And then something she says rouses us. We add it to her character, so that the character grows and changes, and she seems like a living person, inexhaustible.

This of course is one of the qualities that all letter writers possess, and she, because of her unconscious naturalness, her flow and abundance, possesses it far more than the brilliant Walpole, for example, or the reserved and self-conscious Gray. Perhaps in the long run we know her more instinctively, more profoundly, than we know them. We sink deeper down into her, and know by instinct rather than by reason how she will feel; this she will be amused by; that will take her fancy; now she will plunge into melancholy. Her range too is larger than theirs; there is more scope and more diversity. Everything seems to yield its juice—its fun, its enjoyment; or to feed her meditations. She has a robust appetite; nothing shocks her; she gets nourishment from whatever is set before her. She is an intellectual, quick to enjoy the wit of La Rochefoucauld, to relish the fine discrimination of Madame de La Fayette. She has a natural dwelling place in books, so that Josephus or Pascal or the absurd long romances of the time are not read by her so much as embedded in her mind. Their verses, their stories rise to her lips along with her own thoughts. But there is a sensibility in her which intensifies this great appetite for many things. It is of course shown at its most extreme, its most irrational, in her love for her daughter. She loves her as an elderly man loves a young mistress who tortures him. It was a passion that was twisted and morbid; it caused her many humiliations; sometimes it made her ashamed of herself. For, from the daughter's point of view it was exhausting, was embarrassing to be the object of such intense emotion; and she could not always respond. She feared that her mother was making her ridiculous in the eyes of her friends. Also she felt that she was not like that. She was different; colder, more fastidious, less robust. Her mother was ignoring the real daughter in this flood of adoration for a daughter who did not exist. She was forced to curb her; to assert her own identity. It was inevitable that Madame de Sévigné, with her exacerbated sensibility, should feel hurt.

Sometimes, therefore, Madame de Sévigné weeps. The daughter does not love her. That is a thought so bitter, and a fear so perpetual and so profound, that life loses its savour; she has recourse to sages, to poets to console her; and reflects with sadness upon the vanity of life; and how death will come. Then, too, she is agitated beyond what is right or reasonable, because a letter has not reached her. Then she knows that she has been absurd; and realizes that she is boring her friends with this obsession. What is worse, she has bored her daughter. And then when the bitter drop has fallen, up bubbles quicker and quicker the ebullition of that robust vitality, of that irrepressible quick enjoyment, that natural relish for life, as if she instinctively repaired her failure by fluttering all her feathers; by making every facet glitter. She shakes herself out of her glooms; makes fun of "les D'Hacquevilles"; collects a handful of gossip; the latest news of the King and Madame de Maintenon; how Charles has fallen in love; how the ridiculous Mademoiselle de Plessis has been foolish again; when she wanted a handkerchief to spit into, the silly woman tweaked her nose; or describes how she has been amusing herself by amazing the simple little girl who lives at the end of the park— la petite personne—with stories of kings and countries, of all that great world that she who has lived in the thick of it knows so well. At last, comforted, assured for the time being at least of her daughter's love, she lets herself relax; and throwing off all disguises, tells her daughter how nothing in the world pleases her so well as solitude. She is happiest alone in the country. She loves rambling alone in her woods. She loves going out by herself at night. She loves hiding from callers. She loves walking among her trees and musing. She loves the gardener's chatter; she loves planting. She loves the gipsy girl who dances, as her own daughter used to dance, but not of course so exquisitely.

It is natural to use the present tense, because we live in her presence. We are very little conscious of a disturbing medium between us—that she is living, after all, by means of written words. But now and then with the sound of her voice in our ears and its rhythm rising and falling within us, we become aware, with some sudden phrase, about spring, about a country neighbour, something struck off in a flash, that we are, of course, being addressed by one of the great mistresses of the art of speech.

Then we listen for a time, consciously. How, we wonder, does she contrive to make us follow every word of the story of the cook who killed himself because the fish failed to come in time for the royal dinner party; or the scene of the haymaking; or the anecdote of the servant whom she dismissed in a sudden rage; how does she achieve this order, this perfection of composition? Did she practise her art? It seems not. Did she tear up and correct? There is no record of any painstaking or effort. She says again and again that she writes her letters as she speaks. She begins one as she sends off another; there is the page on her desk and she fills it, in the intervals of all her other avocations. People are interrupting; servants are coming for orders. She entertains; she is at the beck and call of her friends. It seems then that she must have been so imbued with good sense, by the age she lived in, by the company she kept—La Rochefoucauld's wisdom, Madame de La Fayette's conversation, by hearing now a play by Racine, by reading Montaigne, Rabelais, or Pascal; perhaps by sermons, perhaps by some of those songs that Coulanges was always singing—she must have imbibed so much that was sane and wholesome unconsciously that, when she took up her pen, it followed unconsciously the laws she had learnt by heart. Marie de Rabutin it seems was born into a group where the elements were so richly and happily mixed that it drew out her virtue instead of opposing it. She was helped, not thwarted. Nothing baffled or contracted or withered her. What opposition she encountered was only enough to confirm her judgment. For she was highly conscious of folly, of vice, of pretention. She was a born critic, and a critic whose judgments were inborn, unhesitating. She is always referring her impressions to a standard—hence the incisiveness, the depth and the comedy that make those spontaneous statements so illuminating. There is nothing naive about her. She is by no means a simple spectator. Maxims fall from her pen. She sums up; she judges. But it is done effortlessly. She has inherited the standard and accepts it without effort. She is heir to a tradition, which stands guardian and gives proportion. The gaiety, the colour, the chatter, the many movements of the figures in the foreground have a background. At Les Rochers there is always Paris and the court; at Paris there is Les Rochers, with its solitude, its trees, its peasants. And behind them all again there is virtue, faith, death itself. But this background, while it gives its scale to the moment, is so well established that she is secure. She is free, thus anchored, to explore; to enjoy; to plunge this way and that; to enter wholeheartedly into the myriad humours, pleasures, oddities, and savours of her well nourished, prosperous, delightful present moment.

So she passes with free and stately step from Paris to Brittany from Brittany in her coach and six all across France. She stays with friends on the road; she is attended by a cheerful company of familiars. Wherever she alights she attracts at once the love of some boy or girl; or the exacting admiration of a man of the world like her disagreeable cousin Bussy Rabutin, who cannot rest under her disapproval, but must be assured of her good opinion in spite of all his treachery. The famous and the brilliant also wish to have her company, for she is part of their world; and can take her share in their sophisticated conversations. There is something wise and large and sane about her which draws the confidences of her own son. Feckless and impulsive, the prey of his own weak and charming nature as he is, Charles nurses her with the utmost patience through her rheumatic fever. She laughs at his foibles; knows his failings. She is tolerant and outspoken; nothing need be hidden from her; she knows all that there is to be known of man and his passions.

So she takes her way through the world, and sends her letters, radiant and glowing with all this various traffic from one end of France to the other, twice weekly. As the fourteen volumes so spaciously unfold their story of twenty years it seems that this world is large enough to enclose everything. Here is the garden that Europe has been digging for many centuries; into which so many generations have poured their blood; here it is at last fertilized, bearing flowers. And the flowers are not those rare and solitary blossoms—great men, with their poems, and their conquests. The flowers in this garden are a whole society of full grown men and women from whom want and struggle have been removed; growing together in harmony, each contributing something that the other lacks. By way of proving it, the letters of Madame de Sévigné are often shared by other pens; now her son takes up the pen; the Abbé adds his paragraph; even the simple girl— la petite personne—is not afraid to pipe up on the same page. The month of May, 1678, at Les Rochers in Brittany, thus echoes with different voices. There are the birds singing; Pilois is planting; Madame de Sévigné roams the woods alone; her daughter is entertaining politicians in Provence; not very far away Monsieur de Rochefoucauld is engaged in telling the truth with Madame de La Fayette to prune his words; Racine is finishing the play which soon they will all be hearing together; and discussing afterwards with the King and that lady whom in the private language of their set they call Quanto. The voices mingle; they are all talking together in the garden in 1678. But what was happening outside?

"NOT ONE OF US"[10]

First published in 1942

Professor Peck does not apologize for writing a new life of Shelley, nor does he give any reason for doing what has been so thoroughly done already, nor are the new documents that have come into his hands of any great importance. And yet nobody is going to complain that here are two more thick, illustrated, careful and conscientious volumes devoted to the retelling of a story which everyone knows by heart. There are some stories which have to be retold by each generation, not that we have anything new to add to them, but because of some queer quality in them which makes them not only Shelley's story but our own. Eminent and durable they stand on the skyline, a mark past which we sail, which moves as we move and yet remains the same.

Many such changes of orientation toward Shelley have been recorded. In his own lifetime all except five people looked upon him, Shelley said, "as a rare prodigy of crime and pollution, whose look even might infect." Sixty years later he was canonized by Edward Dowden. By Matthew Arnold he was again reduced to the ordinary human scale. How many biographers and essayists have since absolved him or sentenced him, it is impossible to say. And now comes our turn to make up our minds what manner of man Shelley was; so that we read Professor Peck's volumes, not to find out new facts, but to get Shelley more sharply outlined

---

10 A review of *Shelley; His Life and Work*, by Walter Edwin Peck, October 1927.

against the shifting image of ourselves.

If such is our purpose, never was there a biographer who gave his readers more opportunity to fulfil it than Professor Peck. He is singularly dispassionate, and yet not colourless. He has opinions, but he does not obtrude them. His attitude to Shelley is kind but not condescending. He does not rhapsodize, but at the same time he does not scold. There are only two points which he seems to plead with any personal partiality; one, that Harriet was a much wronged woman; the other, that the political importance of Shelley's poetry is not rated sufficiently high. Perhaps we could spare the careful analysis of so many poems. We scarcely need to know how many times mountains and precipices are mentioned in the course of Shelley's works. But as a chronicler of great learning and lucidity, Professor Peck is admirable. Here, he seems to say, is all that is actually known about Shelley's life. In October he did this in November he did that; now it was that he wrote this poem it was here that he met that friend. And, moulding the enormous mass of the Shelley papers with dexterous fingers, he contrives tactfully to embed dates and facts in feelings, in comments, in what Shelley wrote, in what Mary wrote, in what other people wrote about them, so that we seem to be breasting the full current of Shelley's life and get the illusion that we are, this time, seeing Shelley, not through the rosy glasses or the livid glasses which sentiment and prudery have fixed on our forerunners' noses, but plainly, as he was. In this, of course, we are mistaken; glasses we wear, though we cannot see them. But the illusion of seeing Shelley plain is sufficiently exhilarating to tempt us to try to fix it while it lasts.

There is an image of Shelley's personal appearance in everybody's picture gallery. He was a lean, large-boned boy, much freckled, with big, rather prominent blue eyes. His dress was careless, of course, but it was distinguished; "he wore his clothes like a gentleman." He was courteous and gentle in manner, but he spoke in a shrill, harsh voice and soon rose to the heights of excitement. Nobody could overlook the presence of this discordant character in the room, and his presence was strangely disturbing. It was not merely that he might do something extreme, he might, somehow, make whoever was there appear absurd. From the earliest days normal people had noticed his abnormality and had done their best, following some obscure instinct of self-preservation, to make Shelley either toe the line or else quit the society of the respectable. At Eton they called him "mad Shelley" and pelted him with muddy balls. At Oxford he spilt acid over his tutor's carpet, "a new purchase, which he thus completely destroyed," and for other and more serious differences of opinion he was expelled.

After that he became the champion of every down-trodden cause and person. Now it was an embankment; now a publisher; now the Irish nation; now three poor weavers condemned for treason; now a flock of neglected sheep. Spinsters of all sorts who were oppressed or aspiring found in him their leader. The first years of his youth thus were spent in dropping seditious pamphlets into old women's hoods; in shooting scabby sheep to put them out of their misery; in raising money; in writing pamphlets; in rowing out to sea and dropping bottles into the water which when broken open by the Town Clerk of Barnstable were found to contain a seditious paper, "the contents of which the mayor has not yet been able to ascertain." In all these wanderings and peregrinations he was accompanied by a woman, or perhaps by two women, who either had young children at the breast or were shortly expecting to become mothers. And one of them, it is said, could not contain her amusement when she saw the pamphlet dropped into the old woman's hood, but burst out laughing.

The picture is familiar enough; the only thing that changes is our attitude toward it. Shelley, excitable, uncompromising, atheistical, throwing his pamphlets into the sea in the belief that he is going to reform the world, has become a figure which is half heroic and wholly delightful. On the other hand, the world that Shelley fought has become ridiculous. Somehow the untidy, shrill-voiced boy, with his violence and his oddity has succeeded in making Eton and Oxford, the English government, the Town Clerk and Mayor of Barnstable, the country gentlemen of Sussex and innumerable obscure people whom we might call generically, after Mary's censorious friends, the Booths and the Baxters—Shelley has succeeded in making all these look absurd.

But, unfortunately, though one may make bodies and institutions look absurd, it is extremely difficult to make private men and women look anything so simple. Human relationships are too complex; human nature is too subtle. Thus contact with Shelley turned Harriet Westbrook, who should have been the happy mother of a commonplace family, into a muddled and bewildered woman, who wanted both to reform the world and yet to possess a coach and bonnets, and was finally drawn from the Serpentine on a winter's morning, drowned in her despair. And Mary and Miss Hitchener, and Godwin and Claire, and Hogg and Emilia Viviani, and Sophia Stacey and Jane Williams—there is nothing tragic about them, perhaps; there is, indeed, much that is ridiculous. Still, their association with Shelley does not lead to any clear and triumphant conclusion. Was he right? Were they right? The whole relationship is muddy and obscure; it baffles; it teases.

One is reminded of the private life of another man whose power of conviction was even greater than Shelley's, and more destructive of normal human happiness. One remembers Tolstoy and his wife. The alliance of the intense belief of genius with the easy-going non-belief or compromise of ordinary humanity must, it seems, lead to disaster and to disaster of a lingering and petty kind in which the worst side of both natures is revealed. But while Tolstoy might have wrought out his philosophy alone or in a monastery, Shelley was driven by something yielding and enthusiastic in his temperament to entangle himself with men and women. "I think one is always in love with something or other," he wrote. But this "something or other" besides lodging in poetry and metaphysics and the good of society in general, had its dwelling in the bodies of human beings of the opposite sex. He saw "the likeness of what is perhaps eternal" in the eyes of Mary. Then it vanished, to appear in the eyes of Emilia; then there it was again manifesting itself indisputably in Sophia Stacey or in Jane Williams. What is the lover to do when the will o' the wisp shifts its quarters? One must go on, said Shelley, until one is stopped. And what is to stop one? Not, if one is Shelley, the conventions and superstitions which bind the baser part of mankind; not the Booths and the Baxters. Oxford might expel him, England might exile him, but still, in spite of disaster and derision, he sought the "likeness of what is perhaps eternal"; he went on being in love.

But as the object of his love was a hybrid creature, half human, half divine, so the manner of his love partook of the same ambiguous nature. There was something inhuman about Shelley. Godwin, in answer to Shelley's first letter, noticed it. He complained of the "generalizing character" of Shelley's style, which, he said, had the effect of making him "not an individual character" to him. Mary Shelley, musing over her life when Shelley was dead, exclaimed, "What a strange life mine has been. Love, youth, fear and fearlessness led me early from the regular routine of life and I united myself to this being who, not one of *us*, though like us, was pursued by numberless miseries and annoyances, in all of which I shared." Shelley was "not one of us." He was, even to his wife, a "being," some one who came and went like a ghost, seeking the eternal. Of the transitory, he had little notion. The joys and sorrows, from whose threads are woven the warm cocoon of private life in which most men live, had no hold upon him. A strange formality stiffens his letters; there is no intimacy in them and no fun.

At the same time it is perfectly true, and Professor Peck does well to emphasize the fact, that Shelley loved humanity if he did not love this Harriet or that Mary. A sense of the wretchedness of human beings burnt in him as brightly and as persistently as his sense of the divine beauty of nature. He loved the clouds and the mountains and the rivers more passionately than any other man loved them; but at the foot of the mountain he always saw a ruined cottage; there were criminals in chains, hoeing up the weeds in the pavement of St. Peter's Square; there was an old woman shaking with ague on the banks of the lovely Thames. Then he would thrust aside his writing, dismiss his dreams and trudge off to physic the poor with medicine or with soup. Inevitably there collected round him, as time went on, the oddest assortment of pensioners and protégés. He took on himself the charge of deserted women and other people's children; he paid other persons' debts and planned their journeys and settled their relationships. The most ethereal of poets was the most practical of men.

Hence, says Professor Peck, from this union of poetry and humanity springs the true value of Shelley's poetry. It was the poetry of a man who was not a "pure poet," but a poet with a passion for reforming the wrongs of men. Had he lived, he would have reconciled poetry and the statement of "the necessity of certain immediate reforms in politics, society and government." He died too young to be able to deliver his message; and the difficulty of his poetry arises from the fact that the conflict between poetry and politics rages there unresolved. We may not agree with Professor Peck's definition, yet we have only to read Shelley again to come up against the difficulty of which he speaks. It lies partly in the disconcerting fact that we had thought his poetry so good and we find it indeed so poor. How are we to account for the fact that we remember him as a great poet and find him on opening his pages a bad one? The explanation seems to be that he was not a "pure poet." He did not concentrate his meaning in a small space; there is nothing in Shelley's poetry as rich and compact as the odes of Keats. His taste could be sentimental; he had all the vices of the album makers; he was unreal, strained, verbose. The lines which Professor Peck quotes with admiration: "Good night? No, love! The night is ill," seems to us a proof of it. But if we pass from the lyrics, with all their exquisite beauty, and read ourselves into one of the longer poems, *Epipsychidion* or *Prometheus Unbound*, where the faults have space to lose themselves, we again become convinced of his greatness. And here again we are confronted by a difficulty. For if we were asked to extract the teaching from these poems we should be at a loss. We can hardly say what reform in "politics, society and government" they advocate. Their greatness seems to lie in nothing so definite as a philosophy, in nothing so pure as perfection of expression. It lies rather in a state of being. We come through skeins of clouds and gusts of whirlwind out into a space of pure calm, of intense and windless serenity. Defensibly or not, we make a distinction—*The Skylark*, the *Ode To The West Wind* are poems; the *Prometheus*, the *Epipsychidion* are poetry.

So if we outline our relationship to Shelley from the vantage ground Of 1927 we shall find that his England is a barbarous place where they imprison journalists for being disrespectful to the Prince Regent, stand men in stocks for publishing attacks upon the Scriptures, execute weavers upon the suspicion of treason, and, without giving proof of strict religious belief themselves, expel a boy from Oxford for avowing his atheism. Politically, then, Shelley's England has already receded, and his fight, valiant though it is, seems to be with monsters who are a little out of date, and therefore slightly ridiculous. But privately he is much closer to us. For alongside the public battle wages, from generation to generation, another fight which is as important as the other, though much less is said about it. Husband fights with wife and son with father. The poor fight the rich and the employer fights the employed. There is a perpetual effort on the one hand to make all these relationships more reasonable, less painful and less servile; on the other, to keep them as they are. Shelley, both as son and as husband, fought for reason and freedom in private life, and his experiments, disastrous as they were in many ways, have helped us to greater sincerity and happiness in our own conflicts. The Sir Timothys of Sussex are no longer so prompt to cut their sons off with a shilling; the Booths and the Baxters are no longer quite so sure that an unmarried wife is an unmitigated demon. The grasp of convention upon private life is no longer quite so coarse or quite so callous because of Shelley's successes and failures.

So we see Shelley through our particular pair of spectacles—a shrill, charming, angular boy; a champion riding out against the forces of superstition and brutality with heroic courage; at the same time blind, inconsiderate, obtuse to other persons' feelings. Rapt in his extraordinary vision, ascending to the very heights of existence, he seems, as Mary said, "a being," "not one of us," but better and higher and aloof and apart. Suddenly there comes a knock at the door; the Hunts and seven children are at Leghorn; Lord Byron has been rude to them; Hunt is cut to the heart. Shelley must be off at once to see that they are comfortable. And, rousing himself from his rapture, Shelley goes.

TWO ANTIQUARIES:
WALPOLE AND COLE

First published in 1942

Since to criticize the Yale edition of Horace Walpole's letters to Cole is impossible, for there cannot in the whole universe exist a single human being whose praise or blame of such minute and monumental learning can be of any value—if such exists his knowledge has been tapped already—the only course for the reader is to say nothing about the learning and the industry, the devotion and the skill which have created these two huge volumes, and to record merely such fleeting thoughts as have formed in the mind from a single reading. To encourage our selves, let us assert, though not with entire confidence, that books after all exist to be read—even the most learned of editors would to some extent at least agree with that. But how, the question immediately arises, can we read this magnificent instalment— for these are but the first two volumes of this edition in which Mr. Lewis will give us the complete correspondence—of our old friend Horace Walpole's letters? Ought not the presses to have issued in a supplementary pocket a supplementary pair of eyes? Then, with the usual pair fixed upon the text, the additional pair could range the notes, thus sweeping together into one haul not only what Horace is saying to Cole and what Cole is saying to Horace, but a multitude of minor men and matters: for example, Thomas Farmer, who ran away and left two girls with child; Thomas Wood, who was never drunk but had a bad constitution and was therefore left fifty pounds and bed and furniture in Cole's will; Cole's broken leg, how it was broken, and why it was badly mended; Birch, who had (it is thought) an apoplectic fit riding in the Hampstead Road, fell from his horse, and died; Thomas Western (1695-1754), who was one of the pall-bearers at the funeral of Cole's father; Cole's niece, the daughter of a wholesale cheesemonger; John Woodyer, a man of placid disposition and great probity; Mrs. Allen Hopkins, who was born Mary Thornhill; and, Lord Montfort, who—but if we want to know more about that nobleman, his lions and tigers and his "high-spirited and riotous behaviour," we must look it up for ourselves in the Harwicke *mss.* in the British Museum. There are limits even to Mr. Lewis.

This little haul, taken at random, is enough to show how great a strain the new method of editing lays upon the eye. But if the brain is at first inclined to jib at such perpetual solicitations, and to beg to be allowed to read the text in peace, it adjusts itself by degrees; grudgingly admits that many of these little facts are to the point; and finally becomes not merely a convert but a supplicant—asks not for less but for more and more and more. Why, to take one instance only, is not the name of Cole's temporary cook's sister divulged? Thomas Wood was his servant; Thomas was left fifty pounds and allowed Cole's coach to run away; Thomas's younger brother James, known as "Jem," ran errands successfully and had a child ready to be sworn to him; their sister, Molly, was for one month at least a cook and helped in the kitchen. But there was another sister and, after learning all about the Woods, it is positively painful not to know at least her Christian name.

Yet it may be asked, what has the name of Cole's cook's sister got to do with Horace Walpole? That is a question which it is impossible to answer briefly; but it is proof of the editor's triumph, justification of his system, and a complete vindication of his immense labour that he has convinced us, long before the end, that somehow or other it all hangs together. The only way to read letters is to read them thus stereoscopically. Horace is partly Cole; Cole is partly Horace; Cole's cook is partly Cole; therefore

Horace Walpole is partly Cole's cook's sister. Horace, the whole Horace, is made up of innumerable facts and reflections of facts. Each is infinitely minute; yet each is essential to the other. To elicit them and relate them is out of the question. Let us, then, concentrate for a moment upon the two main figures, in outline.

We have here, then, in conjunction the Honourable Horace Walpole and the Reverend William Cole. But they were two very different people. Cole, it is true, had been at Eton with Horace, where he was called by the famous Walpole group "Tozhy," but he was not a member of that group, and socially he was greatly Walpole's inferior. His father was a farmer, Horace's father was a Prime Minister. Cole's niece was the daughter of a cheesemonger; Horace's niece married a Prince of the Blood Royal. But Cole was a man of solid good sense who made no bones of this disparity, and, after leaving Eton and Cambridge, he had become, in his quiet frequently flooded parsonage, one of the first antiquaries of the time. It was this common passion that brought the two friends together again.

For some reason, obscurely hidden in the psychology of the human race, the middle years of that eighteenth century which seems now a haven of bright calm and serene civilization, affected some who actually lived in it with a longing to escape— from its politics, from its wars, from its follies, from its drabness and its dullness, to the superior charms of the Middle Ages. "I . . . hope," wrote Cole in 1765, "by the latter end of the week to be among my admired friends of the twelfth or thirteenth century. Indeed you judge very right concerning my indifference about what is going forward in the world, where I live in it as though I was no way concerned about it except in paying, with my contemporaries, the usual taxes and impositions. In good truth I am very indifferent about my Lord Bute or Mr. Pitt, as I have long been convinced and satisfied in my own mind that all oppositions are from the ins and the outs, and that power and wealth and dignity are the things struggled for, not the good of the whole . . . I hope what I have said will not be offensive."

Only one weekly newspaper, the *Cambridge Chronicle*, brought him news of the present moment. There at Bletchley or at Milton he sat secluded, wrapped up from the least draught, for he was terribly subject to sore throats; sometimes issuing forth to conduct a service, for he was, incidentally, a clergyman; driving occasionally to Cambridge to hobnob with his cronies; but always returning with delight to his study, where he copied maps, filled in coats of arms, and pored assiduously over those budgets of old manuscripts which were, as he said, "wife and children" to him. Now and again, it is true, he looked out of the window at the antics of his dog, for whose future he was careful to provide, or at those guinea fowl whose eggs he begged off Horace—for "I have so few amusements and can see these creatures from my study window when I can't stir out of my room."

But neither dog nor guinea fowl seriously distracted him. The hundred and fourteen folio volumes left by him to the British Museum testify to his professional industry. And it was precisely that quality—his professional industry—that brought the two so dissimilar men together. For Horace Walpole was by temperament an amateur. He was not, Cole admitted, "a true, genuine antiquary"; nor did he think himself one. "Then I have a wicked quality in an antiquary, nay one that annihilates the essence; that is, I cannot bring myself to a habit of minute accuracy about very indifferent points," Horace admitted. " . . . I bequeath free leave of correction to the microscopic intellects of my continuators." But he had what Cole lacked—imagination, taste, style, in addition to a passion for the romantic past, so long as that romantic past was also a civilized past, for mere "bumps in the ground" or "barrows and tumuli and Roman camps" bored him to death. Above all, he had a purse long enough to give visible and tangible expression—in prints, in gates, in Gothic temples, in bowers, in old manuscripts, in a thousand gimcracks and "brittle transitory relics" to the smouldering and inarticulate passion that drove the professional antiquary to delve like some indefatigable mole underground in the darkness of the past. Horace liked his brittle relics to be pretty, and to be authentic, and he was always eager to be put on the track of more.

The greater part of the correspondence thus is concerned with antiquaries' gossip; with parish registers and cartularies; with coats of arms and the Christian names of bishops; with the marriages of kings' daughters; skeletons and prints; old gold rings found in a field; dates and genealogies; antique chairs in Fen farmhouses; bits of stained glass and old Apostle spoons. For Horace was furnishing Strawberry Hill; and Cole was prodigiously adept at stuffing it, until there was scarcely room to stick another knife or fork, and the gorged owner of all this priceless lumber had to cry out: "I shudder when the bell rings at the gate. It is as bad as keeping an inn." All the week he was plagued with staring crowds.

Were this all it would be, and indeed it sometimes is, a little monotonous. But they were two very different men. They struck unexpected sparks in one another. Cole's Walpole was not Conway's Walpole; nor was Walpole's Cole the good-natured old parson of the diary. Cole, of course, stressed the antiquary in Walpole; but he also brought out very clearly the limits of the antiquary in Walpole. Against Cole's monolithic passion his own appears frivolous and flimsy. On the other hand, in contrast with Cole's slow-plodding pen, his own shows its mettle. He cannot flash, it is true—the subject, say, the names of Edward the Fourth's daughters, forbids it—yet how sweetly English sings on his side of the page, now in a colloquialism—"a more flannel climate"—that Cole would never have ventured; now in a strain of natural music —"Methinks as we grow old, our only business here is to adorn the graves of our friends or to dig our own." That strain was called forth by the death of their common friend, Thomas Gray. It was a death that struck at Cole's heart, too, but produced no such echo in that robust organ. At the mere threat of Conway's death, Horace was all of a twitter—his nerves were "so aspen." It was a threat only; "Still has it operated such a revolution in my mind, as no time, *at my age*, can efface. I have had dreams in which I thought I wished for fame— ... I feel, I feel it was confined to the memory of those I love"—to which Cole replies: "For both your sakes I hope he will soon get well again. It is a misfortune to have so much sensibility in one's nature as you are endued with: sufficient are one's own distresses without the additional encumbrance of those of one's friends."

Nevertheless, Cole was by no means without distresses of his own. There was that terrible occasion when the horses ran away and his hat blew off and he sat with his legs in the air anticipating either death at the tollgate or a bad cold. Mercifully both were spared him. Again, he suffered tortures when, showing Dr. Gulston his prints, he begged him, as a matter of form, to take any he liked; whereupon Gulston—"that Algerine hog"—filled his portfolio with the most priceless. It is true that Cole made him pay for them in the end, but it was a most distressing business. And then what an agony it was when some fellow antiquaries dined with him, and, confined with the gout, he had to let them visit his study alone, to find next morning that an octavo volume, and a borrowed volume at that, was missing! "The Master is too honourable to take such a step," but—he had his suspicions. And what was he to do? To confess the loss or to conceal it? To conceal it seemed better, and yet, if the owner found out, "I am undone." Horace was all sympathy. He loathed the whole tribe of antiquaries—"numskulls" he called them mumbling manuscripts with their toothless jaws. "Their understandings seem as much in ruins as the things they describe," he wrote. "I love antiquities, but I scarce ever knew an antiquary who knew how to write upon them."

He had all the aristocrat's contempt for the professional drudge, and no desire whatsoever to be included among the sacred band of professional authors. "They are always in earnest, and think their profession serious, and dwell upon trifles, and reverence learning," he snapped out. And yet, when writing to Cole he could confess what to a man of his own class he would have concealed—that he, too, reverenced learning when it was real, and admired no one more than a poet if he were genuine. "A page in a great author humbles me to the dust," he wrote. And after deriding his contemporaries added, "Don't think me scornful. Recollect that I have seen Pope, and lived with Gray."

Certainly Cole's obscure but bulky form revealed a side of Horace Walpole that was lost in the glitter of the great world. With that solid man of no social gift but prodigious erudition Horace showed himself not an antiquary, not a poet, not an historian, but what he was—the aristocrat of letters, the born expert who knew the sham intellect from the genuine as surely as the antiquary knew the faked genealogy from the authentic. When Horace Walpole praised Pope and Gray he knew what he was saying and meant it; and his shame at being hoisted into such high society as theirs rings true. "I know not how others feel on such occasions, but if anyone happens to praise me, all my faults gush into my face, and make me turn my eyes inward and outward with horror. What am I but a poor old skeleton, tottering towards the grave, and conscious of ten thousand weaknesses, follies, and worse! And for talents, what are mine, but trifling and superficial; and, compared with those of men of real genius, most diminutive! . . . Does it become us, at past threescore each, to be saying fine things to one another? Consider how soon we shall both be nothing!" That is a tone of voice that he does not use in speaking—for his writing voice was a speaking voice—to his friends in the great world.

Again, Cole's High Church and Tory convictions when they touched a very different vein in Walpole sometimes caused explosions. Once or twice the friends almost came to blows over religion. The Church of England had a substantial place in Cole's esteem. But to Walpole, "Church and presbytery are human nonsense invented by knaves to govern fools. *Exalted notions of church matters* are contradictions in terms to the lowliness and humility of the gospel. There is nothing sublime but the Divinity. Nothing is sacred but as His work. A tree or a brute stone is

323

more respectable as such, than a mortal called an archbishop, or an edifice called a church, which are the puny and perishable productions of men . . . A Gothic church or convent fill one with romantic dreams—but for the mysterious, the Church in the abstract, it is a jargon that means nothing or a great deal too much, and I reject it and its apostles from Athanasius to Bishop Keene." Those were outspoken words to a friend who wore a black coat. Yet they were not suffered to break up an intimacy of forty years. Cole, to whom Walpole's little weaknesses were not unknown, contented himself by commenting sardonically at the end of the letter upon the lowliness and humility of the aristocracy, observed that "Mr. Walpole is piqued, I can see, at my reflections on Abbot's flattery"; but in his reply to Mr. Walpole he referred only to the weather, Mr. Tyson, and the gout.

Horace's politics were equally detestable to Cole. He was, in writing at least, a red-hot republican, the bitter enemy of all those Tory principles that Cole revered. That, again, was a difference that sometimes raised the temperature of the letters to fever heat—happily for us, for it allows us, reading over their shoulders, to see Horace Walpole roused —the dilettante become a man of action, chafing at his own inactivity "sitting with one's arms folded" in a chair; deploring his country's danger; remembering that if Cole is a country clergyman, he is a Walpole; the son of a Prime Minister; that his father's son might have done more than fill Strawberry Hill with Gothic ornaments; and that his father's reputation is extremely dear to him. And yet did not gossip whisper that he was not his father's son, and was there not, somewhere deep within him, an uneasy suspicion that there was a blot on his scutcheon, a freakish strain in his clear Norfolk blood?

Whoever his father may have been, his mother nature had somehow queered the pitch of that very complex human being who was called Horace Walpole. He was not simple; he was not single. As Cole noted with antiquarian particularity, Mr. Walpole's letter of Friday, May 21St, 1762, was sealed with a "seal of red wax, a cupid with a large mask of a monkey's face. An antique. Oval." The cupid and the monkey had each set their stamp on Horace Walpole's wax. He was mischievous and obscene; he gibbered and mocked and pelted the holy shrines with nutshells. And yet with what a grace he did it— with what ease and brilliancy and wit! In body, too, he was a contradiction—lean as a grasshopper, yet tough as steel. He was lapped in luxury, yet never wore a great-coat, ate and drank as little as a fasting friar, and walked on wet grass in slippers. He fribbled away his time collecting bric-a-brac and drinking tea with old ladies; yet wrote the best letters in the language in the midst of the chatter; knew everyone; went everywhere; and, as he said, "lived post." He seemed sometimes as heartless as a monkey; drove Chatterton, so people said, to suicide, and allowed old Madame du Deffand to die alone in despair. And yet who but Cupid wrote when Gray was dead, "I treated him insolently; he loved me and I did not think he did"? Or again, "One loves to find people care for one, when they can have no view in it"? But it is futile to make such contradictions clash. There were a thousand subtler impressions stamped on the wax of Horace Walpole, and it is only posterity, for whom he had a great affection, who will be able, when they have read all that he wrote to Mann and Conway and Gray and the sisters Berry and Madame du Deffand and a score of others; and what they wrote to him; and the innumerable notes at the bottom of the page about cooks and scullions and gardeners and old women in inns —it is only they who will be able, when Mr. Lewis has brought his magnificent work to an end, to say what indeed Horace Walpole was. Meanwhile, we, who only catch a fleeting glimpse and set down hastily what we make of it, can testify that he is the best company in the world—the most amusing, the most intriguing—the strangest mixture of ape and Cupid that ever was.

MIDDLEBROW

This letter was Written,
But not Sent to The New Statesman.
First published in 1942

TO THE EDITOR OF
THE "NEW STATESMAN"

Sir,

Will you allow me to draw your attention to the fact that in a review of a book by me (October) your reviewer omitted to use the word Highbrow? The review, save for that omission, gave me so much pleasure that I am driven to ask you, at the risk of appearing unduly egotistical, whether your reviewer, a man of obvious intelligence, intended to deny my claim to that title? I say "claim," for surely I may claim that title when a great critic, who is also a great novelist, a rare and enviable combination, always calls me a highbrow when he condescends to notice my work in a great newspaper; and, further, always finds space to inform not only myself, who know it already, but the whole British Empire, who hang on his words, that I live in Bloomsbury? Is your critic unaware of that fact too? Or does he, for all his intelligence, maintain that it is unnecessary in reviewing a book to add the postal address of the writer?

His answer to these questions, though of real value to me, is of no possible interest to the public at large. Of that I am well aware. But since larger issues are involved, since the Battle of the Brows troubles, I am told, the evening air, since the finest minds of our age have lately been engaged in debating, not without that passion which befits a noble cause, what a highbrow is and what a lowbrow, which is better and which is worse, may I take this opportunity to express my opinion and at the same time draw attention to certain aspects of the question which seem to me to have been unfortunately overlooked?

Now there can be no two opinions as to what a highbrow is. He is the man or woman of thoroughbred intelligence who rides his mind at a gallop across country in pursuit of an idea. That is why I have always been so proud to be called highbrow. That is why, if I could be more of a highbrow I would. I honour and respect highbrows. Some of my relations have been highbrows; and some, but by no means all, of my friends. To be a highbrow, a complete and representative highbrow, a highbrow like Shakespeare, Dickens, Byron, Shelley, Keats, Charlotte Bronte, Scott, Jane Austen, Flaubert, Hardy or Henry James—to name a few highbrows from the same profession chosen at random—is of course beyond the wildest dreams of my imagination. And, though I would cheerfully lay myself down in the dust and kiss the print of their feet, no person of sense will deny that this passionate preoccupation of theirs—riding across country in pursuit of ideas—often leads to disaster. Undoubtedly, they come fearful croppers. Take Shelley—what a mess he made of his life! And Byron, getting into bed with first one woman and then with another and dying in the mud at Missolonghi. Look at Keats, loving poetry and Fanny Brawne so intemperately that he pined and died of consumption at the age of twenty-six. Charlotte Bronte again—I have beep assured on good authority that Charlotte Bronte was, with the possible exception of Emily, the worst governess in the British Isles. Then there was Scott— he went bankrupt, and left, together with a few magnificent novels, one house, Abbotsford, which is perhaps the ugliest in the whole Empire. But surely these instances are enough—I need not further labour the point that highbrows, for some reason or another, are wholly incapable of dealing successfully with what is called real life. That is why, and here I come to a point that is often surprisingly ignored, they honour so wholeheartedly and depend so completely upon those who are called lowbrows. By a lowbrow is meant of course a man or a woman of thoroughbred vitality who rides his body in pursuit of a living at a gallop across life. That is why I honour and respect lowbrows—and I have never known a highbrow who did not. In so far as I am a highbrow (and my imperfections in that line are well known to me) I love lowbrows; I study them; I always sit next the conductor in an omnibus and try to get him to tell me what it is like—being a conductor. In whatever company I am I always try to know what it is like—being a conductor, being a woman with ten children and thirty-five shillings a week, being a stockbroker, being an admiral, being a bank clerk, being a dressmaker, being a duchess, being a miner, being a cook, being a prostitute. All that lowbrows do is of surpassing interest and wonder to me, because, in so far as I am a highbrow, I cannot do things myself.

This brings me to another point which is also surprisingly overlooked. Lowbrows need highbrows and honour them just as much as highbrows need lowbrows and honour them. This too is not a matter that requires much demonstration. You have only to stroll along the Strand on a wet winter's night and watch the crowds lining up to get into the movies. These lowbrows are waiting, after the day's work, in the rain, sometimes for hours, to get into the cheap seats and sit in hot theatres in order to see what their lives look like. Since they are lowbrows, engaged magnificently and adventurously in riding full tilt from one end of life to the other in pursuit of a living, they cannot see themselves doing it. Yet nothing interests them more. Nothing matters to them more. It is one of the prime necessities of life to them—to be shown what life looks like. And the highbrows, of course, are the only people who can show them. Since they are the only people who do not do things, they are the only people who can see things being done. This is so—and so it is I am certain; nevertheless we are told—the air buzzes with it by night, the press booms with it by day, the very donkeys in the fields do nothing but bray it, the very curs in the streets do nothing but bark it—"Highbrows hate lowbrows! Lowbrows hate highbrows!"—when highbrows need lowbrows, when lowbrows need highbrows, when they cannot exist apart, when one is the complement and other side of the other! How has such a lie come into existence? Who has set this malicious gossip afloat?

There can be no doubt about that either. It is the doing of the middlebrows. They are the people, I confess, that I seldom regard with entire cordiality. They are the go-betweens; they are the busy-bodies who run from one to the other with their tittle tattle and make all the mischief—the middlebrows, I repeat. But what, you may ask, is a middlebrow? And that, to tell the truth, is no easy question to answer. They are neither one thing nor the other. They are not highbrows, whose brows are high; nor lowbrows, whose brows are low. Their brows are betwixt and between. They do not live in Bloomsbury which is on high ground; nor in Chelsea, which is on low ground. Since they must live somewhere presumably, they live perhaps in South Kensington, which is betwixt and between. The middlebrow is the man, or woman, of middlebred intelligence who ambles and saunters now on this side of the hedge, now on that, in pursuit of no single object, neither art itself nor life itself, but both mixed indistinguishably, and rather nastily, with money, fame, power, or prestige. The middlebrow curries favour with both sides equally. He goes to the lowbrows and tells them that while he is not quite one of them, he is almost their friend. Next moment he rings up the highbrows and asks them with equal geniality whether he may not come to tea. Now there are highbrows—I myself have known duchesses who were highbrows, also charwomen, and they have both told me with that vigour of language which so often unites the aristocracy with the working classes, that they would rather sit in the coal cellar, together, than in the drawing-room with middlebrows and pour out tea. I have myself been asked—but may I, for the sake of brevity, cast this scene which is only partly fictitious, into the form of fiction?—I myself, then, have been asked to come and "see" them—how strange a passion theirs is for being "seen"! They ring me up, therefore, at about eleven in the morning, and ask me to come to tea. I go to my wardrobe and consider, rather lugubriously, what is the right thing to wear? We highbrows may be smart, or we may be shabby; but we never have the right thing to wear. I proceed to ask next: What is the right thing to say? Which is the right knife to use? What is the right book to praise? All these are things I do not know for myself. We highbrows read what we like and do what we like and praise what we like. We also know what we dislike—for example, thin bread and butter tea. The difficulty of eating thin bread and butter in white kid gloves has always seemed to me one of life's more insuperable problems. Then I dislike bound volumes of the classics behind plate glass. Then I distrust people who call both Shakespeare and Wordsworth equally "Bill"—it is a habit moreover that leads to confusion. And in the matter of clothes, I like people either to dress very well; or to dress very badly; I dislike the correct thing in clothes. Then there is the question of games. Being a highbrow I do not play them. But I love watching people play who have a passion for games. These middlebrows pat balls about; they poke their bats and muff their catches at cricket. And when poor Middlebrow mounts on horseback and that animal breaks into a canter, to me there is no sadder sight in all Rotten Row. To put it in a nutshell (in order to get on with the story) that tea party was not wholly a success, nor altogether a failure; for Middlebrow, who writes, following me to the door, clapped me briskly on the back, and said "I'm sending you my book!" (Or did he call it "stuff?") And his book comes—sure enough, though called, so symbolically, *Keepaway*, [Keepaway is the name of a preparation used to distract the male dog from the female at certain seasons] it comes. And I read a page here, and I read a page there (I am breakfasting, as usual, in bed). And it is not well written; nor is it badly written. It is not proper, nor is it improper—in short it is betwixt and between. Now if there is any sort of book for which I have, perhaps, an imperfect sympathy, it is the betwixt and between. And so, though I suffer from the gout of a morning— but if one's ancestors for two or three centuries have tumbled into bed dead drunk one has deserved a touch of that malady— I rise. I dress. I proceed weakly to the window. I take that book in my swollen right hand and toss it gently over the hedge into the field. The hungry sheep—did I remember to say that this part of the story takes place in the country?— the hungry sheep look up but are not fed.

But to have done with fiction and its tendency to lapse into poetry—I will now report a perfectly prosaic conversation in words of one syllable. I often ask my friends the lowbrows, over our muffins and honey, why it is that while we, the highbrows, never buy a middlebrow book, or go to a middlebrow lecture, or read, unless we are paid for doing so, a middlebrow review, they, on the contrary, take these middlebrow activities so seriously? Why, I ask (not of course on the wireless), are you so damnably modest? Do you think that a description of your lives, as they are, is too sordid and too mean to be beautiful? Is that why you prefer the middlebrow version of what they have the impudence to call real humanity?—this mixture of geniality and sentiment stuck together with a sticky slime of calves-foot jelly? The truth, if you would only believe it, is much more beautiful than any lie. Then again, I continue, how can you let the middlebrows teach you how to write?—you, who write so beautifully when you write naturally, that I would give both my hands to write as you do—for which reason I never attempt it, but do my best to learn the art of writing as a highbrow should. And again, I press on, brandishing a muffin on the point of a tea spoon, how dare the middlebrows teach you how to read—Shakespeare for instance? All you have to do is to read him. The Cambridge edition is both good and cheap. If you find *Hamlet* difficult, ask him to tea. He is a highbrow. Ask Ophelia to meet him. She is a lowbrow. Talk to them, as you talk to me, and you will know more about Shakespeare than all the middlebrows in the world can teach you—I do not think, by the way, from certain phrases that Shakespeare liked middlebrows, or Pope either.

To all this the lowbrows reply—but I cannot imitate their style of talking—that they consider themselves to be common people without education. It is very kind of the middlebrows to try to teach them culture. And after all, the lowbrows continue, middlebrows, like other people, have to make money. There must be money in teaching and in writing books about Shakespeare. We all have to earn our livings nowadays, my friends the lowbrows remind me. I quite agree. Even those of us whose Aunts came a cropper riding in India and left them an annual income of four hundred and rfifty pounds, now reduced, thanks to the war and other luxuries, to little more than two hundred odd, even we have to do that. And we do it, too, by writing about anybody who seems amusing—enough has been written about Shakespeare—Shakespeare hardly pays. We highbrows, I agree, have to earn our livings; but when we have earned enough to live on, then we live. When the middlebrows, on the contrary, have earned enough to live on, they go on earning enough to buy— what are the things that middlebrows always buy? Queen Anne furniture (faked, but none the less expensive); first editions of dead writers, always the worst; pictures, or reproductions from pictures, by dead painters; houses in what is called "the Georgian style"—but never anything new, never a picture by a living painter, or a chair by a living carpenter, or books by living writers, for to buy living art requires living taste. And, as that kind of art and that kind of taste are what middlebrows call "highbrow," "Bloomsbury," poor middlebrow spends vast sums on sham antiques, and has to keep at it scribbling away, year in, year out, while we highbrows ring each other up, and are off for a day's jaunt into the country. That is the worst of course of living in a set—one likes being with one's friends.

Have I then made my point clear, sir, that the true battle in my opinion lies not between highbrow and lowbrow, but between highbrows and lowbrows joined together in blood brotherhood against the bloodless and pernicious pest who comes between? If the B.B.C. stood for anything but the Betwixt and Between Company they would use their control of the air not to stir strife between brothers, but to broadcast the fact that highbrows and lowbrows must band together to exterminate a pest which is the bane of all thinking and living. It may be, to quote from your advertisement columns, that "terrifically sensitive" lady novelists overestimate the dampness and dinginess of this fungoid growth. But all I can say is that when, lapsing into that stream which people call, so oddly, consciousness, and gathering wool from the sheep that have been mentioned above, I ramble round my garden in the suburbs, middlebrow seems to me to be everywhere. "What's that?" I cry. "Middlebrow on the cabbages? Middlebrow infecting that poor old sheep? And what about the moon?" I look up and, behold, the moon is under eclipse. "Middlebrow at it again!" I exclaim. "Middlebrow obscuring, dulling, tarnishing and coarsening even the silver edge of Heaven's own scythe." (I "draw near to poetry," see advt.) And then my thoughts, as Freud assures us thoughts will do, rush (Middlebrow's saunter and simper, out of respect for the Censor) to sex, and I ask of the sea-gulls who are crying on desolate sea sands and of the farm hands who are coming home rather drunk to their wives, what will become of us, men and women, if Middlwbrow has his way with us, and there is only a middle sex but no husbands or wives? The next remark I address with the utmost humility to the Prime Minister. "What, sir," I demand, "will be the fate of the British Empire and of our Dominions Across the Seas if Middlebrows prevail? Will you not, sir, read a pronouncement of an authoritative nature from Broadcasting House?"

Such are the thoughts, such are the fancies that visit "cultured invalidish ladies with private means" (see advt.) when they stroll in their suburban gardens and look at the cabbages and at the red brick villas that have been built by middlebrows so that middlebrows may look at the view. Such are the thoughts "at once gay and tragic and deeply feminine" (see advt.) of one who has not yet "been driven out of Bloomsbury" (advt. again), a place where lowbrows and highbrows live happily together on equal terms and priests are not, nor priestesses, and, to be quite frank, the adjective "priestly" is neither often heard nor held in high esteem. Such are the thoughts of one who will stay in Bloomsbury until the Duke of Bedford, rightly concerned for the respectability of his squares, raises the rent so high that Bloomsbury is safe for middlebrows to live in. Then she will leave.

May I conclude, as I began, by thanking your reviewer for his very courteous and interesting review, but may I tell him that though he did not, for reasons best known to himself, call me a highbrow, there is no name in the world that I prefer? I ask nothing better than that all reviewers, for ever, and everywhere, should call me a highbrow. I will do my best to oblige them. If they like to add Bloomsbury, W.C.1, that is the correct postal address, and my telephone number is in the Directory. But if your reviewer, or any other reviewer, dares hint that I live in South Kensington, I will sue him for libel. If any human being, man, woman, dog, cat or half-crushed worm dares call me "middlebrow" I will take my pen and stab him, dead. Yours etc.,

VIRGINIA WOOLF.

Printed in July 2023
by Rotomail Italia S.p.A., Vignate (MI) - Italy